"Forsyth's real life has been almost as thrilling as the stories he's created in his fifteen novels. Forsyth details his many once-in-a-lifetime experiences [and] packs his stories with history both personal and global. **A riveting and refreshing memoir.**"

—*Publishers Weekly*

"We all make mistakes, but starting the Third World War would have been a rather large one. To this day, I still maintain it was not entirely my fault."

For more than forty years, Frederick Forsyth has been writing extraordinary real-world novels, from the groundbreaking *The Day of the Jackal* to the prescient *The Kill List*. Whether writing about the murky world of arms dealers or the intricacies of worldwide drug cartels, every plot has been chillingly plausible because every detail has been minutely researched.

But what most people don't know is that some of his greatest stories of intrigue have been in his own life.

Written with extraordinary charm, warm candor, irreverent wit, and the storytelling skills that have made him one of the most popular writers of our time, *The Outsider* is a memoir like no other.

PRAISE FOR *THE OUTSIDER*

"Acclaimed thriller writer Forsyth delivers a charming autobiography about his real-life adventures around the globe. His tales of derring-do are a pleasure to read, especially when coupled with his self-deprecating humor, but his most endearing quality is his ravenous curiosity, which pulled him from one exotic location to another. Forsyth has seen it all. After living such an exciting life, he has earned his bragging rights."

—*Kirkus Reviews*

"Forsyth applies his clean, journalistic style to his own life. . . . Like his novels, his life has had its moments of drama and intrigue. A very intriguing look at the personal story of the man behind [the] bestselling thrillers."

—*Booklist*

"If there is one memoir to read this autumn, it's Frederick Forsyth's extraordinary life story, *The Outsider*, which reads like a James Bond novel."

—*The Irish Independent*

"Forsyth relates the many fascinating episodes of his life with joie de vivre and a disarming sense of wonder that will ring true with readers of his novels. Also recommended for those unfamiliar with Forsyth's fiction but intrigued by the rich observations and well-earned ruminations of a master of his craft."

—*Library Journal*

"Entertaining and compelling. . . . If you're intrigued by 20th-century history and politics, Cold War spycraft or the life of a foreign correspondent, you'll relish *The Outsider*."

—*BookPage*

"Frederick Forsyth has never let us down in his spy thrillers. Their authenticity rings with truth and action for one very simple reason: Forsyth's own life was every bit as exciting and filled with danger as his characters'. . . . With self-deprecating humor, wit, and the charm of a born storyteller, Forsyth shares his adventures and misadventures with as much zest as his legendary thrillers."

—Bookreporter.com

"This is a raconteur's book. . . . Your host is so genial and so quick to refill your glass that before you know it, you've whiled away a very pleasant evening."

—*The New York Times Book Review*

"Forsyth's memoir is subtitled *My Life in Intrigue*, and that's no lie. While most of us will lead lives of quiet and normality, it's greatly entertaining to read about someone who has enjoyed grander and more memorable exploits."

—*The Rap Sheet*

THE OUTSIDER

My Life in Intrigue

FREDERICK FORSYTH

G. P. Putnam's Sons
New York

G. P. Putnam's Sons
Publishers Since 1838
An imprint of Penguin Random House LLC
375 Hudson Street
New York, New York 10014

The Library of Congress has catalogued the G. P. Putnam's Sons hardcover edition as follows:

Forsyth, Frederick, date.
The outsider : my life in intrigue / Frederick Forsyth.
p.   cm.
ISBN 9780399176074
1. Forsyth, Frederick.   2. Novelists, English—20th century—Biography.   I. Title.
PR6056.O699Z46   2015   2015015842
823'.914—dc23

First G. P. Putnam's Sons hardcover edition / October 2015
First G. P. Putnam's Sons trade paperback edition / October 2016
G. P. Putnam's Sons trade paperback ISBN: 9781101981856

Printed in the United States of America
1   3   5   7   9   10   8   6   4   2

Book design by Lauren Kolm

For my sons,
Stuart and Shane,
in the hopes that I was an OK dad

CONTENTS

PREFACE

We all make mistakes, but starting the Third World War would have been a rather large one. To this day, I still maintain it was not entirely my fault. But I'm getting ahead of myself.

During the course of my life, I've barely escaped the wrath of an arms dealer in Hamburg, been strafed by a MiG during the Nigerian Civil War, and landed during a bloody coup in Guinea-Bissau. The Stasi arrested me, the Israelis regaled me, the IRA prompted a quick move from Ireland to England, and a certain attractive Czech secret police agent—well, her actions were a bit more intimate. And that's just for starters.

All of that I saw from the inside. But all that time, I was, nonetheless, an outsider.

To be honest, I never intended to be a writer at all. Long periods of solitude were first a circumstance, then a preference, and finally a necessity.

After all, writers are odd creatures, and if they try to make a living at it, even more so. There are reasons for this.

The first is that a writer lives half his life inside his own head. In this tiny space, entire worlds are created or erased and probably both. People come into being, work, love, fight, die, and are replaced. Plots are devised, developed, amended, and come to fruition or are frustrated. It is a completely different world from the one outside the window. In children, daydreaming is rebuked; in a writer, it is indispensable.

The result is a need for long periods of peace and quiet, often in complete silence without even gentle music, and these require solitude as an absolute necessity, the first of the reasons behind our oddness.

When you think about it, with the abolition of lighthouse keepers, writing is the only job that has to be undertaken wholly alone. Other professions afford colleagues. The airline captain has his crew, the actor the rest of the cast, the soldier his mates, the office staffer his colleagues grouped around the watercooler. Only the writer closes the door, takes the phone off the hook, draws down the blinds, and withdraws into a private world alone. Man is a gregarious beast and has been since the hunter-gatherers. The hermit is unusual, odd, and sometimes weird.

You may occasionally see a writer out on the town: wining, dining, partying; being affable, sociable, even merry. Beware; this is only half of him. The other half is detached, watching, taking notes. That is the second reason for the oddness—the compulsive detachment.

Behind his mask, the writer is always watching; he cannot help it. He observes, analyzes, takes mental notes, stores nuggets of the talk and behavior around him for later use. Actors do the same for the same reasons—for later use. But the writer has only words to use, more rigorous than the film set or stage, with its colors, movements, gestures, facial expressions, props, and music.

The absolute need for extensive solitude and the permanent detachment from what Malraux called "the human condition" explain why a writer can never really enter in. Membership involves self-revelation, conformity, and obedience. But a writer must be a loner and thus always an outsider.

As a boy, I was obsessed by airplanes and just wanted to be a pilot. But even then, not one of an aircrew. I just wanted to fly single-seaters, which was probably a warning sign, had anyone noticed. But no one did.

Three factors contributed to my later appreciation of silence in an increasingly noisy world, and solitude where the modern world demands jostling crowds. For one thing, I was my parents' firstborn and remained an only child; and they are always slightly different. My parents might have had more children, but the war intervened in 1939, and by the time it was over, it was, for my mother, too late.

So I grew into little boyhood largely alone. A boy alone in his playroom can invent his own games and ensure they are played by his rules and come to their desired conclusion. He becomes accustomed to winning, and on his own terms. The preference for solitude is beginning.

The second factor in my isolation was occasioned by the Second World War itself. My town of Ashford was very close to the coast and the English Channel. Just twenty-two miles across that water was Nazi-occupied France. For a while, the mighty Wehrmacht waited across that strip of gray water for the chance to cross, invade, conquer, and occupy. The bombers of the Luftwaffe droned overhead to raid London, or, fearing the waiting fighters of the Royal Air Force, to turn back and dump their loads anywhere onto Kent. Other raids sought to destroy the great Ashford railway junction just 500 yards from my family's home.

The result was that for most of the war, many of the children of Ashford were evacuated to foster homes far away. Apart from a brief departure during the summer of 1940, I spent the whole war in Ashford, and there was no one else to play with anyway. Not that I minded. This is no poor-little-me narrative. Silence and solitude became not my bane but my dear and lasting friends.

The third factor was the public school (meaning of course the private school) to which I was sent at thirteen. Nowadays Tonbridge School is a fine and humane academy, but back then it had a harsh reputation. The house to which I was allocated, Parkside, was the most brutal of all, its internal philosophy dedicated to bullying and the cane.

Faced with that, a boy has only three choices: to capitulate and become a fawning toady, to fight back, or to withdraw into some mental carapace like a turtle in a shell. You can survive, you just don't enjoy it. I survived.

I recall the leavers' concert in December 1955, when those departing had to stand up and sing the "Carmen Tonbridgiensès," the Tonbridge song. One of the lines records that "I am shut out of the garden, the dusty high road waits." I mimed the words without singing, aware that the "garden" had been a loveless monastic prison and the "dusty high road" was a broad and sunlit path that was going to lead to much fun and many adventures.

So why, eventually, become a writer? It was a fluke. I wanted not to write but to travel the world. I wanted to see it all, from the snows of the Arctic to the sands of the Sahara, from the jungles of Asia to the plains of Africa. Having no private funds, I opted for the job I thought would enable me to do this.

During my boyhood my father took the *Daily Express*, then a broadsheet newspaper owned by Lord Beaverbrook and edited by Arthur Christiansen. Both were extremely proud of their foreign coverage. At the breakfast hour, I would stand at my father's elbow and note the headlines and the datelines. Singapore, Beirut, Moscow. Where were these places? What were they like?

Patient as ever and always encouraging, my dad would take me to the family atlas and point them out. Then to the twenty-four-volume *Collins Encyclopedia*, which would describe the cities, the countries, and the people who lived there. And I vowed that one day I would see them all. I would become a foreign correspondent. And I did, and I saw them.

But it was not the writing, it was the traveling. It was not until I was thirty-one that, home from an African war, and stony-broke as usual, with no job and no chance of one, I hit on the idea of writing a novel to clear my debts. It was a crazy idea.

There are several ways of making quick money, but in the general list, writing a novel rates well below robbing a bank. But I did not know that and I suppose I must have got something right. My publisher told me, to my complete surprise, that it seemed I could tell a story. And that is what I have done for the past forty-five years, still traveling, no longer to report foreign news stories but to research the material needed for the next novel. That was when solitude and detachment became not a preference but an absolute necessity.

At seventy-six, I think I also remain part journalist, retaining the two other qualities that a reporter must have: insatiable curiosity and a gritty skepticism. Show me a journo who does not care to discover the reason why, and who believes what he is told, and I will show you a bad one.

A journalist should never join the Establishment, no matter how tempting the blandishments. It is our job to hold power to account, not join it. In a world that increasingly obsesses over the gods of power, money, and fame, a journalist and a writer must remain detached, like a bird on a rail, watching, noting, probing, commenting, but never joining. In short, an outsider.

For years I have fended off suggestions that I should pen an autobiography. And I still do. This is not a life story and certainly not a self-justification. But I am aware that I have been to many places and seen many things: some amusing, some gruesome, some moving, some scary.

My life has been blessed by extraordinary good fortune for which I have no explanation. More times than I can count, a lucky break has got me out of a tight spot, or procured me an advantage. Unlike the moaners in every Sunday tabloid, I had two wonderful parents and a happy childhood in the fields of Kent. I managed to fulfill my earlier ambitions to fly and to travel and then, much later, to write stories. The latter has brought enough material success to live comfortably, which is all I ever wanted anyway.

I have been married to two beautiful women and raised two fine sons, while enjoying so far robust good health. For all this, I remain deeply grateful, though to what fate, fortune, or deity I am not quite sure. Perhaps I should make my mind up. After all, I may have to meet Him soon!

WHISPERED WORDS

———◆◆◆———

My father was born in 1906, the eldest son of a frequently absent chief petty officer, Royal Navy, in Chatham, Kent, and emerged at twenty from the Dockyard School to an economy that was creating one job for every ten young men in the labor pool. The other nine were destined for the dole queue.

He had studied to be a naval architect, but as the Great Depression loomed, no one wanted ships to be built. The Hitlerian threat had not yet materialized and there were more merchant ships than anyone needed to carry the diminishing industrial product. After five years scraping a living from little more than odd jobs, he followed the popular advice of the age: Go east, young man. He applied for and secured a post as a rubber planter in Malaya.

Today it would seem strange to appoint a young man with not a word of Malay or knowledge of the Orient to go to the other end of the world to manage many thousands of acres of plantation and a large labor force of Malays and Chinese. But those were the days of empire, when such challenges were perfectly normal.

So he packed his things, said good-bye to his parents, and took ship for Singapore. He learned Malay and the intricacies of estate management and rubber production, and ran his estate for five years. Each day, he wrote a love letter to the girl with whom he had been "walking out," as they called dating back then, and she wrote to him. The next liner from Britain to Singapore brought the week's supply of letters and they came to the estate in Johore on the weekly riverboat.

Life was lonely and isolated, illuminated by the weekly motorcycle ride south through the jungle, out onto the main road, across the causeway, and into Changi for a convivial evening at the planters' club. His estate consisted of a huge tract of rubber trees set in parallel rows and surrounded by jungle, which was home to tigers, black panthers, and the much-feared *hamadryad*, or king cobra. There was no car, because the track to the main road ten miles through the jungle was a narrow, winding line of red laterite and gravel, so he rode a motorcycle.

And there was the village in which the labor force of Chinese tappers lived with their wives and families. And as in any village there were a few craftsmen—a butcher, a baker, a blacksmith, and so forth.

He stuck it out for four years until it became plain there was little enough future in it. Rubber had slumped on the market. European rearmament had not yet started, but the new synthetics were taking more and more market share. The planters were asked to take a 20 percent salary cut as a condition of continued employment. For the bachelors, the choice was either to send for their fiancées to come and join them, or to go home to England. By 1935, he was havering between the two when something happened.

One night his houseboy roused him with a request.

"*Tuan*, the village carpenter is outside. He begs to see you."

The routine was usually rise at five, tour the estate for two hours, then the morning reception when he would sit on the veranda and hear any petitions, complaints, or adjudications in quarrels. Because of the early rise, he turned in at nine p.m., and this request was after ten o'clock. He was about to say "In the morning" when it occurred to him that if it could not wait, it might be serious.

"Bring him in," he said. The houseboy demurred.

"He will not come, *tuan*. He is not worthy."

My father rose, opened the screen door, and went out to the veranda. Outside, the tropical night was like warm velvet and the mosquitoes were voracious. Standing in a pool of light below the veranda was the village carpenter, a Japanese, the only one in the village. My father knew he had a wife and child and they never mixed with anyone. The man bowed deeply.

"It is my son, *tuan*. The boy is very ill. I fear for him."

Dad called for lanterns and they went to the village. The child was about ten and racked with pain from his stomach. His mother, with an agonized face, crouched in the corner.

My father was no doctor, not even a paramedic, but a compulsory course of first aid and a clutch of medical textbooks gave him enough knowledge to recognize acute appendicitis. It was pitch-black and closing on midnight. Changi General Hospital was eighty miles away, but he knew that if appendicitis turned to peritonitis, it would kill.

He ordered his motorcycle brought out, fully fueled. The father used his wife's broad sash, the obi, to fasten the child on the pillion, tied to my father's back, and he set off. He told me later it was a hellish journey, for all the predators hunt at night. It was nearly an hour down the rutted track to the main road, then due south for the causeway.

Dawn was close to breaking some hours later when he rolled into the forecourt of Changi General Hospital, yelling for someone to come and help him. Nursing staff appeared and wheeled the child away. By luck, a British doctor was coming off night shift, but took one look at the boy and rushed him to surgery.

The doctor joined my father for tiffin in the canteen and told him he had been just in time. The appendix was just about to burst, with probably lethal results. But the boy would live and was even then asleep. My father gave the obi back.

After refueling, my father rode back to his estate to reassure the impassive but hollow-eyed parents and catch up with the delayed day's work. A fortnight later, the riverboat brought the mail package, the usual stores, and a small Japanese boy with a shy smile and a scar.

Four days later, the carpenter appeared again, this time in daylight. He was waiting near the bungalow when Dad returned from the latex store for tea. He kept his eyes on the ground as he spoke.

"*Tuan*, my son will live. In my culture when a man owes what I owe you, he must offer the most valuable thing that he has. But I am a poor man and have nothing to offer save one thing. Advice."

Then he raised his eyes and stared my father in the face.

"Leave Malaya, *tuan*. If you value your life, leave Malaya."

To the end of his days in 1991, my father never knew if those words caused his decision or merely reinforced it. But the next year, 1936, instead of sending for his fiancée, he resigned and came home. In 1941, Imperial Japanese forces invaded Malaya. In 1945, of all his contemporaries, not one came home from the camps.

There was nothing spontaneous about the Japanese invasion of Malaya. It was meticulously planned and the imperial forces swept down the peninsula as an unstoppable tide. British and Australian troops were rushed up the spine of the colony to man defensive points along the main roads south. But the Japanese had not come that way.

Out of the rubber estates came scores of sleeper agents, infiltrated years before. On hundreds of bicycles, the Japanese rode south along tiny, unknown jungle tracks, guided by the agents. Others came by sea, leapfrogging down the coast, guided inshore by winking lanterns held by fellow countrymen who knew the coast and all the inlets.

The British and Australians were outflanked over and over again as the Japanese appeared behind them, and in strength, always guided by the agents. It was all over in days and the supposedly impregnable fortress of Singapore was taken from the landward side, her massive guns facing out to sea.

When I was a child but old enough to understand, my father told me this story and swore it was absolutely true and it happened nearly seven years before the invasion of December 1941. But he was never quite certain that his village carpenter was one of those agents, only that had he been taken, he, too, would have died. So perhaps only a few whispered words from a grateful carpenter caused me to appear on this earth at all. Since 1945, the Japanese have been held responsible for many things, but surely not this as well?

A LARGE JAR OF TALC

The spring of 1940 was not a relaxing time to be in East Kent. Hitler had swept across Europe. France was overrun in three weeks. Denmark and Norway were gone; Belgium, Luxembourg, and Holland were swallowed.

The outflanked British army in France had been driven into the sea off Dunkirk and Calais, and only rescued, minus all their equipment, by a miracle of small inshore boats manned by civilians who chugged across the Channel from the English coast and, against all the odds, brought 330,000 of them off the sand dunes.

All Europe was either occupied by Hitler, putting into office servile collaborator governments, or sheltering in their neutrality. The British prime minister had been tossed out, to be replaced by Winston Churchill, who vowed we would fight on. But with what? Britain was completely isolated and alone.

All Kent waited for the invasion, the famed Operation Sea Lion, which, on Eagle Day, would see the German army roar up the beaches to invade, conquer, and occupy.

My father had already volunteered for the army, but was still based in his native Kent and living at home. He and my mother decided that if the invasion came, they would not survive. They would use the last gallon of petrol in the old Wolseley and, with a length of hose, end their lives. But they did not want to take me with them. With my crown of blond curls, I would be accepted by the Nazis as of good Aryan stock and raised in an orphanage. But how to see me safely evacuated somewhere else?

The solution came in one of the customers at my mother's dress shop. She was the principal of the Norland College, the training school of the famous Norland nannies who for decades had gone out to raise the children of the rich and royal worldwide. The institute was at Hothfield, a village outside Ashford. It was going to evacuate to Devon, far away in the southwest. My mother put it to her client: Would they take me with them?

The principal was dubious, but her deputy proposed to her that nannies in training would always need babies to practice on, so why not this one? The deal was done. When the train bearing the Norland Institute steamed out of Ashford, I went with them. May 1940: I was twenty months old.

It is hard to describe in the modern world, or explain to the new generation, the anguish of those parents as Ashford was emptied of its evacuees, seen off by weeping mothers and a few fathers who thought never to see them again. But that was the way it was at Ashford station.

I cannot recall those five months I was in Devon, as class after class of eager young nannies experimented at putting me to bed, getting me up, and constantly changing my nappies. That was before Velcro fastenings and absorbent padding. It was all terry toweling and pins back then.

It seems I could hardly pass wind or let go a few drops before the whole lot came off to be replaced by a new one. And the standby was talc: lots and lots of talc. I must have had the most talc-dusted rear end in the kingdom.

But the Few in their Spitfires and Hurricanes did the job. On September 17, Adolf simply gave up. His vast army on the French coast turned around, took a last look at the white cliffs across the Channel that they would not conquer after all, and marched east. Hitler was preparing his June 1941 invasion of Russia. The landing barges bobbed uselessly at their moorings off Boulogne and Calais.

Sea Lion was off.

Our photographic recce planes noted this and reported back. England was saved, or at least saved to struggle on. But the Luftwaffe bombing raids on London and the southeast would not cease. Most of the evacuated children would stay far from their parents, but at least with a good chance of reunification one day.

My own parents had had enough. They sent for me, and back I came, to spend the rest of the war in the family home in Elwick Road, Ashford. I recall none of this, not the going away, or the ceaseless attention to the nether parts in Devon, or the return. But something must have struck in the subconscious. It took years until I ceased to feel trepidation every time I was approached by a beaming young lady with a large jar of talc.

A LITTLE BOY'S DREAM

The summer of 1944 brought two great excitements to a small boy of five in East Kent. The nightly droning of German bombers overhead, heading from the French coast for the target of London, had ceased as the Royal Air Force won back control of the skies. The rhythmic throb-throb of the V-1 rockets, or "doodlebugs," Hitler's pilotless drones packed with explosives, had not yet started. But by May all the grown-ups were tense. They were expecting the long-awaited Allied invasion of occupied France. That was when the Texan came and parked his tank on my parents' lawn.

At the breakfast hour, he was not there, but when I returned in the midafternoon from kindergarten, there he was. I thought the tank, which turned out to be a Sherman, was immense and hugely exciting. Its tracks were half on the parental lawn, the fence reduced to matchwood, and half on Elwick Road. It simply had to be explored.

It took a chair from the kitchen and a lot of climbing to reach the top of the tracks, and then there was the turret, with its formidable gun. Having reached the top of the turret, I found the hatch open and stared down. A face stared up and there was a muttered conversation down below and a head began to climb toward the light. When a tall, lanky figure detached himself from the metal and towered over me, I recognized that he had to be a cowboy. I had seen them in the Saturday-morning film shows and they all wore tall hats. I was looking at my first Texan in a Stetson.

He sat on the turret, coming eye to eye with me, and said, "Hiya, kid." I replied, "Good afternoon." He seemed to be speaking through his nose, like the cowboys in the movies. He nodded at our home.

"Your house?"

I nodded.

"Waal, tell your paw I'm real sorry about the fence."

He reached into the top pocket of his combat fatigues, produced a wafer of something, unwrapped it, and offered it to me. I did not know what it was, but I took it, as it would have been rude to refuse. He produced another piece, put it in his mouth, and began to chew. I did the same. It tasted of peppermint, but unlike British toffee, it refused to dissolve for swallowing. I had just been introduced to chewing gum.

That tank and its entire crew were convinced that in a few days they would be part of the invasion force that would try to storm Hitler's Atlantic Wall in the massively fortified Pas-de-Calais. Many must have thought they would never come back. In fact they were all wrong.

My Texan was part of a huge decoy army that the Allied commanders had stuffed into East Kent to dupe the German High Command. Secretly they were planning to invade via Normandy, way down south, with another army then crouching under camouflaged canvas miles away from Kent.

The soldiers of the decoy army might go over later, but not on D-Day. Thinking they would be the first shock wave, with terrible casualties, thousands of them were jamming every bar in Kent to the doors, drinking in the final saloon. A week later, a solemn voice on the radio, which was then called the wireless, announced that British, American, and Canadian troops had landed in strength on five beaches in Normandy and were fighting their way inland.

Two days after that, there was an earsplitting rumble from the front garden and the Sherman rolled away. My Texan was gone. No more chewing gum. Under the guidance of my mother, I knelt at the bedside and prayed to Jesus to look after him. It was a month later that I was taken to Hawkinge.

My father was a major in the army, but for the past ten years he had been a member of Ashford's amateur fire brigade. Despite his protests, this put him in a "restricted occupation," meaning he could not be posted abroad and go into combat. The country needed every fireman it had. He insisted on a job and was made a welfare officer, answerable to the War Office and charged with overseeing the living conditions of all the soldiers based in East Kent.

I do not know when he ever slept for those five years. My mother ran the family furrier's shop while Dad spent his days in a khaki uniform and his nights on a fire truck, racing around putting out fires. My point is, he had a car and a cherished petrol allowance, without which he could not have done his day job. Hence the trip across the Weald of Kent to visit the grass-field fighter strip at Hawkinge. It was the base of two squadrons of Spitfires.

Back then the Spitfire was not just a fighter plane, it was a national icon. It still is. And for every small boy, the men who flew them were heroes to surpass any footballer or showbiz personality. While my father conducted his business with the base commander, I was handed over to the pilots.

They made a great fuss of me, thinking perhaps of their own children or kid brothers far away. One of them picked me up under the armpits, swung me high, and dropped me into the cockpit of a Mark 9 Spitfire. I sat on the parachute, overawed, dumbfounded. I sniffed in the odors of petrol, oil, webbing, leather, sweat, and fear—for fear also has an aroma. I studied the controls, the firing button, the instruments; I gripped the control stick. I stared ahead along the endless cowling masking the great Rolls-Royce Merlin engine to the four-bladed propeller, stark against a duck-egg-blue Kentish sky. And in the manner of little boys, I swore a little boy's oath.

Most small boys swear to something they want to be when they grow up, but usually the promise fades and the dream dies. I swore that one day I was going to be one of them. I was going to wear the pale blue uniform with wings on the chest, and fly single-seaters for the RAF. When I was hoisted back out of the cockpit, I had made up my mind what I was going to do: I would be a fighter pilot, and I would fly a Spitfire.

I could not foresee the years of discouragement from schools and peer groups, the mockery and disbelief. When my father drove his little Wolseley saloon back to Ashford, I was lost in thought. A month later, I turned six and the dream did not die.

LEARNING FRENCH

Before the war, my father had been a pillar of the Rotary Club of Ashford. With the departure of so many men into the armed forces or to war work, that was all suspended for the duration. But in 1946 it was restarted, and the next year saw a program of "twinning" with our newly freed neighbors in France. Ashford, beginning with the letter A, was twinned with Amiens in Picardy.

My parents were matched with a French doctor, the Resistance war hero Dr. Colin and his wife. Throughout the occupation, he had remained the doctor assigned to the hundreds of railwaymen living and working in the great rail hub of the Amiens marshaling yards. Permitted his own car and free movement, he had observed many things useful to the Allies across the Channel, and at risk of discovery and execution, had passed them on to the Resistance.

The Colins came to visit in 1947, and the following year invited my parents back. But the shop came first, and they could not take the time off, so I went instead, a pattern that would be repeated for the next four years. Not just for a weekend, but for most of the eight-week summer school vacation.

Like many families of the French bourgeoisie, the Colins had a country house far from the city fumes, buried deep in the countryside of Corrèze in the Massif Central in the middle of France. Thus in July 1948, aged nine, in short trousers and school cap, I accompanied my father on the adventure of crossing the Channel on a ferry. Only at the other side, looking back, could I see for the first time the towering white cliffs of Dover, which the German army had been staring at so long-ingly eight years earlier. Dr. Colin met us at Calais, and my father, pink with embarrassment, was duly embraced and kissed on both cheeks. Then he patted me on the head and reboarded the ferry for home. Real men did not kiss in those days.

Dr. Colin and I boarded the train for Amiens, and I saw for the first time wooden seats in a railway carriage. The doctor had a compli-mentary ticket for first class, but he preferred to travel in third with the working-class people he served.

At Amiens, I met Madame Colin again, and their four children, all in their early twenties and late teens. François, then seventeen, was the wild one, arrested several times by the Gestapo during the occupation and reason for his mother's snow-white hair. Not one of them spoke a word of English, and after three terms at a British prep school, I could just about manage *bonjour* and *merci*. Sign language was coming into its own, but I had been given a primer textbook for the grammar and began to work out what they were saying. Two days later, we all left for Paris and Corrèze.

"Abroad" seemed a very strange but fascinating place. Everything was different—the language, the food, the mannerisms, the customs, and those massive French railway engines. But children, in the manner of learning things, are like blotting paper. They can soak up information. Today, sixty-five years later, stumped by the new Internet-connected, digitalized world, I marvel at children little more than toddlers who can do twenty things with an iPhone that I have a problem switching on.

Dr. Colin was not with us. He had to stay in Amiens and tend to his patients. So Madame and the teenagers traveled south to fulfill the sacred French summer holiday in the country with a small and slightly overwhelmed English boy. We changed trains at Ussel onto a branch line to Egletons and thence by wheezing country bus to the ancient village of Lamazière Basse. It was like going back to the Middle Ages.

The family home was large, old, and decrepit, with falling plaster, a leaky roof, and many rooms, one of which became mine, and where mice ran freely over me as I slept. The lady who lived there was the old family nanny, pensioned off but given a home for the rest of her days. Amazingly, she was English, but had been in France since her girlhood.

A lifelong spinster, Mimi Tunc had served the Colin family for many years, and throughout the entire war had passed for French under the noses of the German authorities, thus escaping internment.

Lamazière Basse was, as said, very old and almost medieval. A few homes, but not many, had electricity. For most, oil lamps sufficed. There were one or two archaic tractors, but no combine harvesters. The crops were scythed by hand and brought home in carts hauled by yoked oxen. In the fields, the peasants at midday would stand to murmur the Angelus, like figures from a Millet painting. Both men and women wore wooden clogs, or *sabots*.

There was a church, packed with attendance by the women and children, while the men discussed the important things of life in the bar-café across the square. The village priest, always called Monsieur l'Abbé, was friendly to me but slightly distant, convinced that as a Protestant I was tragically destined for hell. Up at the château on the hill dwelled Madame de Lamazière, the very old matriarch of the surrounding land. She did not come to church; it came to her in the form of poor Monsieur l'Abbé, sweating up the hill in the summer sun to bring her Mass in her private chapel. The pecking order was very rigid, and even God had to recognize the distinctions.

As my French improved, I made friends with a number of village boys to whom I was an object of extreme curiosity. The summer of 1948 was blazingly hot and our daily magnet was the lake a mile outside the village. There, with rods made from reeds, we could fish for large green frogs, whose back legs, dusted with flour and fried in butter, made an excellent supper.

Lunches were always large and taken outside: hams cured black in the chimney smoke, pâté, crusty bread, butter from the churn, and fruit from the trees. I was taught to sample watered red wine like the other boys, but not the girls. It was at the lake one sweltering day that first summer that I saw Benoît die.

There were about six boys skylarking in the clearing by the water's edge one midday when he appeared, clearly very intoxicated. The village youths murmured to me that he was Benoît, the village drunk. To our fascinated bewilderment, he stripped naked and waded into the lake. He was singing out of tune. We thought he was just going to cool off, waist deep. But he went on walking into the water until he was up to his neck. Then he started to swim, but within a few clumsy strokes his head disappeared.

Among the boys I was the strongest swimmer, so after half a minute it was suggested I should swim out and look for him. So I did. Having reached the point where his head had disappeared, I peered downward. Without a snorkeling mask (unheard of back then), I could see very little. The water was an amber color, and there were tangles of weeds and some lilies. Still unable to see much, I took a deep breath and dived.

About ten feet down, on the bottom, was a pale blob lying on its back. Closer up I could see a trickle of bubbles emerging from his mouth. He clearly was not frolicking, but drowning. As I turned to resurface a hand gripped my left ankle and held it. Above my head, I could see the sun shining through the dim water, but the surface was two feet away and the grip did not slacken. Feeling the onset of panic, I turned and went back down.

Finger by finger, I peeled the dying hand off my ankle. Benoît's eyes were open and he stared at me as my lungs began to hurt. Finally the hand was off my leg and I kicked for the surface. I felt the fingers seeking a second grip, but I kicked again, felt an impact with a face and then shot upward toward the sun.

There was that wonderful inrush of fresh air that all free divers will recognize when they return to the surface, and I began to splash toward the gravel patch under the trees where the village boys waited, openmouthed. I explained what I had seen and one of them ran for the village. But it was half an hour before men appeared with ropes. One stripped to his long johns and went in. Others waded in waist deep, but no farther. The man in the long johns was the only one who could swim. Eventually a connection was made with the object under the water and the body was hauled out by one wrist on the end of a rope.

There was no question of resuscitation even if anyone had known the technique. The boys gathered around before being shooed away. The corpse was bloated and discolored, a trickle of red, either blood or red wine, dribbling from the corner of the mouth. Eventually an oxcart appeared, and what was left of old, drunk Benoît was taken back to the village.

There were no formalities such as an autopsy or inquiry. I suppose

17

the mayor wrote out a death certificate and Monsieur l'Abbé presided over a burial somewhere in the churchyard. I spent four happy summer holidays at Lamazière Basse, and when I returned from the fourth, aged twelve, I could pass for French among the French. It was an asset that would later prove extremely useful many times.

That summer of 1948 was the first time I had seen a human corpse. It would not be the last. Not by about fifty thousand.

LEARNING GERMAN

-------◆◆◆-------

My father was a remarkable man. His formal education was from the Chatham Dockyard School, math-oriented, and in what he knew he was largely self-taught. He was not rich or famous or titled. Just a shopkeeper from Ashford. But he had a kindness and a humanity that were noted by everyone who knew him.

At the very end of the war, being a major serving directly under the War Office, he was summoned to London without explanation. In fact it was for a film show, but this one did not star Betty Grable.

With a hundred others, he sat in a darkened hall inside the ministry to see the first films, taken by the army photographic unit, of British soldiers liberating the concentration camp known as Bergen-Belsen. It marked him forever. He told me much later that after five years of war he had not really understood what he and millions of others had been struggling to defeat and destroy until he saw the horrors of Bergen-Belsen. He did not know there could be such cruelty on earth.

My mother told me that he came home, still in uniform, but instead of changing, he stood for two hours in front of the window, staring out, his back to the room, impervious to her pleading to tell her what was wrong. He just stared in silence. Finally he tore himself away from his thoughts, went upstairs to change, instructing her as he passed: "I never want to meet one again. I never want one in my house." He meant Germans.

It did not last. Later, he mellowed, went to Germany, and met and spoke civilly to many Germans. It is a mark of the man that in 1952, when I was thirteen, he decided to send me to live during the school holidays with a German family. He wanted his only son to learn German, to know the country and the people. When my bewildered mother asked him why, he simply said: "Because it must never happen again."

But he would not, by the summer of 1952, have an exchange visit with a German boy, though there were plenty of such offers available. I would go as a paying guest. There was a struggling British–German Friendship Society and I think it was arranged through them. The family chosen farmed outside Göttingen. This time I flew.

Dad had a friend from his army days who had stayed on and was based with the British Army of the Rhine at the British camp at Osnabrück. He saw me off at Northolt aerodrome outside London; the airplane was an elderly Dakota DC, which droned its way across France and Germany to land at the British base there. Father Gilligan, a jovial Irish padre who had been billeted with us in Ashford, was there to meet me. He drove me to Göttingen and handed me over.

It was very strange to be an English boy in Germany back then. I was an oddity. I had had three years of German at prep school, so at least I had a poor smattering of the language, as opposed to my first visit to France four years earlier, when I knew hardly a word of French. The family was very kind and did everything in their power to make me feel at home. It was an uneventful four weeks, of which I recall only one rather strange encounter.

There was a world gliding championship that year, and it was held at a place called Oerlinghausen. We all went off there for a family day out. My host's interest in flying stemmed from the fact that he had been in the Luftwaffe during the war, as an officer but not a flyer.

The huge expanse of grassland was crowded with gliders in a variety of club markings, waiting their turn to be towed into the air. And there were notable pilots, around whom admiring crowds were grouped. One in particular was clearly very famous and the center of attention. And she was a woman, though I had not a clue who she was.

In fact she was Hanna Reitsch, Luftwaffe test pilot and Hitler's personal aviator. If he doted on her, his admiration was as nothing to the adoration she bore for him.

In April 1945, as the Red Army closed in on the surrounded heart of Berlin, and Hitler, drawn and trembling, moped about his bunker under the Reich Chancellery, Hanna Reitsch, at the controls of a Fieseler Storch, a high-wing monoplane with an extremely short landing and takeoff run, flew into the doomed enclave. With amazing skill, she put it down on an avenue in the Charlottenburg Zoo, switched off, and walked through the shell fire to the bunker.

Because of who she was, she was allowed into the final redoubt where, a few days later, Hitler would blow his brains out, and was ushered into the presence. There she begged the man she admired so much to let her fly him out of the Berlin death trap and down to the Berghof, his fortified home at Berchtesgaden in southern Bavaria. There, she urged him, surrounded by SS last-ditch fanatics, the resistance could continue.

Hitler thanked her, but refused. He was determined to die and bring all Germany down to ruin with him. They were not worthy of him, he explained, one notable exception being Hanna Reitsch.

A friend of my host, another veteran of the Luftwaffe, secured our admission into the admiring circle around the ace aviator. She was beaming and shook hands with my host and his wife and their teenage children. Then she turned to me and held out her hand.

That was when my host made a mistake. "Our young house guest," he said. "*Er ist ein Engländer.*"

The smile froze, the hand was withdrawn. I recall a pair of blazing blue eyes and a voice rising in rage. "*Ein Engländer???*" she squawked, and stalked off.

Like my father, it appeared, she had not quite forgotten, either.

BACK TO GERMANY

The following year, 1953, I returned to Germany. The farming family outside Göttingen could not have me back, so I went to stay with Herr Dewald and his wife and children. He was a schoolteacher in Halle, Westphalia.

Back then Germany still seemed like a country under some form of occupation, even though the German Federal Republic had been formed under the chancellorship of Konrad Adenauer in 1949. But the old Germany was divided into East and West, with the capital of West Germany not at Berlin but in Bonn, a small town on the Rhine, chosen because it was Chancellor Adenauer's hometown.

The reason for the impression of occupation was the omnipresence of the NATO forces, which were there not to occupy but to defend; it was NATO that held the line against the expansionist Soviet bloc, which had, until his death in March, been in the grip of the brutal tyrant Joseph Stalin. Westphalia was in the British Zone, which was studded with British Army camps and air bases. This force was simply known as the British Army of the Rhine, and its vehicles could often be seen speeding through the streets. The invasion threat from east of the Iron Curtain was seen as very real.

The eastern third of Germany was behind that Iron Curtain and part of the Soviet empire. It was known as East Germany or, weirdly, the German Democratic Republic. It was very far from being democratic, being a harsh dictatorship with a nominal German Communist government eager to do the bidding of the real masters, the twenty-two divisions of the Red Army and the Soviet embassy. The Western powers retained, by treaty, only one enclave, the encircled West Berlin, stuck eighty miles inside East Germany.

The infamous Berlin Wall, completing the encirclement of West Berlin, would not go up until 1961 to prevent the constant flow of East German graduates pouring out of the technical colleges and universities via West Berlin to seek a better life in West Germany. But the general air of threat after the Berlin Blockade of 1948–49, which nearly sparked World War III, meant that the British Army, far from being resented by the Germans, was much appreciated.

In my own class, I had a more practical use as a guest with a German family. Using my stiff blue passport, I could enter a British base, go to the on-site duty-free shop, and buy real coffee, which, after years of drinking bitter substitutes, ranked with gold dust.

I arrived in Halle after the break for the Easter holidays of British schools, but before that of German schools. As Herr Dewald was a teacher and his children were still at school, it was thought practical that I should attend the German school until its holidays began a fortnight later. Here I was, very much a figure of curiosity, the first Britisher they had ever seen and presumed to have fanged teeth or at least a forked tail. There was considerable mutual relief that we all looked much the same. Both in the Dewald home and at the high school, my German was improving rapidly.

A characteristic of German society that I was introduced to, and that somewhat bewildered me, was the worship of nature, the open countryside. Having been brought up amid the fields and woods of Kent, I pretty much accepted Mother Nature as just being there, with no need to adulate it. But the Germans made great play of going on long walks through it. These were called "Wandering Days." The whole school, age group by age group, would be lined up to go on these country hikes. During the first I ever went on, I noticed something strange.

While a similar group of British kids would simply amble along in an untidy mass, the German children within half a mile had somehow formed themselves into a column, rank upon rank, three abreast. Then the walking slowly transformed, with all the feet coming up and down in unison until we were marching.

This was soon accompanied by singing, specifically a song I can remember sixty years later. It started "Whom God wishes truly to favor He sends out into the wide world to see His miracles in mountain, forest, and field." All good, healthy stuff.

After a while, I noted a stick had gone up into the air at the head of the column, held high so that we could all march behind it. There was no flag, but soon a hat appeared on the stick, like a sort of banner.

We were now deep in the forest, marching down a sandy track behind our leader, singing away, when far ahead a jeep appeared, speeding toward us. It was a British Army vehicle; I could make out the regimental insignia on the front mudguard, and it was clearly not going to stop.

The children broke ranks and jumped to one side to let it pass. It was open-topped, with a redheaded corporal driving and a sergeant beside him. As it swept past, the corporal leaned out and shouted something in a clear East London accent. As the tail disappeared down the track and the sand and dust settled, the German children gathered eagerly around me to ask, "Fritz, what was that the soldier called out to us?" I felt it wise to be diplomatic.

"He said, 'Have a happy Wandering Day,'" I reported.

They were delighted. "Ach, Fritz," I was told, "your British soldiers are so nice."

I had not the heart to tell them what he had really shouted. It was: "Practicing for the next time, are we, lads?"

There is simply no substitute for Cockney humor, and obviously a certain amount of reconciliation was yet to be achieved.

I spent a third vacation with a German family the next year—the Dewalds again—and by 1954 I could pass for a German in Germany. That, too, was to prove extremely useful when, a decade later, I was posted for a year to live in East Berlin and, after shaking my secret police "tail," used to disappear into the heart of East Germany.

LANGUAGES

————◆◆◆————

It is sometimes thought that to speak a foreign language—really speak it rather than just get by with fifty words, a phrase book, and a lot of gestures—it suffices to master grammar and vocabulary. Not so: those are two, but there are, in all, three further aspects to passing unnoticed in a foreign language.

Third, there is the accent. The British are spectacularly useless at mimicking foreign accents, and there is absolutely no substitute for starting young and living with a family in the foreign country involved, with the one proviso that the family should speak hardly a word of the student's language. With English now the common language of virtually the whole world, this is harder and harder. Everyone wants to practice their English.

But after the accent comes the slang. Perfect, academic language is an immediate giveaway—because every people sprinkles its native language with phrases that appear in no dictionary or guidebook and simply cannot be translated word for word. We do not even notice how often we do this, but it is constant. Listen in a crowded bar or at a lively dining table, and it will become clear that in almost every sentence a speaker will use a colloquialism that will never be taught in any language class.

The last aspect is even harder to quantify or imitate. It is the body language. All foreign languages and the speaking of them are accompanied by facial expressions and hand gestures that are probably unique to that language group and are picked up by children as they watch their parents and schoolteachers.

Thus, when in 1951, at the age of thirteen, I went to Tonbridge School to try for a scholarship in modern languages, I recall the senior teacher in French, Mr. A. E. Foster (always known in the absence of political correctness as Frog Foster), sitting in some bemusement, facing a small boy jabbering away in French complete with colloquialisms and gestures. A few days later, Mr. Logie Bruce Lockhart had the same experience in German. I got the scholarship and transferred to the upper school in September.

A year later, having swotted hard at Latin, history, geography, and the hated math and science, I collected my Ordinary Levels, and at fifteen, three Advanced Levels—all in languages.

But Tonbridge, whatever its failings, was academically excellent and, discovering a teacher who had served on the Arctic convoys to Russia and spoke Russian, offered a third language. The choice was Russian or Spanish. I chose Russian on the grounds that it would be much harder than Spanish, which I could learn later.

The summer of 1954 would entail O-Level Russian, and my dad thought some holiday tutelage might help. Somehow he tracked down a pair of Russian princesses in Paris who tutored in Russian and took in young paying guests. Their services were much patronized by the Royal Navy (I think it was a Navy contact who recommended them).

So that spring I was sent over during the school holidays to reside for three weeks at their apartment in Paris.

They were the Princesses Dadiani and they were actually Georgian, but pillars of the White Russian community of Paris. They were completely divorced from planet Earth and charmingly dotty. But huge fun.

Their world had more or less stopped when, in 1921, as the White forces lost the civil war to the Red Soviet army, they were evacuated by their father, the last king of Georgia, and arrived with only a suitcase of jewelry in Paris, which was then teeming with refugees from the Russian aristocracy.

Over thirty years later, they were still convinced that the Georgian people would rise any day, throw off the Soviet yoke, and restore them to their palaces and oil wells. The jewels had lasted about five years—they had no taste for economizing—so after that, they took in paying guests. They had a contract with the Royal Navy, who sent them midshipmen and sub-lieutenants, whom they much favored because the Navy paid promptly and had manners.

Their flat was frequented by counts, dukes, and the occasional prince, who either drove taxis or appeared as artists or singers at the opera. They always appeared to be clearing up after a party or preparing for the next one.

At Easter they took me to High Mass at the extremely impressive Russian Orthodox cathedral, which was then followed by the father and mother of all parties. I was plied with incredibly sweet Russian Easter delicacies and a vodka that felt like an explosion in the pit of the stomach.

It had nothing to do with the stuff in a modern bottle shop. It was thick and viscous, and each slug had to be downed in a single gulp, accompanied by *Christos voskressiya*, or "Christ is risen."

I never recall any formal lessons in Russian. I and the other three young Navy men simply had to pick it up by listening and asking questions. But I recall the princesses with affection. Those three weeks helped me to get O-Level Russian in the summer exams and, years later, to listen to Russians talking in East Berlin while pretending to understand not a word.

And the following year, in the summer of 1955, which was a very busy time, I would have need of their sofa.

A STEP NEARER TO THE STARS

———◆◆◆———

It must have been a small advertisement in one of the flying magazines that I spent much time devouring, but I do not now recall which one. It introduced me to a new scheme being offered by the Royal Air Force—the concept of the RAF Flying Scholarship. The idea was that if you could pass all the tests, the RAF would pay for a young enthusiast to go to his local flying club and learn to fly to private pilot's license level. Of course, I applied at once. That was in spring 1955.

The RAF had no intention of wasting its money subsidizing young men with defective eyesight or other flaws that meant they would never fly anyway. The point was to help eager youngsters develop the flying bug and later join up. The first thing that arrived at my parental home in Ashford was a small buff envelope requiring me to attend a thorough medical examination at RAF Hornchurch, a base in Essex. There was also a rail pass.

If I thought the tests would involve just a few minutes with a stethoscope on the chest or some taps to the kneecap, I was much mistaken. Hornchurch was a five-day residential course designed to pull you to pieces and see if the tiniest flaw could be detected. I arrived with a small suitcase, changed into boxer shorts and overalls, presuming myself to be impeccably fit, and then they got started.

For two days, it was just the physical. One after another, young applicants who were not there for the scholarship but, older than I was, were trying to get accepted for flying training, were sent home, disappointed. The medics and the opticians discovered color-blindness, lack of night vision, farsightedness, myopia, or some other eye defect that the applicant had lived with and never suspected.

Others had a shadow on the lungs, fallen arches in the feet, something wrong somewhere, something less than a hundred percent. Day three was dedicated to reflexes, reaction speed to emergencies, dexterity, hand-eye coordination. Day four was for initiative exercises. Two white lines on the parade ground to represent a chasm. Some poles, ropes, and an oil drum. Get the team safely over the gulf.

The last day was interviews in the morning, with time left over to go home in the afternoon. I kept quiet about the languages, for fear they would accept me but for the education branch or even intelligence. Three officers, two with wings on the chest. Bored stiff. All right, lad. Why do you want to fly?

For heaven's sake. Why did I want to lose my virginity? Because it sounded fun and I was sixteen and life was racing by. But no humor, please. Not in front of a board of officers. So serious answers and an assurance that I had been mad about flying since being plonked into a Spitfire cockpit at the age of five. Several raised eyebrows and one amused grin. Several trick questions about modern fighter planes, which I could answer easily, because I had been studying them for years.

Yes, sir, I had been at Farnborough that day when John Derry, at the controls of the prototype de Havilland 110, had plunged into the hillside. No more grins; some serious sideways glances, but approving. Then dismissed. Cannot salute; no flat hat. But I would have one someday.

Five days later, another buff envelope. Report to RAF Kenley to be kitted out with a flying suit, boots, a leather helmet. Then start at Blue Bell Hill Flying Club, Rochester, in June. One technical problem: school started in May. I could do it, but I needed transport.

Dad came to the rescue again. He bought me a secondhand Douglas Vespa scooter. It was British-built, licensed from the Italian Vespa company, and it was a load of rubbish. It had a kick-start pedal and would cough for fifty kicks before sparking into life. Still, it was my first motorized transport. With a learner's license and a red L-plate front and back, it was legal on the road. Dad ran me to Blue Bell Hill to get introduced and see what I would be learning on.

It was a silver Tiger Moth, a biplane like something out of the First World War, and the standard workhorse of flying schools back then. Open cockpit, a speaking tube to communicate with the instructor, wind-in-the-hair sort of stuff. Marvelous, intoxicating. The only problem was Tonbridge School. The authorities there had already made plain my passion for flying was juvenile madness. I would never get permission. So I got a shed instead.

Of course it was not on school grounds. It was down in Tonbridge town, on one of those small gardens called allotments, leased for a peppercorn rent by the municipality to those with no garden but who wished to raise their own vegetables. The kindly gardener allowed me to keep the Vespa in it, out of sight and out of the rain.

Back at Parkside for what I hoped would be my last term, I had no more exams to pass, so I was put down for GCE S Levels. The S stood for state scholarship, but it was a forlorn hope. State scholarships were means-tested, and my father could now afford university fees without state help, so it would never be awarded. But no one wanted me hanging idly around. Actually I had another exam in mind—my private pilot's license. But I would not take that until August 26, the day after my seventeenth birthday. Still, I had thirty hours of prepaid flying tuition waiting for me up at Rochester and could certainly not wait for school to break up. So I amazed Parkside by becoming a cross-country runner.

Until then I had loathed cross-country running, usually awarded as a punishment for some misdemeanor, or practiced by those stringy youths who resembled stick insects. I was still short and stocky and would not start to shoot up until the next year. I regarded cross-country as pure misery. Yet I suddenly started volunteering for it, and not just the five-mile junior run but the eight-mile senior cross. My one condition: I would run alone.

So, twice a week I would don white shorts and a spotless T-shirt and jog out the gates to the street. It took fifteen minutes to get to the allotment shed, where I would put on the canvas flying suit, boots, and leather helmet. Thus disguised, I could putter past the school gates and out on the highway to Blue Bell Hill and its flying club.

After six hours' dual instruction, I went solo and experienced the intoxication of flying free, high over the winding Medway, looking down on Rochester and its towering medieval cathedral. Up there I could roll and twist among the clouds, turning, climbing, diving, ripping off the helmet, keeping only the goggles to protect the eyes.

In my boyish imagination, I was over the fields of Flanders, circa 1916, in formation with Bishop, Ball, Mannock, and McCudden, with a cheery wave for the French aces Guynemer and Garros, hunting for the Germans Von Richthofen, Boelcke, and Immelmann. I had read all about them, researched their stories, their victories, and, one by one, their deaths. By the end of school term, I had logged twenty-seven of my permitted thirty hours, saving three for the final tests at the end of August.

Parkside never solved the riddle of the cross-country running schoolboy. The bullying ebbed away, as there were now other new boys to persecute. The caning continued. I think I managed to collect seventy-four strokes from the rattan cane over my three and a half years, always administered to me in the bending position, my head under a table, protected only by thin pajamas.

I never contrived to develop those strange deviances so often attributed to the English, but only two things in their place: the ability to take pain in silence and a contempt for harsh and arbitrary authority.

Summer term ended in July 1955. Blue Bell Hill promised to welcome me back for the flying tests in late August. Meanwhile, one of my few mates at Parkside, John Gordon, and I decided to hitchhike from Newhaven on the Sussex coast across France to Ventimiglia on the Italian border, via the length of the Côte d'Azur. John was fifteen to my sixteen. We thought it might be an adventure. It was.

A LONG HIKE

Hitchhiking is rare nowadays, but back in 1955, for a youngster with no money, it was common. Middle-aged men, mindful of their own impecunious teenage years, would take pity on the figure by the roadside with right fist extended, thumb erect, slow down, pull over, and ask the face appearing in the passenger window where he was heading.

National Servicemen in their uniforms, heading home to Mum and Dad with a weekend pass or struggling back to camp, could usually expect some help. Most middle-aged men had once done it themselves. John Gordon and I, though we did not know it, had an even bigger advantage than a uniform.

John had an aunt who lived in Cooden, close to the Sussex coast and not far from Newhaven. There was a ferry across to Dieppe. I ran down to Cooden on the Vespa and the aunt took us to Newhaven the following morning for the first ferry. We had two return tickets and a very tiny budget.

We firmly expected to sleep rough in sheds, outbuildings, and even ditches, and eat the cheapest of foods, probably bread and cheese. We were in tough hiking boots, short khaki drill pants, knee-high socks, and canvas shirts. Those, plus a haversack. I had taken the precaution of tacking a Union Jack onto the back of my rucksack. We would march in single file, with me at the rear so that motorists coming up behind could see it clearly. It turned out to be the game changer.

By midmorning, we were out of the Dieppe ferry terminal and heading for the highway to Paris when a car swerved up behind, tooted, and a voice asked—in French, of course—where we were heading. I replied in French, and within seconds the haversacks were in the boot. John telescoped into the rear seat and I was beside the driver, answering his question as to how I spoke such fluent French. Then we learned the reason for the rapid pickup.

In 1944, only eleven years before our hiking jaunt, the Allied armies curved out of Normandy and proceeded to liberate France. The British and Canadians turned north for Holland and Belgium, passing through all of northern France. Anyone over twenty-five would clearly have remembered the German occupation and the liberation. It was the British flag that did it.

There were no motorways back then, just the usual Route Nationale, narrow and winding, with one traffic lane on each side and occasionally a central and pretty lethal overtaking lane, disputed by cars approaching each other at a hundred miles an hour. It was encouraging if the driver would stop looking sideways and keep his eyes on the road ahead. In three rapid lifts, I believe we made it to Paris ahead of the boat train.

Once in the city, we took the Metro and arrived unannounced at the flat of the Princesses Dadiani. Completely unfazed, as if teenage hitchhikers were always turning up at their door, the lovely ladies welcomed us in and gave us supper. At ten, I parked John on the sofa and went back into the night.

I had worked out that there was a very long haul from Paris south to Marseille and there was one way that, if it worked, would be a terrific way of covering the distance in a single day. Every day, thousands of trucks—big snorting rigs with trailers we would now call juggernauts—brought fruit and vegetables from the subtropical south, the Midi, to replenish the stomach of Paris. And then they went back empty.

The gigantic fresh-produce market they made for was in the district called Les Halles, long since moved to the outer suburbs. But then it was right at the heart of Paris, a square kilometer of sheds and warehouses, blazing with light and activity through the night, its bars, restaurants, and bistros the haunt of the workers and the social night owls. I began to inquire and had no luck.

I went from café to café, asking perfectly politely if anyone was a truck driver heading south in the morning. The answer was always no, until the proprietors chased me out for not spending anything. Then I got a tap on the shoulder from someone who had followed me out to the pavement.

It was a small and scruffy market worker, an Algerian, who said he had a friend who was exactly what I sought and who was sleeping at his small flat a few hundred yards away. I should follow him and he would lead me there. Like a fool, I fell for it.

The streets became narrower and dirtier, mere alleys between blocks of slum. Finally he led me through a door and up one flight of stairs. He unlocked his own bed-sitter and gestured me inside. The filthy little room was empty. I turned. He had closed the door and locked it. He gave me a snaggle-toothed smile and gestured at the grubby bed.

I reckoned there was not much point in calling for help. This was obviously not that kind of community. I shook my head. He gestured again, adding in French, "Pants down, over the bed." I just said, "*Non.*"

He ceased smiling, fumbled at his flies, and produced his penis. It was semi-tumescent. He repeated his instruction.

I am not homophobic but just have a personal aversion to sodomy. I repeated "*Non*" and then added, "I'm leaving." Then he produced a knife. It was a lock knife that needed two hands to open it. The blade was curved; I assumed it was used mainly for cutting fruit. But it would do just as well on a human body.

By great good fortune, my father, several years before, when I used to camp out in the fields of Kent, had given me a hunting knife, horn-handled, with seven inches of Toledo-steel blade. It was for paunching and skinning rabbits brought down with my air rifle, for cutting twigs for the campfire, or trimming branches for a hide.

I was carrying it horizontally across the small of my back. I fumbled under my shirt. The Algerian thought I was loosening my belt. When the hunting knife came out, his eyes widened and he came forward.

There was a scuffle—quite short, really. A few seconds and it was over. I found myself in the doorway, the door open, my hand on the handle. The market porter's knife was on the floor. He had sustained a long gash to the right bicep, about which he was making rather a fuss. In Arabic. I saw little point in waiting around in case he had friends elsewhere in the flophouse, so legged it down the stairs and out into the alley.

The incident was not entirely without benefit, because on my way back to the streetlights, I came across what I needed, a sort of elephants' graveyard; row after row of parked juggernauts, waiting for the dawn. The drivers were saving their overnight allowances by bedding down in their cabs. I found one relieving himself against the rear wheel of his truck, and when he had finished, approached him with my problem. He thought it over.

"It's not allowed," he said. "Company policy, no hitchhikers. It's more than my job's worth."

But again, luck cut in. He was from Marseille, which had never been occupied by the Germans. But his wife was from the north and her father had been in the Resistance in Amiens. He was in jail, destined for execution, when Group Captain Pickard led his Mosquitoes on the Amiens jail raid. They had ripped open the cell block with precision bombing and destroyed the outer wall. His father-in-law had escaped and was still alive.

"I'll have to lock you in for the whole trip," he said. "If we are caught, you say you stowed away during the night while I slept. Agreed? OK, be back here at six."

It was still dark at six, but the graveyard was slowly stirring. Our new friend cleared a space at the rear of the trailer, near the door, piling the empty crates further to the front to create a cubbyhole about eight feet by eight. Once John and I were curled up inside, he locked the doors and went to his cab. By six thirty, we were rolling.

There was a distinctive odor to the crates that had once contained his cargo. Melons. At seven, in the southern suburbs, the sun rose. By eight, we were out on the Route Nationale Eight, heading for Marseille, eleven hours away. By nine, it was getting hot; by ten, it was a small furnace. By eleven, the melon smell had become an overpowering stench. John was as white as a sheet and complaining of advancing nausea. By midday, he was on his knees by the door trying to deposit what remained of his Russian supper through the crack where the doors joined the floor. The stench of the melons joined that of human puke in a heady cocktail.

There was no way to contact the driver, way up front in his cabin. At one, he pulled into a roadside halt for fuel and lunch, but with other drivers milling around, he did not approach the trailer or let us out. After half an hour, he resumed the run south, but we had not a clue where we were and John was very sick indeed. He had ceased bringing up and was just moaning.

At first he thought he was going to die, and then feared he wouldn't. I was lucky in having a fairly strong stomach, whether for open boats on an angry sea or journeys by road. And I had just spent June throwing a Tiger Moth all over the sky above Rochester. Our misery ended around six p.m., when the truck pulled onto a wayside lay-by and we were let out.

John retired to the verge to put his head in his hands. I produced a map of France from my haversack, and the driver pointed out where we were. South of Avignon, but north of Marseille. I thanked him profusely, we shook hands, and he left, presumably to head for his melon farm and a large bucket of disinfectant.

But such is the recovery of the young that within half an hour we were up and marching along the verge. By eight, as the sun set, we had found a farm with a friendly barn full of straw and hay. Despite being ravenously hungry, we collapsed in the bales and slept for ten hours.

On the following day, we discovered as we marched, rigid thumbs erect for a lift, that the Union Jack did not work anymore. The Midi had never been occupied. It was part of Vichy France, notorious for its enthusiastic collaboration with the Germans. Even the Allied invasion of August 1944 was seen locally as an assault rather than a liberation. No cars stopped. We turned along the coast at Marseille, and for three weeks, thousands of cars, vans, and trucks sped by without stopping.

We lived off crusty baguette bread and cheap cheese, slaking our thirst and filling our water bottles at the public drinking fountains in the villages. There was no Corniche Littorale motorway (where hitch-hiking would have been forbidden, anyway), but just the shoreside road that wended through every village and hamlet as well as the great cities of Toulon, Nice, and Cannes.

Marching along it, we found tiny non-tourist bays and creeks, where we could strip off and dunk our overheated bodies in crystal-clear cool water. We slept in the workers' sheds in the olive groves and once on the cool marble of a mausoleum in a cemetery. We saw the grandeur of Monaco and Monte Carlo, where all the cars seemed to be Rolls-Royces and where I would many years later be the guest of Prince Albert. Finally, we came to the Italian border at Ventimiglia.

Just to say we had been to Italy, we went across and trudged to San Remo. Then time and money ran out. We had just enough for two third-class tickets back to Marseille, and there we bought just one single ticket for Paris. We spent the whole journey in the lavatory. Three times, a ticket inspector came to the door and rapped. Each time, I opened a fraction, explained in French that I was not very well and had the ticket clipped. Each time, John stood on the lavatory seat behind the door and out of sight.

We hitched back to Dieppe and used our return halves to get to Newhaven. No mobile phones back then, so we used a public phone booth and four one-penny coins to alert John's aunt to our presence, and then waited to be collected.

We were very brown and rock-hard. We had each grown an inch, and still, in old age, laugh at some of the tricks we got up to. The fifties were a good, carefree, and uncomplicated time to be a teenager, before drugs and worries and political correctness. Materially, we had infinitely less than what youngsters have today, but I think we were happier.

A few years back, a friend from the same generation—one of the teenagers of National Service, who got by with very few rules and regulations, minimal bureaucracy, basic but healthy food, good manners, and masses of walking—remarked to me: "You know, we had the best of the last and the last of the best." And that got it all in a single sentence.

But it was mid-August and I wanted something badly. I wanted that private pilot's license. So the day after my seventeenth birthday, I Vespa-ed back to Rochester Flying Club.

And since that holiday, John Gordon has never been able to contemplate a melon, and I have never carried a blade.

A SILLY REVENGE

The flying test was almost a routine. Everything about it had already been covered during tuition.

First came a triangular navigation exercise in which I had to give a running commentary to the instructor in the front cockpit, describing what I was doing and why. The technology for nav exercises in a Tiger Moth was basic and there were two. They were called eyeballs.

A map had already been prepared, with the route marked in felt pen, folded, and strapped with elastic bands to my left thigh. Identification of where one was could be achieved by putting my head over the rim of the cockpit and looking down. Location and direction depended on recognizing main roads, railway lines, and above all rivers, with their distinctive curves. Towns and cities were identified by castle, cathedral, or other obvious features.

There was one elderly member of the club who was so nearsighted that he used to swoop down to fly alongside railway trains and read the destination board on the side of the front carriage. One imagines commuters might be somewhat surprised to lift their gaze from the crossword to see a biplane outside the window and an old codger peering down at them. But no one seemed to mind. It was a rather carefree age.

After the nav test, we repaired to the clubhouse for a sandwich lunch, then did the general competence hour. This involved the usual basic maneuvers—climb, dive, turn, wingover, sideslip, and several pretended emergencies. The routine was for the instructor to suddenly shut down the power and say, "You have a complete engine failure. What are you going to do?"

The response was to look around for a large, flat green field away from woods, large trees, or buildings; with the landing field selected, assess wind direction and speed; glide down behind the idly turning propeller; line up as if for a real landing; and approach the unwary farmer's best wheat crop. At the last minute, the instructor would ram the power back on and the Tiger Moth would surge upward and away.

Landing back at Blue Bell Hill, I was told that I had passed and my license would be "in the bag." The written test, a two-hour paper exam, I had completed before going to France. But I noticed that of my thirty hours of flying time so generously prepaid by the RAF, there were still forty-five minutes left. I asked for them as a last solo flight, and, with a shrug, was granted them. There was something else I wanted to do.

Tonbridge town was easy to find by following the river Medway, which flows right through it. Short of the town, I dropped down into the shallow valley between the school playing fields and Hildenborough, through which I had pretended to jog so many times.

I came up out of the valley and approached over the two playing fields known as Martins and Le Flemings. I think I was about six feet up. There was a quick blip to clear the line of elms between Le Flemings and the first X1 cricket pitch, the sacred turf of the Head. Then the school buildings were ahead of me: School House, where the headmaster lived, and Old Big School, the big assembly hall.

The school was still on holiday and therefore empty of boys, or, at that hour on a summer afternoon, they would have been playing cricket on the Head. A face appeared at a window in School House, staring openmouthed at the approaching propeller. It might have been the headmaster, the kindly but ineffectual Reverend Laurence Waddy, but I was never later in a position to ask.

The owner of the face threw himself to the floor as the Tiger Moth climbed the wall of the Old Big School, nearly clipped the roof, rolled to the north, missed the pepper pot on the chapel roof by a few feet, and climbed away into a clear blue sky.

Having completed my asinine gesture to a place I was yearning to leave, I flew back to Rochester, hoping no sharp-eyed citizen of Tonbridge had noted my registration number and reported me, for then I would have been finished.

School would reconvene in a fortnight, and to please my father I had agreed to complete the last term of the year and leave at Christmas. At the start of term, I half expected to be summoned to report to the headmaster, but no one said a thing.

A fortnight later, my private pilot's license arrived from the ministry at my parents' home in Ashford. I mailed my flying kit back to RAF Kenley and have never flown a Tiger Moth since, until I was given a ride and the controls at the age of seventy-six at Lasherden airfield in Kent. And she is still a great little airplane.

A GENTLEMAN OF CLARE

When I returned to Tonbridge in early September 1955, I thought I faced a term of filling in time. The previous summer, I had fulfilled my wager with my father whereby if I could pass every exam they could throw at me, he would get me out of there. With great luck, I had managed my O Levels at fourteen and my A Levels at fifteen, about three years earlier than required. In this, my fluent French and German, provided by the prescience of my parents, had been invaluable.

In summer term 1955, I had at sixteen sat for a state scholarship, or S Level. I think I passed, but state scholarships were means-tested and it was judged that my parents could put me through university unaided by the state, so no scholarship was awarded. But Dad did not want to be the only shopkeeper on Ashford High Street whose son left school at sixteen, so he begged me to stay on the extra term and leave at seventeen. I agreed, but idleness was not exactly what Tonbridge had in mind.

My obsession with warplanes and flying magazines brought nothing but frowns, and I was soon required to attend a long interview with a gentleman from the Public Schools Appointments Bureau, who came down for a day to look over the winter leavers. He was genial enough, a bit of a Colonel Blimp type, and he sought to interest me in becoming "something in the City."

Eyes alight with enthusiasm, he proposed an interview with Shell-BP or a major bank. There might even be an opening as a stockbroker. There was no point in protesting. I feigned enthusiasm, took his numerous career brochures, and slipped away. But I had fooled no one. Strings were pulled in the background, and I was secured an interview at Clare College, Cambridge. With the master, no less. For my schoolmasters, this was close to a visit to Parnassus.

I was furnished with a rail warrant to London and another from London to Cambridge, return. I set off, crossed London by bus, arrived at Cambridge station, and walked to Clare College, nestling by the River Cam, and presented myself at the appointed hour. I was in school uniform, but without the absurd straw boater, which I had been allowed not to wear. A porter showed me up to the master's study.

The luminary behind the desk was studying a file. It appeared to be about me. He clucked several times, raised his head, and beamed.

"Still sixteen," he said. "Fluent in two languages and conversational in Russian. Sounds like the Foreign Office."

It was not a question, so I said nothing. Undeterred, his beam never faltered.

"So, do you want to try for the Foreign Office, young man?"

"No, Master."

"Ah, well, never mind. So why do you want to come to Clare?"

There are times when dissimulation has no point and straight-up honesty is the best policy. I decided this was one.

"Actually, Master, I don't."

This time, the beam did falter. It was replaced not by anger but by an intrigued puzzlement.

"Then what are you doing here?"

"Tonbridge sent me, Master."

"Yes, I see that." He gestured at the file on his desk, which had clearly preceded me. "In that case, what do you want to do when you leave school?"

"I am going to join the Air Force, Master. I want to be a fighter pilot."

He rose and came round the desk, the seraphic beam back in place. He wrapped an arm around my shoulders and guided me back to the door, which he opened.

"Then may I wish you the very best of good fortune. And thank you."

The good wishes were agreeable, but . . .

"Why 'thank you,' Master?"

"Because, young man, you have just given me the shortest and most honest interview I have ever had in this room."

I made my way back to the station, thence to London and on to Tonbridge. A week later, his report arrived, and I went under a very large and very black cloud. But tenacity is a rather British trait, and Tonbridge certainly had it. They sent for my father.

I was not in the room, but he told me about it later. There were four of them: the headmaster (whose summer repose I had ruined), my housemaster, the head of studies, and the chaplain. He said it was like a summons to the high court. They were all in their scholastic robes, graduates of Oxford and Cambridge. The shopkeeper they confronted came from Chatham Dockyard and they knew it.

The lecture was not hostile but deeply earnest. His son, they told him, was making a grievous mistake. Brilliant exam results stemming from an expensive education. The sort of background that could one day, after two more years at Tonbridge, result in an exhibition, possibly even an open major, to Oxford or Cambridge. A first-class degree could open the doors to the Civil Service. Why, his son might even be able to return as a junior master at Tonbridge, something they clearly regarded as the pinnacle of achievement.

And in the face of all this, the lad had some weird dream of becoming little more than a mechanic. It was all very *infra dignitatem*—beneath one's dignity, a Latin phrase my dad had never heard.

In the raging snobbery of those days, it seemed that Dartmouth College (Royal Navy) or Royal Military Academy Sandhurst (Army, good regiment, of course) was just acceptable, but volunteering for boot camp, RAF, was distinctly bizarre. It was his (my father's) clear duty to do everything in his power to dissuade his son from avoiding those last two years at school and inexplicably declining to go to Cambridge.

My dad heard them out, one after the other. Then he spoke very briefly. He said, "Gentlemen, if my son wants to become a British fighter pilot, I intend to give him every conceivable support and encouragement of which I am able. Good day to you."

Then he left, drove back to Ashford, and reopened his shop. He was a great man. I left school that December, still under a cloud.

LEARNING SPANISH

Even over the Christmas break, my father had made plain that, at seventeen and three months, I would have no chance of getting into the Royal Air Force when the permissible age was eighteen. I would be wise to wait until I was at least seventeen and a half before trying.

He also made plain he was not having me mooning about the house doing nothing. Some activity had to be found to fill in the first three months of 1956. We made a study of the terms of the scholarship I had won five years earlier to Tonbridge. Founded by the long-gone Mr. Knightly, the Knightly Scholarship involved a large sum of deposited money that, with sound investment, should (and did) generate enough to create one bursary per year. But if there was a surplus, it would be lodged in a separate fund.

This extra fund could, with the permission of the governors, be used to allow a student to study an extra language during his last year at school. It did not insist that he must be at the school to do this. I made an application to be allowed to take a course in Spanish, with costs paid for by the fund.

The bemused governors, who had never received such an application, found the fund was brimming from so many years of non-use and needed depleting. A little more research disclosed that Granada University in Andalusia, in southern Spain, offered a three-month spring course for foreigners to study Spanish language and culture. Again, the governors conceded the point and paid the course fee, plus a personal allowance of six pounds per week while away from home. In early January, I left for Spain.

The course was not actually held in Granada, but at Málaga, on the coast. Back then the sprawling city of modern Málaga was just a seaside town famous for two things. Before the war (the Spanish Civil War, the conflict that still consumed Spain), the matador Carlos Arruza had performed in the Málaga ring, while suffering from flu and a raging temperature, a *corrida* so spectacular that he had been awarded two ears, the tail, and one hoof from the dead bull, a feat never matched since.

And Pablo Picasso, who was still alive and painting, but in exile in France after bitterly opposing Franco and painting *Guernica*, had been born there. If it had an airport, it must have been a small municipal field and not on any international route. I flew to Gibraltar, hefted my suitcase across the border on foot, and took the wheezing old coastal bus from La Linea to Málaga. In Gibraltar, I exchanged all the sterling pounds I had into pesetas at the remarkable rate of two hundred to one pound. I did not know enough to realize that I had become a wealthy young man by Spanish standards.

What today is the sprawling Costa del Sol chain of tourist resorts did not exist. Between Málaga and La Linea were four small fishing villages: Torremolinos, Fuengirola, Marbella, and Estepona. Today's huge motorway was a narrow track, with one lane on each side. But as the verges were very pitted, every driver rode the center line, swerving at the last minute with much hooting, shouting, and gestures. I was entering a very different and fascinating new culture.

At Málaga, I reported to the local branch of Granada University and met the course director, Don Andres Oliva. He was truly cultivated, a real traditional *caballero*, a gent. I quickly learned that the fifty or so students on the course were all to be lodged in one communal hostel. It became also rapidly plain that as they were Americans, Canadians, British, Germans, Danes, Swedes, and others, they would all have one common language—English. And that was what would be used in the hostel. But that was not what I had come for. I wanted to lodge with a Spanish family that spoke no English, and took my problem to Don Andres.

He considered it with quiet but surprised approval, remarked that no one had ever requested this before, but promised to ask around. Twenty-four hours later, he told me he had found a family content to take in a paying guest.

The lady concerned was Doña Concha Lamotte, Viuda de Morales. When deciphered, that meant Madame Concepcion (or Conchita or Concha) Lamotte, Viuda (widow) of the late Señor Morales. It transpired she was French by birth but in the thirties had married Señor Morales. He had been executed by the Communists during the civil war, and his widow had raised her two children alone.

Not surprisingly, she loathed the Communists and adored General Franco, who in 1936 had landed with his Moroccan troops just down the coast to start the civil war as the Republic fell into Communist hands. Franco, of course, was by 1956 dictator of Spain, running a pretty extreme right-wing government.

I took my grip and walked from the hostel to the Lamotte apartment beside the old Miramar Hotel, and introduced myself. My lodging was three pounds per week, but Spain then was so extraordinarily cheap that the other three pounds of my weekly allowance would be more than enough pocket money. I would have a room of my own and eat all meals with the family.

Madame's children were her son, at seventeen the same age as me while also awaiting his call-up into the armed forces, and her daughter, two years older and engaged to be married. They spoke not a word of English and had never seen an Englishman, let alone a Protestant. I spoke no Spanish, but I had a grammar primer, and mercifully Madame could just remember her native French and help me out when we got really stuck.

Málaga back then was still a sleepy, quaint, and intensely traditional community. Each evening, the girls of the respectable classes not yet "spoken for" would slowly parade the length of the palm-lined *paseo*, duly chaperoned by a mother or aunt. From the sidelines, they could be observed by the young men not yet engaged. It was a marriage market of great decorum.

The girls would have high ivory combs in their hair, draped with a black lace shawl, the *mantilla*. The young men often wore the short jacket, the *traje corto*, and the wide-brimmed black or dove-gray hat known as the *cordobés*.

If or when a young man saw a girl he really fancied, he would ask around for her name. When he had it, he would go to his father, who would then inquire about the girl's own father, and if he was also of a respectable family in a good house and with a worthy profession, the two fathers would meet to confer over a possible union of their offspring. There was no question of the youngsters meeting for a chat.

The girl's father would then invite the young man to his house for tea. As tea was served, the girl's mother and possibly a bevy of aunts, all agog with curiosity, would sit with the girl on one side of the room, and the young guest and his father on the other. It must have been a very stilted occasion, with all sides pretending it was just a cup of neighborly tea.

In fact, both sides were sizing up the other. Courtship was carried on with the eyes. The young people never touched. If impressions were favorable, the father would later consult with his wife and invite the boy to join them for Mass the following Sunday.

While he had seen her during the *paseo* when she caught his eye, that first stilted cup of tea would be for the girl her first sight of her new admirer. Her curiosity must have been immense. My new friend Miguel Morales told me all this because he had been through it via his sister.

As chastity was total, there had to be some release valve, and this was the bordello, of which there were many. At the top of the range, these were also pretty dignified establishments. It was far from impossible for the mayor and the chief of police to take a glass of sherry with a leading madam, who was also a pillar of the community (not to consort with wives, of course) and a donor to good causes such as the church and the orphanage, to which her girls, if they were careless, might one day contribute.

From a vantage point sixty years later, it is hard to imagine all this, but that was the way it was. The chief of police was not run ragged by overwork, because crime was very rare and violent crime just about unheard of. The occasional knife fight might take place among the Gypsies, or *gitanos*, who lived in a camp out of town and who made a living either tending horses or giving demonstrations of flamenco at private soirées, or in cafés with a hat passed round. And that was before the gawping tourists arrived.

To get in trouble with the police, a troublemaker would really have to work at it, but political opposition was a serious concern, and police tolerance was nonexistent. But that seemed to be the way the people liked it. They had experienced four years of war and cruelty in the late thirties when the Phalangists (Fascists) fought the Communists, and they did not want it back.

Life was cheap, the prices minimal. For ten pesetas, one could have two large schooners of fine sherry, attended by enough free tapas to constitute a good dinner.

The scholastic course was 160 lectures. I attended the first in January and the last at the end of March. I would have missed that as well, but for the fact that a foreign student peered at me nursing a large bumper of amontillado at a café table on the day before and asked me if I was the missing English student. Then she told me about the final exam the following day.

Without a hope of passing it, I showed up and met an amused and sardonic Don Andres Oliva. I noticed something quite quickly. The hostel students spoke a grammatically perfect but stilted and awfully accented Spanish. I was rattling away in torrents of street Spanish with an Andalusian accent. Don Andres had to exercise all his self-control not to burst out laughing.

The examination turned out to be one single essay in Spanish on a subject of the student's choosing, drawn from the five headings of the language, literature, culture, geography, and history of Spain. And there I had a problem. I did not know anything about any of them. So I chose history.

But that proposed a further problem. Recalling our history lessons at school, it appeared that every time British and Spanish history made contact, we were fighting each other, especially in 1588. That was when King Philip II sent his Armada up the English Channel to invade and subdue the heretical Protestant English. The Devonian sea dog Francis Drake, a former pirate along the Spanish Main off Central

America, was instrumental in the Spanish fleet's destruction. It was not very diplomatic, but it was the only story I knew that involved a bit of Spanish history. If only I could have stuck to the conquistadors.

Legend has it that when the sails of the Armada hove over the horizon, Drake was on the expanse of greensward outside Plymouth known as Plymouth Hoe playing bowls. He is supposed to have told those who came to warn him that he would finish his game before taking on the might of Spain.

Then arose the third problem. They play *boules* in France, virtually the same thing, but no bowls in Spain. So, despite all the Spanish I had learned, I did not know how to say "bowls." The exam markers must have been somewhat bewildered to be told that when the Armada appeared, Francis Drake was playing with his balls.

Anyway, these Andalusian scholars must have been intensely tolerant, for five days later they actually gave me a diploma in Hispanic studies. At the inevitable sherry party, I protested to Don Andres that it was wholly unmerited. He smiled somewhat sadly and said, "Frederico, mine is not a rich country. We need these foreign course fees. So when you get home, please tell everyone what good value this course is."

And I did. At least, I wrote to the governors of Tonbridge to recommend the Granada University's Málaga course as an excellent avenue for future holders of the Knightly Scholarship to perfect their Spanish. But after the reception, I had to leave, because my father had arrived with my mother in tow, was lodged in the Marbella Club Hotel, and wanted to see me.

It was all because someone else, a neighbor from Ashford, had perchance seen me imbibing sherry, again in the heat of the day, at a street café. He had asked me what I had been doing and, being a bit lightheaded from the sherry and the blazing sun, I told him. He had scurried back to his hotel and rung Ashford with the news. That was what brought my parents on the next plane to Gibraltar.

I had not spent the middle 158 lectures sitting drinking sherry. After my arrival in January, I investigated what I had really come for. Bullfighting.

During my last year at school, I had come across and devoured Ernest Hemingway's classic *Death in the Afternoon*, and had become fascinated by this brutal but incredibly testosterone-fueled spectacle on the sand of the arena beneath a glaring sun: a lethal pitting of a man against half a ton of truly wild animal. I had followed up Hemingway with Ibáñez's *Blood and Sand* and various other books. And I was determined to see it.

In Spain, winter is the close-down season for the *corrida*—which simply means "the running." But in the deep south, it is still warm and sunny even in January, February, and March—or it used to be. That was the time for the *novilladas*.

A fighting bull suitable for a full-fledged *corrida* is usually five years old. Until he trots out of the dark pen beneath the stands for his last twenty minutes on earth, he has led an idyllic life roaming free on the vast ranches with a herd of lady friends and all the lush grass he can eat. Not for him a miserable abattoir at barely a year old. But he is emphatically not sweet-tempered.

Any talk that a fighting bull has to be provoked to charge is nonsense. He will charge at anything not on four legs. That is why the *vaqueros* on the ranches have to be mounted. Any human descending to the ground on two legs is committing suicide. Because the bull is nearsighted and sees in monochrome, it is not the "red" that he is charging, but the cape, flickering and taunting him. When he has hit it and felt no impact, he turns and charges again. And again. If the matador remains motionless beside the cape in his hands, he should get away with it. Some do, some don't, because those huge horns are absolutely deadly.

While it is still a calf, or *becerro*, the bull will probably be tested once and briefly so that it does not remember later what happened. The point is to see if, when taunted by a cape, it will run straight and true or turn away. If the latter, then it will be for the knackers' yard. But if it charges, it will go back to the ranch to spend four more years coming to full maturity.

But at three it is called a *novillo*, and in the deep south, *corridas* featuring only *novillos* take place. They are mainly for young matadors who have not yet graduated to the great summer festivals. These are what I wanted to see in Málaga. The *novillo* may not be as big as a five-year-old, but he is still a very dangerous brute. When I made inquiries at Málaga's famous bullring for the spring program, I discovered something interesting. There was a training school there as well. I signed up at once.

Basically, it was under the tutelage of a retired matador with a heavy limp. He had stopped one horn too many and his hip had never healed. This did not prevent him teaching, because the matador is not supposed to run around much anyway.

The school met in the mornings, out on the sand of the arena, beneath the empty stands: about half a dozen young aspirants with hopes of one day starring in the big festivals of Granada, Seville, or Madrid. A teenager could still look up and imagine those stands thronged with swooning señoritas and hear the clang of the *paso doble* and the roared *olé*s that greet an impressive passage of capework. Then Don Pepe ended the daydreaming and introduced us to the two capes: the *capa* and the *muleta*.

The *capa* came first, a heavy canvas semicircle, magenta on one side and yellow on the other. The surprising weight of the *capa* explains why matadors have immensely strong wrists. The *muleta*, a smaller bright scarlet cloth splayed on a sword and a wooden stick, used only for the third and last section of the encounter, would come later.

There was of course no real bull. They are expensive and not to be wasted on apprentices. The contraption that charged was a construction of two wheels on a frame. At the front of the frame was a set of two real horns from a long-dead Miura, fearsome artifacts about a yard wide, each with needle tips that would really hurt if they hit you.

Behind the frame were two long shafts, and the whole thing was raced across the sand by two boys earning themselves a bit of pocket money. At the start of the charge they held the ends of the shafts high, so that the horns were dipped low, for that is how a bull really charges.

As the horns went through the cape, the running boys would thrust downward on the shafts, causing the horns to swerve upward as the bull sought to gore and toss his enemy. After several mornings, it became plain I was never going to make a matador. As the horn tips swept up toward the genitalia, I tended to step sideways. This caused great merriment.

The matador is supposed to stay absolutely still, his feet planted, and sway his hips like a ballet dancer, so that the rising horn almost brushes the fabric of his trousers. My father later averred that he would have taken a ten-foot leap. But my single step was enough to earn a mocking cheer from the Spanish teenagers and a grin from Don Pepe. Toward the end of my stay, I completed the lessons but gave up any hope of ever going further.

That was when the neighbors from Ashford spotted me at the café and rang my father. Within days, my parents were in the Marbella Club, then a small private hotel out on the Marbella road. My dad came to collect me from Madame Lamotte's flat after the diploma ceremony. He told me never to reveal to my mother that I had been in a bullring. She would attain her gray hair one day without any help from me.

The only other thing of interest during those ten weeks in the hot, sunny spring of 1956 was a torrid affair with a thirty-five-year-old German countess. She frequented the training sessions, and later taught me many things a lad should know as he steps out on life's bumpy road.

She had the quaint habit of singing the "Horst Wessel Song" during coitus. At the time, I did not know what it was, and only a year later learned it was the marching song of the Nazis. This probably meant she had been involved during the war with something deeply unpleasant, which would explain her migration to Spain, which, under Franco, was tolerant of that sort of thing.

My folks spent a week at the Marbella Club, then we all left for Gibraltar and the ferry for Tangier.

TANGIER AND COMMANDOS

Tangier in 1956 was an extraordinary place, my first taste of Africa and the world of Islam. Morocco had been, until very recently, a French colony, but Tangier was under tripartite administration between the British (the post office), the French (police and law courts), and the Spanish (general administration).

There was a vigorous independence movement called Istiqlal, which rioted elsewhere, but the Tangerines are known for their civility and tolerance, so Tangier was spared the rioting, at least while we were there.

It had a fascinating old quarter called the Medina and a large covered market, the souk, where tourists could browse for bargains in perfect safety. I recall that the French were not liked, as they represented the law and punishment, while we were identified as British, so it was smiles all around. As we ran only the post office, our sole visible presence was the little red vans delivering letters.

Tangier was also a free port into which freight ships would arrive to unload out-of-bond cargo immune from even French or Spanish taxes.

The cargoes underpinned the smuggling operation, which was considerable. Lined up at the quay was a line of lean gray Second World War motor torpedo boats, war surplus bought cheap but easily able to outrun the motorboats of the Spanish customs across the water.

Thus, each evening as the sun set, they would slip mooring and head toward the Spanish coast, loaded with perfume, toilet soap, silk stockings, and, above all, cigarettes, mainly Camels and Lucky Strikes, which were contraband but highly prized and therefore expensive in Spain.

They would cruise through the darkness slowly, lights doused, engines rumbling quietly, until the first flashlight on the shore indicated where the mule trains were waiting. Then it was a fast run to shore, frantic hands discharging the cargo before the arrival of the Guardia Civil, and the mules lumbering away into the olive groves. A fast run back out of Spanish territorial waters and a slow cruise home brought them back to Tangier by dawn.

The going rate was fifty pounds for a deckhand per trip, which was a lot of money back then, so I went down to see if anyone would take me on, but was rebuffed. No vacancies. The jobs were extremely sought after, despite twenty years in a Franco jail if caught, and anyway I had had no seamanship.

Otherwise, Tangier was noted for the sumptuous palace occupied by Woolworth heiress Barbara Hutton. It was also a magnet for elderly European gays, because the Moroccan boys were numerous, willing, and cheap.

My parents played the tourist out of the El Minzah Hotel, but I could not, like them, retire to bed at ten p.m., so I would steal back out and explore the bars and dives of the port quarter. It was here I met the Marine Commandos.

There was a British warship moored in the outer harbor on what is called a "flying the flag" mission. The idea was to spread pro-British goodwill along the African coast. It was in a dockside bar that I came across a group of Marines who were having terrible trouble making themselves plain to the bar staff, who spoke only Moorish Arabic and Spanish.

I tried to help and was promptly press-ganged as unit interpreter by the senior sergeant. They were all from Glasgow, from, I believe, Gallowgate, or the Gorbals: about five feet tall and just as wide.

The problem was not between English and Spanish. That was easy. It was between English and Glaswegian. I could not understand a word they said. Eventually a corporal was discovered whom I could decipher and the three-language enigma was solved. We moved from bar to bar as they spent their shore leave and accrued pay on pints of beer and triple-scotch chasers.

Another problem, and quite a big one on a goodwill mission, was that they tended to leave each bar looking as if a bomb had gone off. I solved this by suggesting a gratuity for the staff. Contrary to rumor, Glaswegians are not stingy. When I explained the Tangerines were dirt poor, the Marines chipped in generously. But I explained to the bar staff that the extra money was the house-repair budget. Smiles all around.

Each morning, I was decanted from a taxi outside the El Minzah at about five, just in time for a short nap before joining my parents for breakfast at eight.

On the third day, the Royal Navy warship weighed anchor and cruised off, taking the commandos to continue their friendship-building mission somewhere else.

After six days, my parents and I went back by ferry to Gibraltar and then by plane to London. I had reached seventeen and a half and needed to get on with the serious task of wangling my way into the Royal Air Force. But in three months, all on the tab of the late Mr. Knightly, I had learned fluent Spanish, collected a Granada University diploma, learned how to handle a cape in the face of two charging horns, discovered what to do in bed with a lady, and developed a rock-hard head for alcohol. I was out on the "dusty high road" referred to in the Tonbridge School song and enjoying every minute of it.

LEOPARD-SKIN SOLUTION

———•◆•———

April 1956 seemed to be racing by, and still I could not persuade the Air Force to let me in. It was a very odd position to be in. Compulsory National Service was not popular and it was becoming even less so as the mood toward a fully professional army, navy, and air force strengthened.

The rumors grew that by 1960 it would be abolished. All my contemporaries were seeking ways of delaying their call-up until abolition. Some invented maladies that would enable them to fail the medical. Much of a generation claimed to have flat feet, fallen arches, defective vision, or shortage of breath. If they were all to be believed, one would conclude the young manhood of Britain was the unfittest on earth.

And yet I was trying to get in against an oncoming tide of youngsters trying to get out. I went to two recruiting offices in East Kent, and in each the result was the same. The flight sergeant in each welcomed me with something approaching disbelief, a surprise compounded on learning I was not trying to sign up for a whole career but just for the two-year National Service that everyone was trying to avoid.

There was a reason for this. I did not want to spend a working lifetime in a blue uniform if I could not fly. In fact, the RAF was extremely generous in that regard. If you failed the selection tests, you could leave immediately, but I did not know that.

In each office, the senior NCO beamed a welcome, drew out a long form, and began to fill it in. Everything went swimmingly until the query about date of birth. When I gave it, there were several seconds of mental arithmetic, then the sad smile as the form was torn up.

"Nice try, son," they said. "Come back when you are eighteen."

It was my father who cracked it. Ashford had an Air Cadet Corps and the corps had a band, and up front marched the big drummer, in both senses. He was a big lad, and jutting out from his chest was the big drum. But he had no leopard-skin tabard or poncho. Everyone knows that the big drummer has to have his leopard skin.

Dad was a furrier, and in his basement store he had a magnificent leopard skin, deposited for safekeeping before the war by someone who had never come back and probably never would. He took it from the chilled vault, trimmed it, backed it with red baize, cut a slit for the drummer's head, and presented it to the corps.

The drummer was in seventh heaven and the corps commander deeply grateful. The point was, the corps had a patron in the form of a retired air marshal who lived out at Tenterden. He rang my father to express his appreciation. The conversation ended with the perfunctory "If there's anything I can ever do . . ."

"Well, as a matter of fact, there is," said my father.

The warmth at the other end dropped several degrees. "Yes . . . ?"

"I have a son."

"Good."

"He wants to join the Air Force."

"Excellent."

"There's a problem, Air Marshal. He's just a couple of weeks too young."

There was a thoughtful pause, then, "Leave it to me."

This is where the luck came in, though only later did I discover the story behind the story.

During the war, the air marshal had been a group captain commanding an air base in the middle of Iraq called Habbaniyah. Serving under him was a certain junior officer, a flight lieutenant. In the intervening years, the group captain had become an air marshal retired to Tenterden. The flight lieutenant had become a group captain and director of personnel at the ministry. To this day, I have a fantasy of the conversation between them. Something along the lines of:

"Now look here, Farnsbarns, stop faffing about and send this lad his papers, we'll say no more about the missing petrol coupons."

Something like that. Anyway, a week later, my call-up papers arrived. The usual buff envelope headed by the letters OHMS. On Her Majesty's Service. I was to report to RAF Hornchurch for aircrew selection tests.

I have little doubt no one knew that I had already done that once, and the presumption was that I would fail and that would solve the problem. After all, only about one in a hundred National Servicemen passed. There was a sound reason for this.

Since the end of the Second World War, the procedure had been that those getting their wings during National Service would go back to Civvy Street but remain on the roll of the Auxiliary Air Force, flying at weekends with one intensive two-week refresher course per year.

But it was becoming very plain that weekend warriors were not going to be any match for the Soviet Union's MiGs and Sukhois if it came to World War III. The economists in London were even then pointing out that training someone to fly fighters—which took two years, anyway—then losing him a fortnight later, was a waste of money.

Awarding a boy a flying scholarship was going to cost the Air Ministry thirty hours in a Tiger Moth at six pounds per hour. From zero to wings on a single-seater jet, even back then, cost over one hundred thousand pounds. The system continued but unwillingly, sustained only by the inertia of all bureaucracies.

The only thing the men in blue could really do was to ensure that National Service trainee pilots were as few as possible and were "chopped" (discarded) for the slightest inadequacy. I had only one ace in the hole. I had been through the Hornchurch tests the previous year and knew what to do and what was expected.

So I took my rail pass and went up there for the second time. I made no mention of the earlier visit and divulged to the interview board only that I had my pilot's license, but not how I got it. They assumed my father had paid for it and approved the enthusiasm. I also implied I was only a National Serviceman because if I could not fly, I did not wish for a life behind a desk. The two officers with wings nodded at that as well. The one with a uniform unadorned by wings looked glum, but two outvote one.

A week after returning home, I got the last buff envelope. No mention of being seventeen and a half. It had just got lost. I was ordered to report in civilian clothes with one small suitcase to RAF Cardington, Bedfordshire, the "kitting out" base for new recruits, all branches. At last I was in.

I'M JESUS CHRIST

Cardington had once been the base of the barrage balloons that had floated over British cities to deter the bombers of the Luftwaffe. The gigantic hangars that housed them proved perfect for the masses of stores needed to transform a generation of young men from civilians to aircraftsmen.

There was a day of filling out forms, then haircuts. The mid-fifties were the age of the mods (moderns) and rockers (bikers). The former had short hair, wore suits, and rode scooters. The rockers had long, greasy hair, wore leathers, and rode motorbikes. When they met, they fought in "rumbles," gang fights that consumed the seaside resorts, to the outrage of the citizens. Out in the early May sunshine, rows of service barbers gleefully wielded their electric clippers, reducing everyone to (very) short backs and sides.

There were several thousand young men on the camp, well over 99 percent extremely "bolshy," a short form of *Bolshevik*, meaning seriously truculent. After shearing, everyone passed down the long lines of trestle tables in the hangars, to be issued with boots, socks, undershorts, undershirts, shirts, trousers, blouses, and berets. After everyone changed back in the dormitory huts, the civilian clothes were packed in suitcases and mailed home. There was one exception: a very small group destined for flying training and thus immediate junior officer status. There were eighteen of us in a single hut trying to survive the week. Because of the shirts.

All our uniforms were of very scratchy serge, but the shirts were different. Those destined to be airmen, or "erks," had shirts of the same rough serge. Those destined for officer cadet status were issued shirts in lawn, a type of soft cotton. It was a dead giveaway.

As soon as we emerged for "chow" in the eating hall, it was plain to all that if you really wished to thump an officer, the next two days would provide the last chance. We retired to our hut, and more or less barricaded ourselves in.

You could tell very quickly who had been to boarding school and who not. The former immediately grabbed the beds farthest from the door, standard dormitory lore. When the NCOs came in at the crack of dawn to waken the exhausted and fast-asleep youngsters, they would start bed-tipping nearest the door. Those at the far end had a few seconds to wake up and get vertical with a bleary but cheerful "Morning, Sarge." It helped the day start without a tangle of sheets, blankets, and bed frame. It also meant you did not have to put the whole thing back together again.

The senior NCOs knew perfectly well we were targeted by the rest of the intake and, to be fair to them, stuck fairly close to us. Two days after kitting out, the "soft shirts" were ordered to assemble with kit bags near Main Gate. We were off to boot camp. Even though we were destined for a flying training base, there was still the ritual of twelve weeks of basic training.

That would mean endless polishing of metal buttons, leather boots, pressing of uniforms, marching and counter-marching, rifle drill, running, obstacle courses, physical training, and saluting just about everything but the trees.

A blue bus showed up and took us to the nearest rail station. In the late afternoon, we were decanted from a branch line on a wayside halt in the middle of the wilds of Lincolnshire, at a place called Kirton Lindsey.

As we stood blinking in the sunlight on the platform, surrounded by our kit bags, a small corporal strutted up and planted himself in front of me. I am no giant, but he was much shorter. He wore his flat hat well forward, with the black plastic peak just above the tip of his nose. This meant that to see where he was going, he had to hold himself like a ramrod, extracting the most height from his tiny frame.

Even so, he had trouble glancing upward. I was aware of two malevolent sultanas glaring up from beneath the cap's peak. Then he spoke in a shrill and outraged squeak. I learned later he was always outraged.

"Do you know who I am?" he screeched.

"No, Corporal, I don't."

"Well, I'm Jesus Christ, that's who I am. And that's how you'll bleeding well treat me."

The tone was set. I had met my first British junior NCO. Corporal Davis.

The twelve weeks of boot camp passed quietly. We polished and marched, attended the gymnasium and the rifle range, practiced with .303 rifles and submachine guns, marched again, polished again, and saluted everything. And there was the drill. Hour after hour of it. Up two three, down two three, general salute, present arms, trail arms, port arms, shoulder arms, left turn, right wheel, halt, quick march. AttenSHUN.

Honestly, we were not a success. Some of us had been in the cadet force at school and pretty much knew the ropes. Others were new to it and quite bewildered. Our course leader was the oldest at twenty-six, with university and a doctorate in chemistry behind him. I was the Benjamin, six months younger than the next youngest.

Our drill sergeant was not the monster of comedy films, but a kindly flight sergeant who treated us like wayward nephews. At that age, everyone over forty seems elderly. He tried so hard to turn us out like the Brigade of Guards and failed nobly. Once, after we had ended up at the edge of the parade ground in a tangle of limbs, he actually burst into tears. It is a terrible thing to see a grown man cry. (Well, it used to be.) Though we had a few shillings a week pocket money, we took him down to the local pub, the First and Last, and got him well plastered.

Finally, there was a passing-out parade and we prepared for the next camp and what we had come for—basic flying training. At this point, we divided. The six trainee navigators went off to one training school and the remaining pilots to another. We spent one last evening in the First and Last, downing foaming pint after pint, singing really bawdy songs, knowing the villagers, wives, and all were listening in the neighboring bar, pretending to be shocked while missing not a word, and laughing their heads off.

Then we were gone, the pilots across country to RAF Ternhill in Shropshire. With the transfer came elevation from cadet to junior officer, specifically acting pilot officer. The reason for "acting" was that if you flunked out, you could still be busted back to airman.

But, failing that, the scratchy serge was replaced by the smooth *barathea*, the beret by a peaked cap. There seemed to be an almost invisible ring around each sleeve, other ranks had to throw up a salute as you passed and men old enough to be your father called you "sir." And the pay went up to a staggering twenty-three pounds a week, three pounds basic plus twenty pounds "flying pay." I would not earn that much again for five years.

I think we all enjoyed our nine months at Ternhill in the lovely Shropshire countryside. Sleeping quarters were in a row of Nissen huts, but divided so that we each had a small bed-sitter, which gave some privacy for the first time since parental home. Eating was in the grand officers' mess building, with stewards to wait table.

Much has been written to the detriment of National Service, but it accomplished three functions that nothing else could. It brought young men from every part of the country together to meet and share living quarters, travel, adventures, and camaraderie: youngsters who from Kent in the southeast to Carlisle in the northwest would never have met each other. It bonded them together and helped unify the nation.

Second, it also brought together youths from every social group and background and broadened a lot of horizons. It taught those of a privileged background never to look down on anyone else, ever.

And it took millions who had never left the parental home, who would only graduate after marriage to the marital home away from Mummy's apron strings to an all-male environment where they stood on their own two feet—or else.

The airplane on which we trained was the Provost, made by Hunting Percival, now long gone. It was a bulky, fixed-undercarriage side-by-side two-seater, powered by a single rotary engine. It was stable, docile, and without vice. It introduced us to aerobatics and very rarely stalled and fell out of the sky. I do not recall that anyone was "chopped" on the Provost, though two of our dozen fell ill and had to be retarded until the next course. And two others joined us from earlier courses. We clocked up 120 hours on the Provost before a final flying test and passing-out parade. Then we had a fortnight's home leave with our parents before reporting to Advanced Flying Training School at RAF Worksop in north Nottinghamshire. At last, single-seat jets.

VAMPIRE

———— ·✦· ————

So we reconvened in high summer of 1956 at RAF Worksop, most of us at Retford station, the better off in their own cars. Mike Porter came from Scotland in his hugely admired MG TF sports car, Anthony Preston from his Saxmundham, Suffolk, home in his four-seater convertible MG Tourer, which, as he was the only teetotaler, would soon become the safest way home from the pub on a Saturday night.

There were no more Nissen huts to live in. We were now lodged in the huge officers' mess, each with a spacious room and each with a "batman," or personal valet. My own was a civilian who had served at that air base since the war. It felt strange to be looked after by a man old enough to be my father.

There was a first-night dinner in the spacious dining hall; then we all convened in the bar to meet our new commanding officer, the wing commander (flying), and the instructors. Each of us longed for the morning when we would go down to the hangars to be introduced to what we all longed to fly. The de Havilland Vampire.

It was a flight sergeant who finally led us around the corner of the hangar, and there she was. We just stared and almost salivated. We felt we had come so far and passed so many tests, and there she was. A Mark 9 single-seater version.

She crouched low on her stubby oleo legs, canopy back, cockpit open. To us, she exuded power and danger. Short elliptical wings, triangular air intakes, a small capsule of a body, and twin booms to sustain the broad tail. Somewhere inside was the de Havilland Goblin engine, which would throw her through the sky at up to 600 miles per hour.

For years after 1945, the Vampire, along with her contemporary the Gloster Meteor, had been the principal frontline fighter of the RAF. Although relegated to an advanced flying trainer, she was in essence just the same. The four Aden cannon had been retained only for the purposes of balance and stoppered at the front end. The gun sight had been removed from the cockpit, but that was all.

We circled, we prowled, we approached as the flight sergeant reeled off the statistics. Length, wingspan, weight, takeoff speed, landing speed, maximum altitude over 40,000 feet, way up in the stratosphere.

Finally we looked into the cockpit and marveled at how small it was. Like a tiny sports car of extraordinary power. Then one of us made an interesting remark.

"Flight, it's got no ejector seat."

And it was true. The larger twin-engined Meteor had been fitted with the Martin-Baker Mk.4 ejector seat, invented after the retro-airplane. The side-by-side twin-seat Vampire T.11 trainer, designed and built specifically for dual instruction, had it. But not the Mark 9, designed and built long before the Martin-Baker, which would hurl a pilot clear of a doomed and falling airplane and save his life.

"That's right, sir," came the sardonic reply from the senior NCO, who would no more fly one of these things than jump off a cliff. "It is the only jet the RAF has ever sent into the sky that has no ejector seat. And no one has ever escaped from a dying Vampire. You either fly in it or die in it."

We retreated to the mess for a rather silent and thoughtful lunch.

But fly in it we did, aware that, with dinghy pack and parachute strapped to your rear end like the bulbous home of a spider on its backside, you could stand up in the cockpit but never get out. The front coaming of the windscreen would jab you in the stomach before the parachute could clear the back of the seat. Like a champagne cork, you were stuck and could only sit back down again.

And that was while stationary on the apron. In the stratosphere, a 300 mph slipstream would simply bend you back until your spine snapped.

We started on the T.11 dual-control version with the instructor in the left-hand seat (always the left-hand seat for the leading pilot, and the right-hander for the copilot).

It was all learning, a huge curve of new expertise to be ingested and assimilated. And the ground instruction—classroom lessons on aerodynamics, meteorology, aviation medicine, the stresses and strains of G-forces up to six times gravity in the turns and dives, the effects of anoxia, or oxygen starvation, if the breathing apparatus packed up.

And the first twenty flights with the instructor at first doing it all, then slowly handing over to the pupil, procedure by procedure, until he was satisfied his trainee could handle it all. Then the transfer to the Mark 9 and first solo.

I was forty-four days short of my nineteenth birthday when I took a single-seat Vampire off the deck, and I believe I was the first and only eighteen-year-old ever to have done so, all because of a leopard-skin poncho.

I sat on the threshold of the runway, engine idling, asking for clear-

Ready . . . Here I am (*left*) in the garden in Ashford aged three in the early war years. RAF Hawkinge and its Spitfires were just down the road (*bottom*).

Steady . . . With my mother and father. My father was a major in the army during the war, but as a member of the fire brigade he was not allowed to go on active service overseas.

Go . . . Off to Blue Bell Hill aged sixteen on my second-hand Vespa and then up into the clouds. The knife in my sock came in handy later when I found myself in a tight spot in Paris.

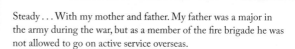

Thanks to my father's efforts, I spent the school holidays abroad learning how to speak French and German like a native. Here I am with Herr and Frau Dewald and their children (*above left*). It was while I was staying with them that I was introduced to Hanna Reitsch (*above right*), Hitler's favourite aviatrix.

Tonbridge School (*right and below*) was not much fun; this is the farewell assembly in Big School in 1952. I hung on until December 1955. At least I had the satisfaction of saying goodbye from the cockpit of a Tiger Moth.

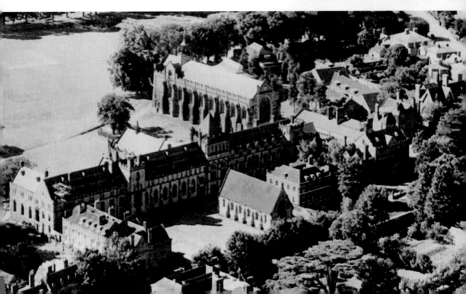

The RAF at seventeen. Heady stuff: flying Vampires in formation. I am number 15 (*above left and right*). Eleven of us made it to the end (*left*). I am second from the right in the back row. Here I am getting my wings (*below left*). I had never been more proud. I was a pilot in the RAF.

To King's Lynn, to work on t[
Eastern Daily Press. I lived in
a flat above a pet shop at the
far end of the ironically name[
Paradise Chambers (*left*). My
mentor, chief reporter Frank
Keeler (*right*), taught me the
importance of checking facts
before you write. Then to
Reuters in London where
Doon Campbell (*far right*) w[
news editor and the inspiratic[
for generations of foreign
correspondents.

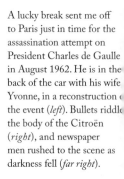

A lucky break sent me off
to Paris just in time for the
assassination attempt on
President Charles de Gaulle
in August 1962. He is in the
back of the car with his wife
Yvonne, in a reconstruction [
the event (*left*). Bullets riddle[
the body of the Citroën
(*right*), and newspaper
men rushed to the scene as
darkness fell (*far right*).

Nobody lasted much
longer than a year in Berlin.
I was there from September
1963 to October 1964 and
lived on the eastern side
of Checkpoint Charlie (*left*).
Kurt Blecha was Press
Secretary to the Politburo,
a nasty piece of work (*right*).
When an American spy plan[
was shot down just outside
Magdeburg, I was the first
journalist on the scene and
managed to get an eye-witne[
account from a local. The thr[
airmen (*see two of them far
right*) had been captured by t[
Russians.

I joined the BBC in 1965, full of enthusiasm—misplaced as it turned out—and in 1967 was sent to Nigeria to cover what turned out to be one of the cruellest African civil wars. Sir David Hunt (*above left*) was the British High Commissioner in Lagos, a snob and a racist. Colonel Yakubu Gowon (*above right*), a Christian from the north, was the puppet head of state. I went to Enugu and met Colonel Emeka Ojukwu (*below*), an Oxford graduate and military governor of Iboland, who had presided over the declaration of the independent state of Biafra in May 1967.

on posters were appearing in Enugu warning of the ...eat of war (*top*). I was with Ojukwu (*right*) when ... soldiers advanced unopposed over the bridge at ...itsha; later they were forced to retreat and blew up ... bridge behind them (*above*).

Having terminated my unhappy relationship with the BBC, I visite Israel in the aftermath of the Six-Day War. I went to a kibbutz at S Boker in the Negev desert to mee David Ben-Gurion (*top*), foundin, father of the state of Israel, one of the greatest men I have ever met. I was also anxious to meet Ezer Weizman, one of the first pilots in the Israeli Air Force. Here he is in 1948 with one of his Czech-produced Messerschmitts, the Avi S-199 (*left*).

A chance meeting in a bar led me the story of the man who drove th truck carrying the explosives that blew up the King David Hotel on 22 July 1946 (*left*).

ance for takeoff, waiting for permission, hearing only the low whine of the Goblin behind the small of my back and the sound of my own breathing and heartbeat inside the rubber mask and the silver "bone-dome" helmet; and vaguely aware that my instructor would be in the tower, gnawing his nails with worry.

"Charlie Delta, clear takeoff."

Slowly forward, with the left hand on the throttle; hear the engine moving up from a low whine to a roaring howl; feel the rumble of the wheels increasing to rapid thuds. Control column neutral, light to the touch. Nose wheel off the tarmac. Ease back. Rumbling gone, airborne.

Three small green lights on the panel ahead, meaning wheel down and locked. Up undercarriage. The lights go red; wheels coming up, but not completely. Red lights out. Wheels fully up. One-third flaps, the takeoff setting up. She's clean, speed rising.

Switch radio channel, acknowledgment from the calm voice in the tower. "Charlie Delta, roger." Then pull back and feel the power, the exhilaration, the adrenaline rush of single-seat jet flight.

One by one, we did it all. Night flying when all England was a vast blaze of lights below, city by city, edged by the pure black of the sea. Instrument flying with a cowl over the head and vision confined to the panel and no glance outside, the instructor alongside checking instrument readings against the world outside. In northern England, there would be cloud, masses of cloud, and once that great ocean of gray cotton wool closes around you, only the instruments will keep you alive and bring you back to a safe landing.

Every emergency procedure was practiced over and over again, from engine flameout to loss of radio.

Sometimes we would find an American bomber out of Lakenheath, patrolling toward the North Sea, formate alongside and give the ally a cheery wave. Other times we would find a Soviet bomber over the ocean, probing the defenses. Another wave, but they never replied.

Summer ended, autumn closed in, the clouds thickened, we used the clear patches for aerobatics, pulling Gs until the vision narrowed to a tunnel and gray-out threatened. But we never lost the euphoria. Until November.

You fly in it or die in it, the grizzled flight sergeant had said. And then Derek Brett and his instructor Jonah Jones died in it.

Ironically, it was in a twin-seat T.11 with an ejector seat that they died. They were in dense cloud over the Pennines, coming home on a radio-controlled tower-guided descent called an ACR-7. They were ordered to fly away from the base down to 12,000 feet, then turn through 180 degrees and fly back toward the base until final landing instructions. But on the turn, they were at 2,000 feet, not twelve. A simple misreading of the altimeter. But the Pennines are 3,000 feet high.

In the tower, the radio communications simply stopped. The last known position was noted and an alarm put out. It was the mountain rescue team that found the wreckage the next day. But dinner had been taken in dead silence.

When a fighter impacts a mountainside at thirty mph, there is virtually nothing left but a crater and some bits of metal. The scythe-bladed compressor wheel is right behind the cockpit. Still spinning at several thousand rpm; it just comes off the axle and churns forward until it reaches the ground ahead.

The mountain rescue men brought down two stretchers with body bags, and the morticians did what they could when transferring the contents to coffins. The family of Flight Lieutenant Jones elected to take his coffin home. Flying Officer Derek Brett was buried at Retford church cemetery nearby.

He was a man on a permanent commission, hence his elevated rank. He was older than most of us, married with a baby son. Formerly in air traffic control branch, he had lusted to fly and passed all the tests, joining us at Worksop as others dropped out or were "chopped." Our original twelve from Kirton Lindsey were down to six, but increased to about a dozen by late joiners from earlier courses.

It was on a bleak winter's day of sheeting rain that eight of us, chosen for equal height, carried Derek's coffin to the Retford grave and stood in the downpour as the obsequies were completed. Then we went back to Worksop and flew again.

I think that in the lives of most young men there comes a moment when the boy simply has to grow up and become a man. For most of us, it was the day we buried Derek Brett. We realized this thing, this Vampire, was not just a great-fun sports car loaned by a generous queen for us to amuse ourselves over the north of England. It was ten tons of aluminum and steel that, if not treated with respect, would kill you.

The remainder of us all got our wings and there was a parade in late March 1958. It was sheeting rain again, so the parade was in the largest hangar on the base. An air vice marshal came up from London, and one by one took the bright white stitched-wings emblems off a cushion held beside him and pinned them on our chests. Until then, it was the proudest moment of my life.

The thing about wings is that they are yours and yours alone. You cannot inherit them from an indulgent father; you cannot buy them in Savile Row; you cannot win them in a lucky draw; you cannot marry them along with a pretty girl; you cannot steal them on a shoplifting spree. You cannot even earn them in a team event. You fight and you struggle, you study and you learn, you practice and you persevere, and finally you do it alone, high above the clouds, in a single-seater.

I could have stayed on, signed the extension, or increased the National Service commission to a direct (eight-year) commission or even a permanent (twenty-year) career. But I only wanted to fly.

I wanted to be assigned to a Hunter squadron. The swept-wing supersonic Hawker Hunter was then the main frontline fighter of the RAF. I was told very bluntly that there was no hope of a Hunter unit. They were for the alumni of Cranwell College, the lifetimers. At best I would get the left-hand (copilot) seat in a Hastings cargo plane on the mail run to Malta; at worst, and most likely, I would drive a desk.

So I decided to go for my next choice of career. There was a song back then called "Moon River," and it contained the lines: "Off to see the world. There's such a lot of world to see." Fifty-seven years later, I can agree with that. There is, and 90 percent of it is terrific. I did not have the money to travel, but I knew people who did: the editors of the great daily newspapers. I would become a foreign correspondent.

And finally I had conquered the bug. The little boy on Hawkinge airfield had not flown a Spitfire, but he had done the rest. He had got his wings. So I opted to leave.

But I still had four weeks of terminal leave and I still had my RAF ID card. There was one more adventure to be attempted. I could still use that card to hitchhike to the Middle East, which I yearned to see. I made my way down to the great Transport Command base at Lyneham, Wiltshire. There I mooned about the officers' mess until I found a friendly pilot who would be flying out to Malta as captain of a Blackburn Beverley the next morning. Could he fit in an extra passenger? Why not? (Things were much more informal back then.)

So I showed up on the flight line that thirty-first of March and found the Beverley was taking a replacement jet engine out to Luqa, the big RAF base on Malta. There were three other passengers hitching a ride. One was an air vice marshal, a second was an army captain, just appointed aide-de-camp to the British governor, and the third was a schoolboy of eighteen joining his parents on the staff of the High Commission.

The lumbering freighter took off and waddled its way across France to the French air base at Salon, outside Marseille. There we refueled and set off again. Not for long. Out over the Mediterranean, there was a loud bang and the starboard inner engine blew up. It simply disintegrated. Through the portholes of the passenger compartment, we watched several cylinders with pistons attached tumbling lazily down the slipstream.

The skipper, Flight Sergeant Farmer, did brilliantly. He would have closed the engine down, but there was nothing to close. Just a large munch-sized bite out of the starboard wing. Running across the void were the fuel lines to the outer engine. If that went as well, there would be a one-way flight straight down to the ocean, where, with the huge jet engine in the hold, we would sink like a stone. The right wing was suffused with extinguisher foam, the Beverley dived to the surface of the sea, and we limped back to Salon.

The schoolboy brought up, the air vice marshal prayed, and the exquisitely turned-out army man just sniffed, which I took to be his comment on the RAF generally.

Back at Salon, there was a major turnout of fire trucks, which were not needed. The RAF presence there was a tiny unit of three: one officer and two NCOs. And there was one further problem. The following day was April 1, the fortieth anniversary of the RAF, founded in 1918. There would be a huge party at Luqa, where we were supposed to be.

The air vice marshal insisted we had to have one anyway. He pulled rank, emptied the RAF reserve of francs, and we set off for Salon town. I recall that much good red wine was drunk, I interpreted into French and back, and we all ended up in a friendly bordello, where I think that schoolboy grew up a bit to a round of applause while the army officer just sniffed.

It took three days for a substitute Beverley to be flown out from Lyneham, and eventually we made it to Luqa. But it was not to be my week. That evening, a sailor was knifed in the gut. It was the first of the rioting led by local politician Dom Mintoff, seeking independence. Everyone was confined to the base. I tried my hitchhiking again and found a skipper prepared to offer me a lift to Cyprus. So I took it.

At Nicosia, I got short shrift. The island had been consumed by the EOKA, another independence-seeking group, but for the moment there was a cease-fire operating. I was told there was no room for a spare body hanging about the mess, so the education officer noticed a free offer by Middle East Airlines for a cultural weekend in Beirut. So I took that, too, and was deposited in Lebanon. Unfortunately there was another revolution brewing there as well.

I was taking a stroll through the souk, drinking in the local color, when there was a sound like tearing calico, and two bodies, riddled with machine gun fire, fell through the awning of a fruit stall. Unbeknownst to me, the Druze tribesmen had come over the Chouf Mountains and launched what turned out to be the civil war against the government of President Chamoun.

I went back to the St. George's Club, to find the British press corps lining the bar (where else?), so I gave them my first contribution to the media, an eyewitness account of what was going on outside. The grateful reptiles stood me several rounds of drinks as they filed their copy with long-shouted phone calls to London.

Unfortunately, I was so squiffy I went outside to the swimming pool, fell asleep, and awoke badly sunburned. Two days later, I took the free MEA flight back to Nicosia. And the cease-fire ended. The war resumed. The commanding officer was incensed to see me again, and with his impetus I found myself on the "rumble" (spare) seat of a Canberra jet bomber heading back to Luqa. From thence, a Hastings freighter took me home to Lyneham without its engines falling off.

I had been away three weeks, experiencing one midair near disaster, one civil war, and two uprisings. So from Lyneham, still in my blue pilot officer's uniform, I hitchhiked back to my parents' home in Kent. But before leaving for the Middle East, and after my decision to leave the service, I had applied for a job in journalism.

My father had consulted the editor of the *Kentish Express* as to how his son should best start. That fine man advised against a weekly like his own, but recommended what he called "the finest provincial daily in England." He referred to the *Eastern Daily Press*, based in Norwich, Norfolk. I applied, secured an interview, and got a job as an apprentice, starting in May. There would be a three-month trial and, if extended, an indenture of three years.

Returning home from Malta, I stripped off my blue uniform for the last time. I was allowed to keep my stainless-steel watch, which kept perfect time until the mid-seventies. After a fortnight with Mum and Dad, I left for Norwich and a new career.

KING'S LYNN

After an initial three weeks at the newspaper's head office in Norwich, I was posted out to the most westerly office within the circulation area, the market and port town of King's Lynn. My trial appointment was confirmed and I spent my three-year indenture there.

The chief reporter was the veteran Frank Keeler, a terrific journalist who became my mentor. He was a stickler for accuracy, dunning into all cubs he ever mentored his personal philosophy: check, check, and check again. Then write. I still do.

On a minuscule salary, I could just afford a scruffy little bed-sitter above a pet-food store on Paradise Parade, the country's most inappropriately named highway. In summer, the minced dog meat stank, but in winter the warmth rising from the caged pets below kept my heating bill down.

There was a lavatory but no bathroom, so for hygiene I had to go to the office, in the attic of which there was an old bath that I brought back into commission and used for three years. There was a kitchen comprising a single gas hob running off a bottle, and a cold-water tap.

I learned to cook eggs just about every known way and not much else. I am still no use in the kitchen and it is the one room I try to avoid.

But at least, using my RAF savings, I had my first sports car, which was my pride and joy. It was an MG TC model, made in 1949, black with scarlet leather seating. Back in 1949, the technology for making paper-thin sheet steel was not known, or when I crashed it, it would have crumpled like a tissue and killed me. But it was built like a truck, which enabled me to survive the crash. But we'll come to that.

The apprenticeship I was serving was devised by the National Council for the Training of Journalists. It involved three years of on-the-job training and night school to study typing, shorthand, libel law, constitution, and theory of journalism, which is a long way from the real thing. At the end, there would be a series of written examination papers and a diploma. Never in the past fifty years has anyone ever asked me for it.

King's Lynn was and remains a bustling market town with rural Norfolk to its east and south, the flat and featureless Fens to the west, and the North Sea outside its ancient harbor and port. The port then played host to a constant stream of small freighters plying their trade between the Norfolk coast and the ports of Western Europe, particularly Germany.

Coverage of news concentrated on the town, its council, magistrate's court, police station, chamber of commerce, and just about every activity concerning the townsfolk, with further supervisory coverage of the surrounding villages. As training for what came later, it was superb.

Reporters on a national paper, let alone an agency, will never meet their readers. For those on a regional or local paper, they are right outside the door, and come in personally to complain about inaccuracies. So the standards have to be high, and they are. I recall one old buffer, puce with outrage, storming into the office to complain that in the results of the cage-bird show at the Corn Exchange, his canary had been wrongly placed. And it really upset him.

In three pleasant but uneventful years, only two episodes remain in the memory. Because of my languages, especially German, Frank asked me to be the new "port reporter" and keep an eye on ships coming and going. On my first summer vacation, unable to afford a holiday, I managed to be taken on as a deckhand on a German freighter called the *Alster*. She plied between King's Lynn and Hamburg. So I spent two weeks on her.

As soon as she docked in Germany, I was off to explore Hamburg, starting with the seamen's zone known as Sankt Pauli. This included the famous Reeperbahn and its surrounding maze of streets and alleys that constituted the red-light district. My deckhand wages did not afford much more than a few beers, but some of these were taken in the old Zillertal, a beer hall famous for its foaming steins of ale and oompah-oompah brass bands. I went there because my father had told me about it.

In the spring of 1939, when I was still a baby, he and a friend from Ashford had treated themselves to a short vacation and picked Hamburg, where they arrived by ferry. They both went to the Zillertal, but on emerging heard a scuffle down a side alley. Peering into the gloom, they observed two Nazi thugs beating up an old Jew.

He and Joe Crotnall may have been just shopkeepers from a small market town who knew nothing of the reality of Germany under the Nazis, but it took them only twenty-four hours to take a dislike to the strutting young men with their armbands and the sign of the broken cross. Neither were Jewish, but they just waded in.

In his time in Chatham Dockyard School, my dad had been a useful middle-weight and his father had once been the boxing, wrestling, and bayonet-fighting champion of the Nore Command, which then contained 50,000 sailors. Anyway, he and Joe Crotnall (who told me the story ten years later) flattened the two assailants. Then, as a crowd gathered, it was time to get out of there. They ran for their car and sped out of Germany into Holland before getting into any more trouble.

I could not know in 1959 that fourteen years later I would also have to get out of Hamburg in a hurry. It seems to be part of our family history. I just contented myself with sightseeing and enjoyed my stay there.

Then in 1960, I crashed the MG and was lucky to survive. It was one in the morning out on the flat Fenland landscape, driving home and of course too fast. A friend was beside me in the passenger seat, the roof was stowed, and we were enjoying the warm summer wind in our hair when we entered the bend.

It was a right-hander and it turned out to be ninety degrees. I think the MG made eighty of those degrees before losing traction and skidding into the left-hand verge, which was actually a steep bank. The thump threw my mate out of the left-hand seat like a cork from a bottle. He was lucky. He landed on a mound of loose sand left behind by workmen, shaken but unhurt. In my case, the steering wheel rammed me back into the seat, and when the car rolled, eight times, several things happened.

My left hand, being on top of the steering wheel, hit the road on the first roll and was crushed. The steel-framed windscreen was snapped off and came back into my mouth. The MG came to rest on its wheels with the driver slumped in the seat in a bit of a mess.

By luck, the accident happened right outside the house of the village policeman. He woke, peered out and down from the top of the bank, saw the wreck, and called an ambulance, which came out from King's Lynn Cottage Hospital.

One of the paramedics found a severed ear in the road, held it up and asked: "Be this yours?" as if detached ears were to be found all over West Norfolk. My friend, still dizzy on his sand pile, says I replied quite calmly: "Yes, put it in a dish." I then passed out into a coma for three days. The ambulance rushed me to emergency, where the first glance by the night-duty sister caused her to think I would not survive till morning. Then luck set in.

The cottage hospital was not a major unit. It handled mainly domestic and agricultural accidents, plus births and winter chills. On that night, Matron was summoned from her bed and began to call in a few favors. The near body in emergency was stripped of clothing and X-rayed as a team of four was assembled.

There was a triangular hole in my skull on the left side with bone fragment embedded inside. A junior surgeon on the staff managed to retrieve the triangle of bone and draw it back into the aperture, where it was supposed to be. Then he bandaged it and hoped it would knit back. It did.

A Dr. Bannerjee worked on my arm. This was long before microsurgery. He put it back where it should have been, sutured the meat back into place, and hoped the blood vessels and nerves would find each other and reconnect. Miraculously they did. Apart from some puckering, the ear has worked perfectly well ever since.

A Mr. Laing, a dental surgeon roused from his bed, worked on my mouth. All five of the top row front teeth had been smashed out and even the roots were in bits. He plucked out every last fragment and sewed the gums closed, leaving tendrils of thread hanging down like something from a horror movie. But the big problem was my left hand. It was pulp.

It just happened that two years earlier, one of the finest orthopedic surgeons in England, after a long and prestigious career in the London teaching hospitals, had retired to his native Norfolk and settled in a village a few miles away. He had met Matron and suggested that, although he was fully retired, if she ever had a really bad one, she could call him. That night, she did. I believe he was called Mr. North. He, too, left his bed and came to the emergency ward.

He would have been perfectly entitled, I was told afterward, to amputate at the wrist. Another surgeon told me later, after seeing the X-rays, that he would have done so. That would have been the unchallengeable decision—a clean, thirty-minute removal of what was left of my hand. The alternative was risky. The trauma was so bad that the young driver could easily die on the slab rather than take a six-hour operation. But he took the risk.

Through the night, the anesthetist constantly checked the life signs, and the surgeon plucked out the tiny fragments and chips of bone and rebuilt the knuckles and metacarpals. He finished around sunrise. His patient was still breathing. Then he took a cup of tea and drove home.

It was three days later that I finally drifted out of a coma. My head was a large ball of bandages, my mouth a gaping hole with no front teeth. My left hand was a globe of plaster of Paris hung up in the air. My haggard father and mother were sitting beside the bed, where they had been for two days. Matron was standing on the other side.

The big worry was that brain damage might have reduced me to a vegetable. But it seems I answered a few simple questions logically, then drifted away for another two days.

Fit young people have amazing powers of recuperation. I was out of commission for about three weeks. My black eyes subsided, the bone fragment in the side of my head resealed itself, and hair began to grow on it. The stitches came out of the gums and the ear reattached. Only the left hand was still a globe of plaster. Finally, Mr. North came back and the plaster was removed.

My hand was still there, uninfected, moving slowly when bidden. Eventually, under the scars, the grip would return, but never quite strong enough to hold a golf club again. But a lot better than a stump. Mr. Laing came back to assure me that a dental plate would give me a better smile than the one before. Dr. Bannerjee was too shy to return to be thanked for his amazing work on my ear. Mr. North would accept nothing from my father save a redecoration of the nurses' hostel, which was accomplished. I remain grateful to them all, though as I was then twenty-one, I doubt any can still be alive.

While I lay in convalescence, I was moved from intensive care to the general ward and found myself next to a middle-aged man recovering from a minor operation, and we got talking as side-by-side patients do, and something very strange took place.

He told me he was a tailor and very diffidently mentioned that he "used to read palms." I had no confidence in that sort of thing, but was intrigued by the phrase "used to." He explained that he had stopped after a nerve-jolting experience. He had agreed to do his fortune-telling hocus-pocus at a village fete.

One of his visitors was a local pillar of the community: wealthy, happily married, healthy, worry-free. Yet in his palm was the unmistakable forecast of his imminent death. He (the narrator beside me) was so horrified, he invented a "fortune" for the man, who left his tent in high good humor.

But the palmist was sufficiently distressed by what he had seen that he went to the vicar and told him. The priest was both horrified and offended, excoriating the palmist and ordering him never to do anything like that again. Two days later, the local notable went to the gun room of his large manor house, took a 12-bore shotgun, and blew his head off. The palmist beside me said he had never told a fortune since.

Of course, it was like a red rag to a bull. I pestered him until he relented. He wanted my left hand, but that was still swathed in bandages. So he studied the less adequate right hand instead. Then he told me what he saw.

I am still unconvinced about this sort of thing. A journalist ought to be a natural skeptic anyway. But I can only report what he said.

He started with my background: birth, family, father's occupation, schooling, the languages, the travels so far, the flying, the lust to see the world, in fact the lot. But I convinced myself he could have learned all this from the staff by cunning questioning. Then he embarked on the future from 1960 onward.

He told me about successes and dangers, triumphs and failures, advances and reverses, wars and horrors, material success and wealth, marriages and sons. And more or less when and how and where I would leave this planet.

And so far, over fifty-five years he has been almost completely accurate. Not unnaturally I am quite curious about the next and last ten years.

Two years later, I took the final exam. I believe I came second in England for that year. I know little of the chap who came first, save that he was from the north of England and chose to remain with his provincial newspaper. I had other ideas.

I had just turned twenty-three; it was autumn 1961. I was heading for London and for Fleet Street, the capital of British journalism, and I still intended to become a foreign correspondent and see the world.

FLEET STREET

I had not the haziest idea which newspaper I wished to join when I took that train down from King's Lynn to London in October 1961. I toyed with the idea of the *Daily Express* because my father had taken it when I was a boy, but I had no inside contacts and no introductions, so I just started at the top end of Fleet Street, near the Law Courts, and began walking. I entered and applied for a job at every press organ I came to.

That was when I discovered Fleet Street was a fortress. It did not seem to want any extra reporters, and certainly not this one. Walking up to the front desk and asking to see the editor was entirely the wrong tactic. The very idea of penetrating the front hall without a confirmed appointment was out of the question.

There were forms to fill out, but pretty clearly they were going to be "binned" as soon as I disappeared out the front door and back onto the street. I had reached the great black-and-chrome edifice of the *Daily Express* by the lunch hour. There was not much point in going on until the editorial staff returned from their liquid lunches. Journalism then had a reputation for heavy smoking and heavy drinking. I repaired for a sandwich and a pint of ale to the Cheshire Cheese pub. It was standing room only.

When the crowd thinned out a bit, I took a stool at the bar and thought things over. I was still on the staff of the *Eastern Daily Press*; I still had my tiny flat. I had my return ticket in my pocket. Then the old luck held.

He was sitting down at the bar in the now almost-empty room, middle-aged, clutching his pint mug, puffing away and staring at me but with a kindly expression.

"You're looking down in the dumps, lad," he said.

I shrugged. "Trying to get a job," I said.

"Any inside contacts?"

"Nope."

He whistled. "Off the street? Not a chance. They don't take walk-ins. Any interviews yet?"

"Nope."

"Any experience?"

"Three years, *Eastern Daily Express*." I added, "Norfolk," in case he did not know, but I had hit a million-to-one lucky shot.

"I trained with the *EDP*," he said. "Long time ago, which office? Norwich?"

"King's Lynn. Under Frank Keeler."

He nearly dropped his pint.

"Frank? Is he still there? We were juniors together. Just after the war."

He held out his hand. We shook and exchanged names. He worked across the road, a veteran of the PA, heading for retirement. The Press Association was and remains the leading news agency in London. I had not thought of an agency, but so what? He led me across the street to the huge gray granite building housing the PA and a range of other companies. Without any ceremony, he walked into the office of the editor in chief.

Mr. Jarvis leaned back in his swivel chair and surveyed the new offering his colleague had brought in. It was difficult to make eye contact, because the lenses of his glasses were as if cut from the bases of shot-glass whiskey tumblers. There were two eyes behind there somewhere and a very broad Lancashire accent. He gave me the same interrogation as his colleague from the pub.

Age? Where from? National Service? Journalistic training? Any other useful qualifications? I mentioned four languages. He stared fixedly, then said:

"Thee's on wrong floor, lad."

He took his phone, dialed a number, and spoke to whoever answered.

"Doon? I think I've got a live one. He's not for me, I've got no vacancies. But he might be for you. Four languages. I'll send him up."

I was led to the lift, said good-bye and thank you to the man I had met only an hour earlier, and as instructed went up two floors. There was a man not much older than me waiting. He led me through swinging doors and down a corridor, knocked, and showed me in.

Doon Campbell was news editor of Reuters, a name so prestigious I had not even thought of it. Not just a few foreign correspondents but an entire agency dedicated to foreign news, reported from their myriad bureaus all over the world. He was actually a very kindly man, but his first, deliberate, impression was of a no-nonsense sergeant-major. Though he had lived and worked in London for many years, his accent might have come out of the Highlands of Scotland a week before. The interrogation was like facing a machine gun. Finally he asked:

"Foreign affairs. Do you study foreign affairs?"

I said I did as best I could from papers, radio, and TV. And that I knew France, Germany, and Spain, with visits to Malta, Cyprus, and Lebanon. He leaned forward, his face close to mine, and snapped, "Where is Bujumbura?"

A day earlier, I would not have had a clue. But on the train down from King's Lynn, I had finished both the papers I had bought on the station and spotted a copy of a magazine folded into the cushions of the seat opposite, abandoned by a previous traveler. It was the American magazine *Time*.

I flicked through it, and in the center was a feature about the Belgian protectorates of Rwanda and Burundi, far away in central Africa. Luck again. I also leaned forward until we were almost nose to nose.

"Why, Mr. Campbell, it's the capital of Burundi." He leaned slowly back. So did I.

"Aye. Aye. So it is. All right, I'll give you a three-month trial. When can you start?"

I knew I would get no Brownie points for walking out on the *EDP* without notice, so I told him I would need to work out my month and could join Reuters in December. He nodded dismissively, and that was that. I had landed a slot in the world's best-regarded agency for foreign news by a series of flukes. I left King's Lynn a month later and moved to a tiny flatlet in Shepherd Market, whence a Number 9 bus would bring me to Fleet Street in twenty minutes.

Reuters started me at the London editorial desk, charged with covering stories of interest only to foreign newspapers far away. In May, I got my break.

The deputy chief of the Paris bureau was diagnosed with a heart murmur and had to be flown home without delay. The British National Health Service was free and the French was not. A head poked around the door of the Home Reporters' room and asked: "Anyone here speak French?"

I was led to the French-language service, whose chief was a real Frenchman called Maurice. My guide asked him, "Does this fellow really speak French?"

Maurice was bent over his typewriter, and without looking up, asked in French: "What do you reckon to the situation in Paris?"

It was back then in a state of crisis. It had just been revealed that President de Gaulle had for months been secretly negotiating with the Algerian resistance at Vichy and had fixed July 1, 1963, for a French pullout from the disastrous Algerian independence war and Algerian independence for the same day. The French extreme right and elements of the elite of the army had declared war on de Gaulle personally. France stood on the verge of coup d'état or revolution.

I let Maurice have a torrent of French, complete with a brace of slang expressions that a pretend speaker would never have known. Maurice had served with the Free French in the war, based at first in London with de Gaulle, then fighting his way across his own homeland as it was liberated under Marshal Juin. But he had married an English girl and settled in London. He stopped typing and looked up.

"You're French born, right?"

"*Non, monsieur*, completely English."

He switched his gaze to the man beside me and dropped back into English.

"Better get him over there. I've never heard a Rosbif talk like that."

My flatlet was on a weekly rent. Living in London, I had given up my car. My possessions were one valise and a haversack. I had no ties. I phoned my parents in Kent and was on the morning flight to Paris. A new chapter was opening that would eventually, and totally unforeseeably, lead to a book called *The Day of the Jackal*.

PARIS AFLAME

The situation I had tried to analyze for Maurice in London was no exaggeration. The uprising against the authoritarian Charles de Gaulle was highly dangerous.

For six years, the Algerians under the FLN had been fighting for independence, getting ever stronger and more dangerous. Successive French governments had poured men, arms, and wealth into the war, with accompanying cruelties on both sides that were pretty hair-raising. Many French soldiers had died, and the mood in France was split down the middle.

In 1958, de Gaulle, who had retired in 1947, or so it was presumed, was recalled as prime minister, and the following year was elected president. In his campaign he had used the magic words: *Algérie française*, "Algeria is French." So the army and the right wing worshipped him. A few weeks into office as premier, he realized the situation was hopeless. France was being bled white in a war it could not win. As president, he began secret negotiations to end it. When that news broke, it was like a nuclear explosion.

In Algeria, vital sections of the army mutinied and marched into exile, taking their weapons with them. Five generals went with them. These were not the raw recruits, but the Foreign Legion and the Paras (Airborne), the cream of the cream. The numerical bulk, the military service inductees, wanted to come home, so they stayed loyal to Paris. But hundreds of French civilians, settled in Algeria, realizing they would be thrown out or at least dispossessed by a new Algerian government, threw in their lot with the rebels who called themselves the Secret Armed Organization, or OAS. Their aims: to assassinate de Gaulle, topple his regime, and install the hard right.

The Paris into which I landed that May 1962 was in turmoil. The biggest Communist Party in Europe, west of the Iron Curtain, was French, completely loyal to Moscow, which had been arming and funding the Algerians. Far-left students marched and clashed violently on the streets of Paris with those supporting the right. Plastic bombs exploded in cafés and restaurants.

Between the warring sides was the newly formed anti-riot police, the CRS, whose methods were not gentle. Almost every street corner featured a couple of them, demanding identity papers, as in a city under occupation. Surrounding de Gaulle's person and keeping him alive were two forces: the Civic Action Service of the counterintelligence arm and his personal squad of four bodyguards, backed by the Gendarmerie Nationale. For a young foreign correspondent, it was some baptism and the peak of all the possible postings.

On arrival, I reported to the bureau chief, the formidable Harold King. He was a legend. Born German, he had fought in the First World War, but for the Kaiser. He emigrated to Britain and naturalized. In 1940, he was Reuters's man in Moscow, following the Red Army deep into Poland before being repatriated to London. Then he followed the Free French into France and became utterly convinced of the claims and policies of Charles de Gaulle. After the liberation, he told Reuters he would head up the Paris bureau or quit. He got Paris.

When de Gaulle resigned in disgust in 1947, he was presumed to be gone forever. Only Harold King, like a Jacobite waiting for the return of the king, insisted de Gaulle would one day return to lead France back to glory, and until it all came true in 1958, King was indulgently regarded as a fantasist. Now in 1962, he was the king (literally) of the Paris foreign press corps. His loyalty to de Gaulle was quietly rewarded with tip-off after tip-off.

I walked into his office, to confront a burly man in his early sixties, glasses perched high on his forehead like accusatory headlights. He was writing, and with one hand gestured that I sit until he was finished. I had been warned about him in London. He was regarded by few with liking, by many with fear, and had a reputation for eating young journalists for breakfast and spitting out the pips. Quite a few in London had been sent back within days of arrival, and hated him.

He finished writing, roared for a copy boy to take his folios to the telex machine, turned his chair to face me, thrust his spectacles even higher on his forehead, where he mostly wore them, and glared at me. Then the interrogation began. This was the ritual that could lead to rejection and a flight back to London. Strangely, he took to me and I became his protégé.

I think the unusual reaction was based on two factors. He perked up when told I had actually volunteered for the RAF instead of fighting to stay out of military service, and then got my wings on Vampires. The other factor was that, while never short of respectful, I declined to be browbeaten. Beneath the gruff exterior, he hated crawlers.

After an hour, he glanced at his watch and asked, "Do you eat?"

"Yes, Mr. King, I do."

Without further ado, he rose and lumbered out of the office. I followed. He had a Citroën at the door, with his loyal driver at the wheel, a perk he insisted on or he would resign. He growled "André" or something at the driver, who set off and deposited us at a restaurant called Chez André, clearly a favorite and regular lunch hole. He was welcomed in and bowed to his regular table.

A new sommelier shimmied up and proposed a bottle of white wine to start with. He raised his specs back to his forehead, stared at the waiter as one contemplating a boll weevil, and growled: "Jeune homme, le vin est rouge" (Young man, wine is red). He was right of course. Wine is red and the other stuff is juice, with or without bubbles.

He did not order, because the staff knew what he would have. He listened to me order in French and then asked me how I had learned it. Spending schoolboy holidays in the depths of the Limousin, in *la France profonde*, or deep France, seemed to please him.

Back then, French lunches lasted nearly three hours. We strolled back into the office at close to four. I did not know it, but I had been, in a way, adopted, and the friendship lasted until he died. The mentoring that Frank Keeler had started in King's Lynn, Harold King completed in Paris, upholding Reuters's house style of rigorous accuracy and complete impartiality—even though he was very partial toward Charles de Gaulle, and the compliment was constantly repaid. He was the only Britisher the French autocrat had any time for.

Because I was the youngest and the most junior, and a single man with no family to hurry home to, Harold King gave me a rather unusual assignment. It was to shadow Charles de Gaulle every time he left the Elysée Palace. I was not the only one.

There was an international corps of media people in permanent attendance tagging along behind his DS 19 Citroën saloon every time he had some journey to make outside the presidential mansion on rue du

Faubourg Saint-Honoré. He knew exactly what we were there for. It was not to cover his visit to the Senate or whatever. It was for that cataclysmic moment when he was assassinated. He knew and he did not give a damn. He despised his enemies and he despised danger. He just shoved his beak of a nose even higher and stalked through.

Whenever his motorcade stopped for whatever function he was attending, the press group split into two and found cafés in which to while away the waiting time. In one group were the British, Americans, Canadians, Nordics, Germans, and all those whose common language was English.

In the other group were the French speakers—French, Belgians, Swiss, and a couple of Québecois. And me. We were often joined by de Gaulle's personal bodyguards, or the pair on duty that day. That was how I got to know Roger Tessier, the Parisian; Henri d'Jouder, the Kabyle from Algeria; and Paul Comiti, the Corsican. I forget the fourth.

Listening to their chitchat and noting the concentric rings of security around the president of France, I became increasingly convinced the OAS would not succeed. There was a large file on every one of them—ex-army mutineers and civilian *pieds-noirs* from Algeria. Their faces, fingerprints, and records were intimately known.

It also became plain—and the security detail was extraordinarily loose-lipped—that the OAS was so penetrated by counterintelligence agents that they could hardly have a four-man conference without their entire conspiracy being quickly "blown" because one of those present was a "grass."

It seemed to me that the only way the OAS would get a bullet through those rings of protection might be if they could find and commission a complete outsider, a professional hit man with no record or dossier known to Paris. Later I would create such a man and call him the Jackal. But that was then. I never really thought to write such a story. So I never told anyone. It was just an idea.

The small flat I had taken on my meager salary was in walking distance of the office, but in the Ninth Arrondissement, home of the Moulin Rouge and Folies Bergère, Place Blanche, Montmartre, and the maze of streets containing hundreds of smaller cabarets and late-night bars. The Ninth was also the red-light district and home of much of the *milieu*, the city's criminal underworld. Being kept awake by the wailing of police sirens was extremely common.

OAS sympathizers also frequented the bars of the Ninth, and so did I. This was largely because the second day shift at the office ended at ten p.m. and I did not need or wish to sleep until well after midnight. So I nursed a beer, stared vacantly at the wall, and listened. That gave me some knowledge of de Gaulle's deadly enemies.

I also developed my "Bertie Wooster mode," an adopted persona based on P. G. Wodehouse's witless hero: helpless, well-meaning, affable, but as dim as a five-watt bulb. Affecting to speak little French and with the usual appalling British accent, it was assumed by both bar staff and customers that I could not understand what they were talking about. The reverse was the case. In the years to come, Bertie would get me out of a lot of trouble. This is because the harmless fool with a British passport is what Europeans want to see and believe.

It was a Friday evening in August when the OAS came closest to killing de Gaulle, and it was at a roundabout in the outer suburb of Petit-Clamart. He was heading from the Elysée Palace to an air base called Villacoublay, where a helicopter awaited him to take him and Madame Yvonne de Gaulle across France to their country home in the east: a mansion called La Boisserie in the village of Colombey-les-deux-Églises.

The couple was in the back of his speeding DS 19. Up front were gendarmerie driver Francis Marroux and the president's son-in-law. The dozen assassins had learned his precise route and were waiting in a side street. They missed because de Gaulle was late, dusk had come early that August 22, the convoy was doing close to ninety mph, and they did not see it until too late. They were going to erupt from the side street, run the limousine off the road, and finish off the inhabitants with submachine-gun fire.

They were too late. As the two motorcyclist outriders screamed past they opened up with full-deflection shots on the speeding car, 120 shots in all. Twelve passed through the car, but failed to stop it. One passed within an inch of the famous nose.

De Gaulle rammed his wife's head into his lap, but remained ram-rod upright. Marroux nearly lost control. Swerved, recovered, and drove on. The follow-up car full of armed guards did the same. At Villacou-blay, the DS 19 slewed to a halt on shredded tires beside the presidential helicopter amid a cluster of panicking air force officers—word had been radioed ahead.

A pretty shattered Madame Yvonne was helped into the 'copter. De Gaulle emerged, shook shards of glass from the lapel of his Savile Row suit (the only British thing he would have about him), and gave his verdict.

"Ils ne savent pas tirer," he sniffed. "They can't shoot straight."

Word reached central Paris about midnight. I and the rest of the press horde got out there and spent the remainder of the night interviewing, observing, and filing stories from local pay phones. Europe's newspapers had already "gone to bed," but an agency works twenty-four hours a day, so there was no rest for AP, UPI, AFP, or Reuters.

That October saw the Cuban Missile Crisis, a hypertense four days when it really looked as if the world might come to thermonuclear war and be wiped out. To be fair to de Gaulle, rightly described as no admirer of the United States since his blazing rows in the war with General Eisenhower, he was the first in Europe to ring Washington and pledge his total support for John F. Kennedy.

I had turned twenty-four, and in January attended the now-famous press conference in the Elysée when de Gaulle vetoed the British application to join the European Economic Community. It was a huge slap in the face to British premier Harold Macmillan, who, in Algeria in the Second World War, had pushed de Gaulle's claims to be the sole leader of the Free French.

His conferences were no press conferences at all. He simply planted five questions with five ultraloyal senior pressmen in the audience, memorized the speech he intended to make in reply, and also memorized the placements of the five so-called questioners, because he could not see them.

Harold King, in the front, was awarded a question to ask. There were, of course, no laptops or mobile phones. The Reuters chief would scribble his press story on a notepad on his knee, tear the pages off, and give them to a runner from his office. The job of the runner was to pelt to the back of the hall and give them to another colleague, who was holding a phone line open to the office.

He would dictate the story to yet another colleague, sitting with headphones in the office, typing furiously, and he would give the sheets to the telex operator, who would send them to London. I was the runner.

I recall the old buzzard peering down in curiosity at the young Englishman crouched below his podium. Because of his extreme myopia, I was about the only person in the room he *could* actually see, and he clearly did not know what I was doing there. In public, he was too vain to wear glasses.

His nearsightedness led to several amusing incidents, at one of which I was present. He was on a provincial tour, always against the frantic advice of his security staff, and he had another habit that drove them mad with worry. All statesmen do it nowadays, but back then I think he invented it.

He would suddenly lean forward, tap the shoulder of his driver, and order him to stop. Then he would climb out and walk straight into the crowd, shaking hands and playing the friend of the common people. Today it is called "pressing the flesh." He called it the *bain de foule*, the bath in the crowd.

On one occasion, as his bodyguards sought desperately to keep up, he plunged on deeper and deeper into the mass, then saw a short, expressionless man in front of him. He seized the fellow's hand and pumped it firmly. Then he moved on. A few yards farther, the same man. He did it again. The problem was that more than a yard away, a face became a blur. The third time he did it, the man reached up and hissed in his ear, "*Monsieur le Président*, will you please stop doing that? That is my f—ing gun hand."

It was Paul Comiti, his Corsican bodyguard, who was unable to go for the shooter under his left armpit if anything happened.

The previous March had seen the execution by firing squad of Colonel Jean-Marie Bastien-Thiry, the leader of the Petit-Clamart attempt, but the OAS did not give up. There were at least three more attempts, and they all failed. One involved a bomb under a pile of workmen's sand beside a country road. It failed to explode, because it had rained the previous night and the would-be killers had not thought to tarpaulin the explosives.

A second involved a sniper high above the parade ground at the École Militaire, where de Gaulle was presiding over a passing-out parade. The intelligence people were tipped off. The sniper, Georges

Watin, the Limper, escaped to South America. A final one had an earthenware jar of geraniums containing a bomb next to a war memorial de Gaulle was due to unveil. In a scene straight from the Pink Panther movies, a kindly gardener, fearing they might wilt, gave them a good hosing and fused the detonator.

In the late summer of 1963, Harold King summoned me, clearly not in a good mood. What had I done wrong? Nothing.

"They want to give you East Berlin, the buggers," he growled. He meant Head Office in London. East Berlin was a peach of an assignment: a one-man office covering East Germany, Czechoslovakia, and Hungary.

Since the building of the now-infamous Berlin Wall in 1961, East Germany had become a pariah state, an outcast from the West. No embassy, consulate, or trade mission. If anything went wrong in the harshest of all the Soviet satellites, there would be no backup, no support at all.

When the Wall went up, all East German presence in the West was expelled, including the East German news agency ADN, which had an office in the Reuters building. East Berlin responded by doing the same, expelling all Western papers and agencies—except one. The Politburo might feed lying rubbish to its own people, but at the top it wanted to know what was really going on. So it retained one Reuters man, with the condition that he live in East Berlin and, if visiting West Berlin, be back through Checkpoint Charlie by midnight. No commuting to the office to work and then going west to spend the night.

"I suppose you're going to take it," grumbled Mr. King.

"If you had just turned twenty-five, wouldn't you?" I asked.

"Too bloody right, I would," he said, then took me out for a slap-up lunch.

Later in September, I packed my traps, had a week's leave with my folks in Kent, and left by train for Paris and Berlin. Most of the passengers alighted when it stopped in West Berlin. I remained seated and watched the Wall drift beneath as the train rolled into the Communist East.

At the Ostbahnhof station, I disembarked, and the man I was replacing, Jack Altman, was there to greet me. He had had a year of it and was yearning to get the hell out.

He had a car, which I would take over, and a spacious flat-cum-office in the Schönhauser Allee, which I would also inhabit. After lunch, he took me to meet the hatchet-faced officials with whom I would have to deal. I noticed that he spoke good German but would never pass for one. In front of officialdom, I made heavy weather of vocabulary and grammar, and affected a clumsy accent. I noticed the officials relaxed at that. This one would be no problem.

He introduced me to the office secretary, Fräulein Erdmute Behrendt, an East German lady who clearly would also be under constant surveillance by the police and the SSD, the formidable Stasi. Two days later, he was gone.

BIG BROTHER

It takes time to accustom oneself to being under surveillance morning, noon, and night. Some people are badly unsettled to know that their office and apartment are heavily bugged; to see the figures in long raincoats pretending to be window-shopping on the streets as they follow you around; to watch the black car with darkened windows moving into position in the rearview mirror on the highway.

My own recourse was to take it as lightheartedly as possible, to realize that even the goons coming up behind are human beings, albeit only just, and we all have a job to do.

It did not take long to find the main "bug" in my office. There was a television, a four-valve model that happened to have five. When I removed the fifth, there was a television repairman on the doorstep within an hour. Before answering the bell, I replaced the fifth valve, then went to make a coffee in the kitchen while he fiddled inside the cabinet. A very puzzled technician left an hour later with profuse apologies for the disturbance.

Opposite the office was an apartment block and, right opposite my own windows, a single black aperture that was never closed and whose lights never came on. The poor mutts sitting beside their telescope must have nearly frozen to death in winter when the night temperature went down to ten below. At Christmas I sent over a bottle of good scotch whiskey and a carton of Rothmans King Size, asking the concierge to send them up to the number I figured had to correspond to the window. That night there was a brief flicker from a butane lighter, and that was all. But it was not all fun and games, and yanking the tiger's tail needed a bit of caution.

One of the nastiest pieces of work in the regime was the press secretary to the Politburo, a certain Kurt Blecha. He had perhaps the falsest smile on earth. But I knew a few things about Master Blecha. One was his birthday, and another was that in the thirties, he had been a red-hot member of the Nazi Party.

Captured in 1943 on the Eastern Front, he had taken no time to convert to communism, being plucked from the freezing prisoner-of-war camp and installed in the retinue of exiled German Communist leader Walter Ulbricht. Blecha returned with the Communist veteran on the tails of the Red Army in 1945 to become part of the puppet government, the most slavish of all the satellite regimes.

At Christmas, Easter, and on his birthday, I sent him an anonymous greeting card at his office. It was bought in East Berlin but typed on a machine in the West Berlin office of Reuters, in case my own machine was checked. It wished him all best, with his Nazi Party membership number writ large and purporting to come from "your old and faithful *Kamaraden*." I never saw him open them, but I hope they worried the hell out of him.

I also learned how to shake the Stasi tail. As the Reuters correspondent, I was allowed through Checkpoint Charlie into West Berlin, but the secret police tail was not. They always pulled over to the curb as I approached the barrier. Once through, I could race down the Kurfürs-tendamm, from there to the Heerstrasse and on to the border leading back into the republic of East Germany at Dreilinden.

It was sometimes thought in the West that Berlin was a border city between East and West. Not so; it was buried eighty miles inside East Germany, with West Berlin surrounded on all sides. Head west out of West Berlin through the Dreilinden crossing point, and you were on the autobahn to West Germany, which was also allowed. Once on it, I could leave the autobahn at the first off-ramp and disappear into the countryside. With a set of shabby local clothes and an East Berlin–registered Wartburg car, eating at roadside halts and sleeping in the car, I could stay off radar for a couple of days.

There were good stories to be had once outside the cage. In theory, everyone was so happy in the workers' paradise that there could not be any dissent to report. The truth was that resentment among workers and students seethed under the surface, occasionally breaking out in strikes and student marches—always short-lived and punished as the Volkspolizei, the People's Police known as VoPos, struck back.

On returning, I would be summoned immediately to the office of Kurt Blecha, who hid his rage behind his smile.

"Where have you been, Herr Forsyth? We were worried about you," was his unconvincing ploy. They felt forced to maintain the fiction that I was free to go anywhere I wanted in their peace-loving freedom state, and being followed was out of the question.

When asked for an explanation, I claimed I was a keen student of church architecture and had been visiting and admiring some of the ecclesiastical gems in East Germany. Back at the flat, I had books to prove it. Blecha assured me this was a highly laudable pastime, but the next time I left would I please tell them so that they could make intro-ductions?

We neither of us believed a word of it, but I kept playing the bumbling ass and he kept beaming his crocodile smile. As for my filed stories of unrest among the supposedly content proletariat, if the regime wondered where I got them from, I let them wonder. I arrived in East Berlin in early October. In late November, the world was hit by a thunderbolt.

THE DEATH OF KENNEDY

It is said that everyone on earth alive at the time recalls where they were and what they were doing when news came through that President John F. Kennedy had been assassinated.

I happened to be dining in West Berlin with a stunning German girl called Annette. We were at the Pariser Café, just around the corner from the Reuters office. It was full, and behind the clatter and chatter there was Muzak playing. Out of nowhere, it stopped and an urgent-sounding voice barked:

"Wir unterbrechen unser Programm für eine wichtige Meldung: auf den Präsidenten Kennedy wurde geschossen."

There was a brief lull in the conversation as the Muzak resumed. It must have been a glitch in the music system. A mistake, a joke. Then the voice came back.

"Wir unterbrechen unser Programm für eine wichtige Meldung: auf den Präsidenten Kennedy wurde geschossen."

Then the world went crazy.

Men stood up and swore repeatedly, women screamed. Tables were overturned. Kennedy had been there in June, speaking at the Wall. It is hard to describe to those who came later how he was hero-worshipped, and in this city of all cities. For me there was one priority above all: to get back to the office and seek to discover East Germany's official reaction. I threw a handful of West marks on the table, ran for the car, and drove through a panicking city to the Wall and Checkpoint Charlie.

The checkpoint was in the American sector of the four-power-divided city, and in their glass booth the GIs were bowed over their radio. You could have driven a herd of buffalo past them and they would not have noticed. The American barrier was up as always. I drove past it and swerved to the East German control sheds. They, too, had heard.

The East German border guards were the hardest of the hard and politically proof-tested before they got the posting. If necessary, they would machine gun anyone trying to climb the Wall to escape to the West.

The story was still recent of Peter Fechter, an eighteen-year-old student who had gotten through the minefield and was halfway up the Wall when the searchlights found him. He was hit by a burst of fire from a watchtower. No one wanted to go through the mines to get him down. In sight of the West Berliners, he hung there on the barbed wire, screaming until he bled out and died.

The only good news about that awful night in 1963 was to see these brutes bleating with panic. They surrounded my car asking: "Herr Forsyth, wird das Krieg bedeuten?" "Will this mean war?"

It was two p.m. in Dallas, eight p.m. in London, and nine p.m. in Berlin when the news came through; ten p.m. when I went through

Charlie. All examinations of my car and my papers were waived. I got back to the office in record time and checked the incoming tapes. That probably made me the best-informed person in East Berlin.

The media concentration was on a panicking America, but that fear was as nothing, compared with the situation on the Iron Curtain. I rang the East German Foreign Ministry for a comment. They were fully awake with desks staffed, but not knowing what to say until told by Moscow. So, terrified voices were asking me rather than the way it should have been.

The point about a Communist state, or any dictatorship, is that independent media are out of the question. So, despite denial after denial, the authorities persisted in the myth that the Reuters man in their midst had some kind of a direct line to the British government. On each of the two occasions I had flown back to the UK during my year in East Berlin, I was given earnest messages for the British Foreign Secretary, whom I had not the slightest intention of visiting, nor he me. When I said I was only going to visit my mum and dad, they tapped the sides of their noses and said, *Ja, ja*, we are men of the world. Wink, wink.

By midmorning, word was coming through that the assassin of Dallas was in handcuffs and was an American Communist. The panic deepened. On the streets, terrified passersby glanced at the skies, expecting to see the bombers of the Strategic Air Command heading east with their nukes. Then Jack Ruby shot and killed Lee Harvey Oswald right in the heart of a police station. If anything was possible to fuel the fires of conspiracy theory, it was that. And indeed the incompetence was pretty hard to believe.

But the United States kept its nerve. The vice president took over and was sworn in. The bombers remained grounded. The panic slowly subsided, to be replaced by grief as the TV pictures flashed of the funeral with the riderless horse. When another shot showed a small boy saluting his father's catafalque, all Berlin, East and West, was in tears. Extraordinary times.

Christmas came. The two Berlins always reminded me of the fairy story of two hostelries, one ablaze with light, feasting, dancing, and laughter; the other, across the street, dark and gloomy. So it was that first and, as it turned out, only Christmas for me in Berlin.

West Berlin lived in a slightly hysterical mood all those years while the Wall stood, aware it could be snuffed out within a night if the order was given in Moscow, like a partygoer drinking in the Last Chance Saloon. That Christmas, it let rip. The East Berliners did their best, but the contrast in prosperity of the two political and economic systems was stark.

It would be another twenty-six years before the Wall finally came down, and two years later the Soviet Union simply imploded. But back then both events were simply inconceivable. Yet in all this grayness and gloom, beyond all the bugged apartments and phone calls, behind the headlights in the rearview mirror, there was one lucky break for the Reuters man, of which I took the fullest advantage.

When East Berlin insisted on keeping the Reuters news service, a deal was struck. East Germany would have to pay 20 percent of the subscription fee in desperately scarce hard Western currency, and 80 percent in virtually worthless East marks. These would be banked in East Berlin. Problem: they could not be exported or converted— at any exchange rate at all. But no one could stop their being spent— locally.

Before I left London to take up the post, the Reuters chief Jerry Long explained all this to me and asked me with a straight face if I could try to reduce the blocked account, which stood at over a million East marks. Even with the office costs and Miss Behrendt's salary, it just kept growing. With an equally straight face, I promised to do what I could.

The problem was, there was almost nothing to buy. In Communist solidarity, Cuba maintained a shop that sold superb cigars for East marks. Cuban produce was banned in the United States, but quite acceptable as a getting-to-know-you offering to an American officer in the West Berlin garrison.

Czechoslovakia produced high-quality long-playing records of classical music, and Hungary very good pigskin luggage. Both maintained a loss-making "prestige" shop in East Berlin. Eventually, even the East German border guards lightened up. They would say nothing about the cargoes going west in the boot of the Wartburg and I would say nothing when a sack of fresh oranges disappeared while I was in the customs shed on the way back. And there was the caviar.

Each Soviet satellite country maintained a prestige restaurant in East Berlin. There was a Haus Budapest with Hungarian cuisine, a Haus Sofia for Bulgaria, and so on. The Haus Moskau served borscht, Stolichnaya vodka . . . and caviar. That first Christmas, I really helped Reuters reduce its surplus marks pile with a mountain of Beluga and enough Stoly to ensure all the bugs in my bedroom could record were the snores.

HELPING OUT THE COUSINS

———◆·◆·◆———

Secret police forces reckon that two or three in the morning is the lowest point of the human spirit, when reactions are at their lowest. That was about the hour that the alarm went off on a certain morning in March 1964.

A direct phone line between the Reuters office in East Berlin and West Berlin or Bonn was forbidden. My colleagues could contact me only by telex, which of course could be monitored by the Stasi, and left a printed record, which could be read later in case a phone call could be so quick that it might be over before they woke up.

But in my office, an alarm bell was fitted to summon me from bed to the machine in case of an emergency. This was definitely an emergency. The Soviets had shot down an American plane outside Magdeburg.

The armed forces hate to have to ask the media for help, but US Air Force HQ at Wiesbaden, West Germany, was in quite a state. I punched out a quick ticker tape asking for more details. While I waited, I got dressed. So far as sleeping was concerned, the night was over.

What came back thirty minutes later made more sense. The downed aircraft was an RB-66, which I knew from my own air force time to be a twin-engined (jet) light bomber converted to photographic reconnaissance. Less politely put, a spy plane, gorged with long-lens cameras pointing down and sideways.

Its mission had been to patrol along the frontier, training angled cameras at something east of the border, inside East Germany. But in this case it had strayed over the border. Any promotion for the navigator was now highly problematic, though that was not his immediate problem.

There had been a quick panic call, then silence. Seconds later, around ten p.m., the blip on the USAF's radar had vanished. At one-thirty, Wiesbaden asked Reuters if their man in East Berlin could find it. The reason they needed to know was the Four-Power Treaty.

Under the terms of the treaty, the Western Allies based in West Berlin had the right to send a patrol car into the Soviet Zone (now East Germany), provided they stated the exact destination. They could not just go a-roving. Without a precise location for their missing spook, they could not leave West Berlin. They also wanted news of the crew: alive, injured, dead, certainly in Soviet hands somewhere.

It was a needle in a haystack, but the orders were clear. Get out there and find it. While waiting for my details, I had packed a gunnysack with bread, cheese, and two flasks of coffee, and written a hasty message for Fräulein Behrendt. Then I left in the Wartburg car for Checkpoint Charlie. As ever with the East Germans, speed was of the essence.

They were methodical and ponderous. They got there in the end but, contrary to spy fiction, they moved like snails. I suspect I was probably in West Berlin before the tail car had got back to the Normannenstrasse HQ to prod the night-duty officer awake. Thirty minutes later, I was out the other side of West Berlin on the westward autobahn and swerved off at the sign to Dessau. From there it was bleak, night-black farmland. I used my pocket compass to keep heading west along B-roads and winding lanes.

Dawn came and the country folk awoke while their city-dwelling masters slept on. The first to appear were farmworkers. I stopped to ask if anyone had heard of a plane belonging to the "Amis" (Americans) coming down nearby. I was completely ignored. At the third halt, instead of saying I was the press from Berlin (official and therefore government), I said "from London." Immediately, the cooperation and helpfulness were unrestrained. I just flashed the British passport to prove my claim and they all tried to help. The denizens of the workers' paradise really hated the place.

At first no one had an inkling, then someone thought it was "over there"—pointing west toward Magdeburg. A group of road workers told me there had been flames in the sky to the west and mentioned a small village, which I found on my road map.

As a watery sun hung over Potsdam behind me, it became clear what the RB-66 had been trying to photograph. Outside Magdeburg, the Soviet army had mounted a huge war-games maneuver ground. I found myself weaving between columns of Russian tanks, half-tracks, jeeps, and trucks of infantry. With an East German–registered car, I leaned out with a broad grin and gave them the V-sign. They responded with the same.

They did not realize that when the first two fingers of the right hand were raised with the palm toward the receiver, it was the Churchillian victory sign. To the British, the other way around means "Up yours." Eventually I parked the Wartburg off the road on a sandy bank and set off through the pine forest on foot. Then I found my charcoal burner.

He was an old man, like something out of a Grimms' fairy tale. I thought he might have a gingerbread house around there somewhere. He considered my request carefully, then nodded.

"*Ja*, it came down over there." I walked on to where he pointed, and there it was. Nose down, tail up, most of its fuselage masked by the pine trees, but with the tail fin jutting up to the sky. It had clearly been hit by air-to-air rockets, and all its ejector seats had been used, so maybe the crew was alive. I marked its exact position and went back to the charcoal burner tending his heap of embers. He was perfectly calm, as one who had lived through two world wars and could cope with the occasional crashing bomber. He showed no nervousness about the authorities, but was interested in my passport. I pointed out and translated the bit in the flyleaf where Her Britannic Majesty "requests and requires" one and all to assist her subject as best they may. Then he spoke quite freely.

There were three crewmen, he said, though he had not seen the first two parachute into the forest. They knew they had been taken prisoner by Russians in jeeps and were lodged in the Soviet army HQ in Magdeburg. His son-in-law, a baker who delivered early bread, had seen them in the jeeps.

The third and last out had landed near him and broken one leg. He was Dutch. No, I said, he was American. The old man tapped his chest on the left side. There was a tab that said "Holland" and two silver bars on the epaulettes. I recalled the US aircrew wore name tags on a white canvas patch, upper chest, left-hand side. So, Captain Holland, the pilot of the falling spy plane, who had ensured his two crewmen were out before ejecting. At the last minute, he landed only two hundred yards from the wreck.

After thirty minutes with my new friend and having delighted him with a pack of Western cigarettes, a universal currency, I had it all.

Then the luck ran out. I was stumbling back to where I had left the car when I heard voices among the pine trees. I dropped to my knees in the undergrowth. Too late.

I heard a barked *"Stoi"* and saw a pair of serge combat trousers ahead of my face. An angry Mongoloid face was staring down at me. These Mongol regiments came from the Russian Far East and have always been used as cannon fodder. I stood up. He was shorter than me, but the tommy gun pointing at my face created its own very persuasive argument.

Surrounded by his mates, I was marched out of the forest to a meadow, where a group of officers was standing around a colonel seated at a trestle table studying a map. One of them looked up, frowned, and came over. He spoke to the soldier in a tongue I could not understand. Certainly not Russian. So, a White Russian officer from a Mongoloid regiment recruited somewhere way out along the Ussuri River. Or maybe the Amur. A long way away.

The soldier explained where I had been found and what I had been doing. The officer spoke in reasonable German and demanded my papers. Figuring the British passport had served its purpose, I offered my East German press accreditation card. He studied it, but the name Forsyth did not mean anything to him, certainly not Scotland.

He asked for an explanation. I dropped into Bertie Wooster mode—hapless, harmless, and very dim. I told him my car had been run off the road and was stuck in a sand drift. I had been told there was a farmer in the woods with a tractor who might pull me out. Then I dropped my car keys and was scrambling around trying to find them when his kindly soldiers guided me out of the forest.

He took my press card and went to show it to the colonel. There was a jabber of Russian. The colonel shrugged and gave him back my card. He clearly had problems more serious than idiot East Germans getting stuck. The captain came back and handed me my press card, and told me to get the hell out of there. I must have been a bit punch-drunk because I said in halting German:

"Herr Captain, it was your trucks that ran me into the sand drift. Your lads couldn't push me out, could they?"

He spat out a stream of orders in the eastern dialect, turned, and went back to his colonel. Six Mongols escorted me back to the Wartburg and pushed. It was not stuck at all, but I kept my foot on the brake, and when I released it, the car shot forward. I turned and waved my thanks at the Mongols, gave them the V sign, and drove away.

I had my story, but how to get it to the West? A laptop would have been useful, but I was forty years too early. It was early evening. I needed a phone and a meal. I needed a hotel. Ten miles later, I found one, a country *gasthof* left over from the past.

Presenting my German ID and speaking like a German, I took a room, pleading car trouble for the lack of reservation, went upstairs, and placed a call to my East Berlin office. Fräulein Behrendt had checked in at nine that morning, read my scrawled message, and was still there. With headphones on, she took down my fifteen-page dispatch.

I told her to transfer the lot to telex tape, but not to connect to West Berlin and Bonn until she had it all and then run it at maximum speed. She got fourteen pages across to the West before the line very predictably went dead and flashed up *Linienstoerung*, or "line disruption." It always did that when the goons did not want something to go through. But as usual, the junior monitors had to check with some senior goon while the story raced through.

I learned later that it had "gone viral," before that phrase was invented. Client newspapers used it across the globe. Wiesbaden was very happy, and a staff car was dispatched to Magdeburg to demand the three crewmen back. (They came home pretty quickly. The nervousness caused by Lee Harvey Oswald was apparently still alive in Moscow.)

I should have driven back to East Berlin that night, but I was bone-tired and hungry. I ate a hearty supper, went back to my room, and slept until morning. After breakfast, I paid up and emerged.

Outside the main door, I was reminded of those society weddings where the bridegroom's mates all line up in two columns, forming a walkway between them.

They were all there. Rural police, city police, forest wardens, People's Police, and at the end, the long leather coats of the ones who took precedence.

The four Stasi were not happy. They had clearly been slow-roasted all night by their masters in Berlin and now they had the swine responsible. One took over my Wartburg, while the other three sandwiched me into the Czech saloon and drove me to their fortress headquarters in Magdeburg.

To be fair, there was no third degree, just a series of very angry interviews and threats. I was not even in a cell but in a bare interview room, with toilet facilities on request. Of course I dropped into Bertie Wooster mode: But, Officer, what have I done wrong? I was only doing my job. Me, a spy? Good Lord no, I wouldn't work for those people: I work for Reuters. I mean, a German correspondent in England would have done exactly the same, wouldn't he? I mean, we all do what we are told to do, don't we? Can I have a widdle?

The senior goon facing me would probably not have had a clue what to do with a hot news story. As he was well over forty, I suspected he had been serving the Nazis twenty years earlier and had switched seamlessly to the Communists. Secret policemen are like that; they'll serve anyone.

Years after Berlin, the pretty vicious DINA, the secret police of the not-so-saintly Salvador Allende of Chile, transferred without a blip to the service of General Pinochet. They even used the same torture chambers. Only the victims changed.

As he had never lived in a free country at all, asking him to agree with what a free journalist would do was simply embarrassing. I just had to hope that my facade of a lucky but gormless fool, and thus too dim to be a spy, would hold up. It did.

I spent a day and a night in that room. In the morning, I was ordered out and escorted upstairs. I thought we might be going to the execution wall, but it was only the car park. I was told to get in and follow the two VoPo motorcycle outriders. The black Tatra brought up the rear.

Someone in Berlin had decided he wanted this whole miserable (for them) affair quashed. We drove fast back to East Berlin, but not via West Berlin. As East German drivers swerved off the highway as the blaring sirens came up behind them, we made record time, driving round West Berlin to enter East Berlin from the south. Many never knew that there was a second border separating East Berlin from East Germany proper. It was to prevent Western tourists who were allowed through Checkpoint Charlie from driving on into East Germany unmonitored.

As we drove up to the pole across the road, one of the motorcyclists explained to the guards that the Wartburg was going through. They would be heading back to Magdeburg. A figure appeared outside my driver's window and tapped. I lowered the window. There was a face, and not a happy one.

"Herr Forsyth," it said, "do not ever come back to Magdeburg."

And do you know? I never have.

OUTBREAK OF WAR

I recall with exact accuracy the date when I almost started the Third World War, for reasons that will become plain. It was April 24, 1964, and it was two o'clock in the morning. I was in my car, twisting and turning my way through the coffin-dark streets of East Berlin back to my flat from a visit to a charming young member of the State Opera Chorus.

I was in a suburb of the sleeping city that I did not know well, and had no map, so I simply headed toward the glow in the sky that was West Berlin, expecting anytime to happen upon a major boulevard that I knew would lead me back to the Stadtmitte district, where the Reuters office was situated.

I was still about a mile from it when I came to another road junction, a crossroads that I needed to go over. Standing foursquare across my path was a Russian soldier. He heard my engine approaching from behind him, turned, and held up a hand in the no-mistake "Halt" signal. Then he turned to face the other way. Because it was chilly, I had the windows up, but now I lowered the driver's-side window and thrust out my head. That was when I heard the low rumble.

As I watched, the first vehicles appeared, coming from the right, meaning the east, and heading across the junction toward the west. They were lorries packed with soldiers, and it was obviously a very large convoy. It just went on and on. I got out of the car and watched for a few minutes. The trucks were then replaced by low-loaders carrying tanks. Nothing else moved. Apart from the Russians, the streets were abandoned.

Wishing to get home, I hung a U-turn and went back, seeking another way past the blockage.

Ten streets farther on, it happened again. Another fur-capped soldier at a crossroads, arms spread, barring traffic from crossing. More armor appeared, moving from east to west, which is to say toward the Wall. Then towed artillery. Now perturbed, I retreated again, found another side street, and continued home. By now, I was zigzagging all over the place, trying to get through.

The third time, the slowly rumbling traffic on the crossing involved more low-loaders but carrying mobile bridges. Then more mechanized infantry with motorcycle outriders. Though no expert, I calculated what I had seen as between four and five divisions of the Soviet army, in full battle order, moving through the darkness toward the Wall.

During the autumn of 1962, world attention had switched to the Cuban Missile Crisis, but it had been the received wisdom for years that if war between the Warsaw Pact and NATO ever came, the spark would come from the embattled and surrounded enclave of West Berlin.

The besieged half city was teeming with spy agencies, agents, infiltrators, and defectors. One West German spy chief, Otto John, had already been snatched from the streets of West Berlin (or so he said, when he later reappeared to explain himself to a skeptical world). In

1948–49, West Berlin had almost been snuffed out when Stalin closed the access motorways and tried to starve the Western outpost into surrender. Only a huge airlift had saved it.

Every day, West Berliners lived in fear of the moment when twenty-two divisions of Soviet-based military in East Germany would get their marching orders. That was why their mood was always slightly hysterical and their partygoing and sexual mores entertainingly louche.

And finally, with Kennedy dead and Khrushchev locked in a power struggle with rivals in the Kremlin, the spring of 1964 was as tense a time as had ever been. Not long before, the Russian tanks of Marshal Konev and the US tanks of General Lucius Clay had been parked barrel to barrel at Checkpoint Charlie with the Reuters man dodging between them.

What I had seen was not merely rolling, it was rolling toward the Wall. In silence, apart from the low rumbling, at two a.m. In rising anguish, I made it back to the Reuters office-cum-apartment and rushed upstairs. The question running through me was simple: What the hell do I do?

There was no question of calling anyone to consult. Telephonically, West Berlin and West Germany were cut off. All the East German ministries were closed.

Do nothing? Say nothing? And what if the worst fears were confirmed by the dawn's early light? Finally I hit upon what I felt was the only thing I could do. Report exactly what I had seen, nothing more, nothing less. No embellishment, no suggestions, no speculation. Just the facts.

So I tapped out the story, watching the yards of hole-punched ticker tape spool out of the telex machine until there was nothing more to say. Then I hit FAST TRANSMIT and watched it disappear toward Bonn.

By four a.m. I was in the kitchen brewing some very strong coffee. I kept returning to the office to check the machine for a response from the Bonn office, but there was none. I suppose their machine was on "automatic on-pass" to London. Actually, it was. I did not know what was going on west of the River Elbe, so I drank coffee and waited for what might become Armageddon as a watery sun rose over Pankow. Only later did they tell me what had been triggered by those yards of punched tape.

It seemed the night staff at Reuters in London had awoken with quite a jolt. In the suburban homes of the top men in Reuters, telephones rang, and the dispatch from East Berlin was read out to them. The story was not sent on to the agency's clients worldwide, and thank heavens for that.

Night-duty officers in the British ministries were roused and they awoke their superiors. It was ten p.m. in Washington when the encrypted calls from London came through. Intelligence agencies were besieged with queries. They were as puzzled as the politicians. There had been no steady deterioration before that date.

Eventually, Moscow was contacted, and bewildered officials in the Kremlin put breakfast on hold to check with their own generals in East Germany. That was when the riddle was solved. Relief surged back across the Continent and the Atlantic. Those about to go to bed did so. Those about to get up did that, too.

A puzzled Soviet commander-in-chief of Warsaw Pact forces in East Germany explained that it was only a rehearsal for the May Day parade, scheduled exactly one week later.

In a rare extension of consideration for the citizens of East Berlin, the Soviets had decided to hold their multi-division military party in the middle of the night, when the streets were empty and, being Communists, it never occurred to them to tell anybody.

Of course, once the banal and ludicrous explanation was out in the open, a rain of derision fell upon the Reuters East Berlin office. My only response was to apologize but with the codicil: Well, you didn't know, either. Which was grumpily conceded. Eventually, it seems a multi-ministry and multi-agency concordat was agreed not to mention it ever again. And so far as I know, from that day to this, it never has been.

HEADLIGHTS

The post of Reuters correspondent for East Germany involved a very large parish: East Germany itself, with compulsory residence in East Berlin, plus Czechoslovakia and Hungary. Visits to Prague and Budapest were not frequent, but mandatory. To Budapest I would always fly, but Prague was close enough for me to motor in my ghastly pink East German Wartburg car. This I did in the midsummer of 1964.

As always, I checked in to the Jalta Hotel on Wenceslas Square and greeted the bugging devices I knew would be somewhere throughout the suite. Elsewhere, crouched over their turning spools, would be the goons of the StB, the Czech secret police. Mr. Stanley Vaterlé, the ever-genial chief of reception, could be relied on to make the right phone call if I handed in my room key and asked for my car key. As I drew out of the guest car park, the StB car would swing in behind me. It was routine procedure, and both parties cheerfully pretended not to notice.

There was a sweltering heat wave that July, and the Jalta had air-conditioning, so after dinner I elected to go down to the basement, where the regime permitted a Western-style disco, which took only Western currency and was patronized by Western businessmen. There were also hostesses, usually university students making pin money on bar tips to help themselves through university or some other college. That night, I met Jana.

She was gorgeous, a twenty-one-year-old who could have stopped traffic on the highway. Her champagne glass was duly topped up; we got talking, then dancing. I was twenty-five; most of the other males were middle-aged, overweight, and beaded with sweat despite the cool air, whether from lust or exercise, it was hard to say.

Dancing till dawn was not quite the Communist way, and at about midnight a voice announced that the joint would close in a few minutes. I paid up and we went to the lobby. If matters were to go further, as I much wished they could, there was no question of my suite upstairs. Each landing had a gorgon behind a desk outside the elevators, noting comings and goings. Western decadence was not on the menu. But I had a car, even if it was an East German horror. And I knew of some lakes outside the city. To my surprise, my suggestion of a night drive was accepted.

I collected my car keys, winked at Stanley, who beamed back, escorted Jana to the Wartburg, and we set off. By then I knew Prague well enough to weave and swerve my way out of downtown, through the suburbs and into the countryside. After thirty minutes, I found the lake. Taking a plaid blanket from the boot, we walked to the water's edge. It was two a.m., but still stiflingly hot. So we stripped down and went into the cool water naked.

We skinny-dipped for half an hour before climbing out and spreading the rug in the long, warm grass. Then, like any healthy young animals, we made love; rather extensively, to my recall. I used to smoke in those days, and after exhausting ourselves, I lay on my back with Jana half-asleep on my left shoulder, watching plumes of blue smoke drift up into the starry sky. Then a remarkable thought occurred to me.

I had never driven through Redland, apart from those times in East Germany when I had deliberately shaken my Stasi "tail" just to annoy them, without the ever-present black-windowed Tatra saloon slotting in two or three cars behind. Even at night, if there were not enough other cars to permit that, and the goons dropped back, pretending not to be there, you could always see the wash of their headlights in the rearview mirror. Except that night: no headlights.

I must have moved in my surprise, for a sleepy voice in the crook of my left arm asked, "What's the matter?" I explained, adding: "Whatever happened to the StB?"

And the sleepy voice replied, "You just made love to it." As I drifted off to sleep, I recall thinking, "If this is the Czech secret police, bring it on." Well, we all have to make a living.

BEER WITH A CAMP GUARD

Weimar is a small, charming town steeped in culture. Composers and writers of world renown worked there centuries ago. But outside Weimar is a hill and on top of the hill is a wood. Unless things have changed, the trees comprising the wood are beeches.

Beech in German is *buchen*, and a wood is called a *wald*. So when the Nazis built a concentration camp in the middle of it they called it Buchenwald, a place of unredeemed horror. After 1949, the East German government decided to preserve it as a place for public visitation. While I was posted there, I motored south from Berlin to see it.

Of course it was a weirdly horrible way to spend a day. There was a car park outside and a place to pay the visitor fee just outside the main gate. Just about everyone else streaming through the gate surmounted by the swastika was in an organized group, quickly taken in tow by the professional guides. Solitaries were rare, for without a running commentary, much would remain unexplained.

There was a school party just ahead of me, so I attached myself to it, and no one seemed to notice. Perhaps the officials thought I was a teacher and the teachers thought I was on the camp staff. I could hear the accompanying lecture quite clearly, and of course understand it. It was all minutely organized along the permitted paths that made up the tour.

We were led past the parade square, with its flogging posts and gallows, through a sample hut (the liberating Allies of 1945 had burned most of them down, as they were infected by disease). We were taken to the crematorium, where the constant stream of corpses had been disposed of, and through the "medical" laboratory where Nazi pseudo-doctors had experimented on living victims. The watch-towers looked down over all of us, only the old machine guns had been removed.

By rote repetition, the commentary was word-perfect, so eventually it became just a drone without inflection or expression. The children were awed into silence as they listened to the explanation of what had been done there.

I noticed that the guides never used the word *Nazi* and never, ever the word *German*. Those responsible had been the "Fascists," even though the Fascists were the Italians. The strong impression being dunned into the children's brains was that the Fascists had in a way, as if from outer space, simply arrived, performed their inhumanities, and then been hounded out to take up residence in their new natural home, Bonn, the capital of West Germany. No one queried this or mentioned that it was actually the Americans who liberated Buchenwald, not the Russians. The whole lecture was a communist tour de force.

By the time it was over and I could escape, thoroughly depressed, back to my car, dusk was falling. At the bottom of the hill, on a side road, there was a country inn, or *gasthof.* I pulled in, parked, went into the bar, and ordered a stein of beer. I sat alone; I wanted to think over what I had seen. It was probably similar to that flickering film my father had seen at the War Office in 1945. He had told me about it; I had read about it, but had never actually seen it (or the remaining evidence of it). Until now. Then there was a power failure, not unusual in rural East Germany.

The landlord came over with a candle. There was only one other drinker in the bar, a middle-aged man a few tables away, glowering over his beer. The host asked if I minded if he joined me to share the candle and relieve the need for two candles. I shrugged and the other drinker came to sit opposite me. The atmosphere by candlelight and with the concentration camp on the hill above us was predictably gloomy, like something from an old Dracula movie.

My new companion did not seem to be drawn from the professional classes; workingman's rough clothes, a pocked and coarse face. After a while in silence, he asked, *"Wo kommst du her?"* (Where do you come from?)

He used the familiar *du* form of address, a familiarity that can be either rudeness or an attempt at camaraderie. He had heard me order in German, so I supposed he meant from which East German city. I did not feel like being German at that moment, so I replied, "Aus London."

He stared at me across the beer glasses, then shook his head. I must be joking, trying to impress.

"Glaub' ich nicht," he said. (Don't believe it.)

Sufficiently irritated, I flicked my blue British passport across the table. He examined it, compared photo and face, and slid it back with something between a mocking smile and a sneer. He jerked his head toward what lay out in the darkness, atop the hill.

"*Und was denkst Du?*" (So, what do you think?)

We both carried on in German. There was something I was beginning not to like.

"What the hell do you think I think?"

He shrugged again, dismissively.

"What happened happened."

It was a long shot but I asked it anyway.

"Were you there? In the old days?" I did not mean as an inmate, I meant on the staff. He shook his head, then confirmed my suspicion.

"Not that one."

So, he had been a camp guard, but at a different concentration camp. And I was sitting opposite him in the half darkness, drinking beer.

It has long been a puzzle to me that I have never resolved. You take a newborn baby, twelve inches of helpless, chubby innocence. You take a toddler, three years old, a bundle of affection. You take a choirboy, ten and possessed of a pure treble voice, a curly blond angel, singing the Te Deum at morning service or helping Dad around the farm. Or you take a fifteen-year-old studying to be an accountant or architect one day.

How on earth do you turn that child in a few years into a savage, cruel monster capable of flogging a tethered man to death or throwing a living child into an incinerator or herding families into a gas chamber? What kind of satanic metamorphosis can achieve that?

But it has happened, not just in Germany, but right across the world, generation after generation. Every torture chamber in every dictatorship in the world is staffed by animals like that. And they were all once gurgling infants.

The lights came on. The landlord came over to snuff out the candle. No need to waste wax. I pushed enough East marks across the table to cover the cost of one beer—mine—and rose to go. The man across the table held out his hand. I left it dangling in midair. I had reached the door when his parting shot reached me.

"Killing is easy, *Engländer*, too damned easy."

Years later, I would discover how right he was.

A VERY UNWISE CHOICE

My departure from East Berlin was not foreseen, but advisable. There were very few places worth visiting after dark. I could stay in, but the television was dire, even though I could pick up West Berlin.

This was strictly forbidden for East Berliners, and locally sold sets had all been tampered with to make reception of the West Berlin programs unobtainable. But thousands had a well-paid freelance "friend" come in to restore the facility. It was wise not to be caught watching the forbidden menu, but in my case they did not even bother.

Or I could read, which I did a lot. Almost my entire literary education, such as it is, comes from that year. Or I could help Reuters's terrible blocked-currency problem by consuming caviar at the Haus Moskau restaurant. Or there was the opera.

One of the few civilized things about the East German government that was not an affectation was their love of music, theater, and opera. The Brecht Theatre was justly famous, but Master Bertolt Brecht was pretty left-wing and I had had enough of that from nine to five. But the State Opera was famous enough to attract international singers and conductors, and the Politburo spent enough foreign currency to indulge it lavishly. Of course, there was the occasional slipup.

One occurred during the opera *Nabucco*, which was immensely popular and always in demand. In it is the Slaves Chorus, where the prisoners sing (in German), "*Teure Heimat, wann seh' ich dich wieder.*" (Beloved homeland, when shall I see you again?) Every time it was played, the entire audience rose and sang along. The Politburo members who attended were gratified by the enthusiasm but bewildered that they never did this for any other aria. Then someone pointed out that for them the "beloved homeland" was not East Germany, but the West. It was their only way of expressing a political opinion. After that, the authorities discontinued *Nabucco*.

And the opera had the pretty chic Opera Café, for after-performance drinking. That was where I met Sigrid, known as Sigi. She was a stunner, and alone. I checked for an escort. There was none. Move-in time.

An East German had to be extremely careful even taking a drink with a Westerner, but Sigi was old enough and sophisticated enough to know what she was doing, and even learning I was from the West but living in East Berlin did not deter her. After a drink, we shared dinner and ended up at my place. She revealed a remarkable figure matched by a rapacity for lovemaking. But on my second date, I realized there was something odd about her.

She claimed she was married to a corporal in the East German army, who would not have had the income to permit her clothes and lifestyle. Moreover, he was permanently based in the garrison at Cottbus, far away on the Czech frontier, and never got any leave. Finally, she refused to let me drive her home, but after hours of fun in bed, insisted that I order a cab from the late-night rank at the Frankfurter Strasse station.

One day I saw the same cabdriver at the station, and for a hefty tip in West marks extracted from him the address to which he had taken her. It was in Pankow, the very blue-chip suburb where the elite of East Germany had their residences. Further discreet inquiries with some of my contacts in West Berlin revealed whose address it was.

I recall driving back into East Berlin through "Charlie" that night with the words of a popular song running through my head. The opening line was: "The party's over, it's time to call it a day."* I had been sleeping with the mistress of the East German defense minister, General Karl-Heinz Hoffmann.

General Hoffmann was not renowned for his sense of humor. I had just turned twenty-six in October 1964 and hoped for a few more birthdays yet to come. Outside of a prison cell, if possible.

I told Reuters I was stressed out and wished to leave rather sharply. Head Office was very understanding; few could take more than a year in that place, and I had just passed twelve months. Within a week, just before the general returned from Warsaw Pact maneuvers in Poland, I had handed over job, office, secretary, and car and was at West Berlin's Tempelhof Airport boarding the British Airways direct flight to London Heathrow.

As the airliner lifted off and both Berlins dropped away beneath the wings, I looked down at the divided city, convinced I would never return to East Germany. As it turned out, I was wrong about that.

---

*From "The Party's Over," lyrics by Betty Comden and Adolph Green, music by Julie Styne.

A MISTAKE WITH AUNTIE

Reuters simply sent me back to Paris to rejoin Harold King, and it was in a silent Paris café in the early spring of 1965 that I watched on a TV screen the state funeral of Winston Churchill.

There must have been a hundred or more around me, all Parisians and not world-famous for their admiration of things British, but they sat in awed silence as the bronze coffin of the old Bulldog was taken to its final resting place in a country churchyard.

I had already made my decision that the future of foreign-sourced news journalism was in radio and television, and that meant the BBC. I got a transfer back to London in April, applied for a job with the BBC, attended the necessary interviews, was accepted, and joined as a staff reporter on the domestic news side that October. As it turned out, that was probably a mistake.

I learned quite quickly that the BBC is not primarily a creator of entertainment, or a reporter and disseminator of hard news like Reuters. Those come second. Primarily the BBC is a vast bureaucracy with the three disadvantages of a bureaucracy. These are a slothlike inertia, an obsession with rank over merit, and a matching obsession with conformism.

Being vast and multitasked, the BBC was divided into more than a score of major divisions, of which only one was the News and Current Affairs Division, which I had joined. That in turn was divided into radio and TV, then Home and Foreign. All starters began in Home Radio, which was to say Broadcasting House on Portland Place, London.

But there was more. It was also and remains at the very core of the Establishment. The calling of a true news and current affairs organization is to hold the Establishment of any country to account, but never to join it.

Then it got worse. The upper echelons of the bureaucracy preferred a devoted servility to the polity of the ruling government, provided it was Labor, and it was.

The icing on the cake was that back then the leadership of the BBC was in turmoil, which prevailed during most of my time there. The former chairman of the Board of Governors had died in office. His deputy, Sir Robert Lusty, presumed the succession to be his. But Labor prime minister Harold Wilson had other ideas. He wanted an even tamer national broadcaster.

Rather than confirming Sir Robert, Wilson transferred his friend and admirer Sir Charles Hill, almost immediately to become Lord Hill, across from the top of BBC's fierce rival Independent TV to chair the BBC board. There was chaos.

Sir Robert Lusty resigned. Several lifelong veterans went with him. The powerful post of director general was held by a former giant of journalism, Sir Hugh Carleton Greene, brother of novelist Graham Greene, who had set up North German Radio after 1945 to teach the old principles of rigor, integrity, and impartiality. He was the last journalist to head the BBC, and thus to protect the News and Current Affairs Division.

The best German news organization for years was the one he left behind him, but twenty years later in London, he was being sabotaged, and eventually he, too, quit in disgust.

As with any ship, when there is chaos on the bridge, vices were adopted belowdecks. Talentless little empire builders proliferated, using all the Machiavellian tricks of office politics instead of a dedication to the business of news. But at the time this was far above my pay grade and seemed of small interest. Only later did I learn about office politics, just as they effectively destroyed me.

Newcomers began by learning the techniques and technology of tape-recorded radio interviews, working out of Broadcasting House under the aegis of the Head of Home Correspondents and Reporters, one Tom Maltby, a good and honorable man.

Then I secured a transfer to TV news, based way up in north London at Alexandra Palace, whence BBC TV News was beamed to the country. This involved learning about reporting directly into a lens, working with cameramen and sound recordists, and being part of a three-man team.

I recall Alexandra Palace, or Ally Pally, with affection. Being away from the hornets' nest, it was informal and clubby, consorting with veteran newsreaders like Robert Dougall and just-arrived young women like Angela Rippon. But I still wanted to go back to foreign reporting and to resume being a foreign correspondent. There were still masses more world I wanted to see.

Still, that summer of 1966, out of Ally Pally, I did cover one good story.

A head came round the door and asked, "Anyone here ever flown in jets?"

"Yes."

"Do you get airsick?"

"No."

"Only we have an invitation to fly with the Red Arrows."

These were and remain the spectacular aerobatic display team of the Royal Air Force, centerpiece of just about every air display, with visits right across Europe and the United States.

"Are you interested?"

Is the chief rabbi Jewish? I was out of the door like a greased ferret.

A DAY WITH THE ARROWS

My assigned cameraman was the really marvelous Peter Beggin, a veteran who had been all over the world with his camera around his neck. We drove in two cars to the West Country and found the base of the Red Arrows display team.

Back then, they were flying the Folland Gnat, a converted trainer with two seats, fore and aft, originally for instructor and pupil. We introduced ourselves and were taken out to survey the Gnat. It was very small and very narrow and, of course, bright red. Near the tails were the canisters that, for the final "bomb-burst" display, would stream long plumes of red, white, and blue smoke.

The tight confines of the cockpit did not worry me, but they were a real squeeze for Peter. He was built like a truck, with immense physical strength, which he was going to need.

His handheld camera was a heavy and bulky Arriflex weighing, I suppose, about ten pounds. Beneath it was a spike, and this would slot into a socket embedded in a canvas harness to be worn around the neck and shoulders. With this in place, he could squint through the lens to film the sky, the horizon, the landscape below, and the rest of the squadron flying in tight formation around him.

The problem was the G-forces we would encounter. Pulling 6 G, that camera would weigh in at sixty pounds, all dragging downward on Peter's shoulders.

We spent the morning in extensive briefings in the crew room, being taught everything that would happen and a variety of emergency procedures if it all went wrong. But if either of us brought up, well, that would just be our problem. No stopping for wax-paper bags. We smiled bravely.

It is perhaps a tribute to the informality of those days that no proof at all was needed that we were fit to fly. No medical, no check for a heart murmur. Our role was clearly to be strapped in, then to sit tight and shut up. The radios were strictly for those terse instructions from team leader to the rest tucked into his wingtips.

Finally we were led out, and we slid into the seats. Peter was third down, starboard side, so he could see the rest of the team in formation round him. I was to fly with the leader.

It took time to get Peter settled in. Two sweating flight sergeants stood on either side of his cockpit, pushing and shoving as he went deeper and deeper. Then the harness. Then the Arriflex into its socket. When the Perspex canopies came down, there seemed to be nothing inside his but him and his camera. We taxied out to takeoff.

The instructions from the leader, coming through my headphones, were very terse: one syllable, two if he felt talkative. All the maneuvers were simply code words and everyone knew exactly what they meant.

There were nine in the team, taking off as a five and a four, then uniting into an arrow formation once airborne. Thus we climbed to about 10,000 feet. The sky was a cloudless blue, the fields of Gloucestershire a patchwork of green. It seemed quite sedate on the way up.

When he was ready, the leader muttered, "Close up." A wingtip appeared a few feet from my left and right eyebrow. I had done formation flying, but this was very close indeed. For twenty minutes, the two wingtips would not move an inch. Across a few feet of racing air, the other two Gnats were as if bolted on. The rest were out behind them.

In deference (I think) to our innocence, the leader began with some gentle barrel rolls and loops. Then the display began.

I heard him say, "Twinkle, twinkle, roll," and the horizon went insane. A twinkle roll is fast, along the axis of the aircraft. The sky went one way, the horizon another, and for a split second Gloucestershire appeared above my head. Then we were back where we started. I looked right and left. The wingtips were still a few inches from my eyebrows.

It went on for about half an hour, then, somehow, we were on final approach, wheels down, flaps at the right setting, green grass flashing past, gentle bumps as the wheels met tarmac.

I had long lost the airfield, except twice, when it was above my head, but the leader had ensured that the whole team hardly left the circuit. That is the point of display flying. The audience has to be able to see it. So it never really leaves their vision. And all the time we had been airborne, the assessors had been watching with powerful field glasses to note any imperfection.

We were assisted out of the cockpits to the wings, then down to the ground. I went over to Peter. He had probably lost several pounds in sweat, but was otherwise impassive. He was probably more concerned for the health of his beloved camera than for himself. How he had taken the strain in the 6-G turns, I shall never know.

We had a "brew" with the Arrows, also soaked in sweat, said our good-byes, and motored back to Ally Pally. I was dying to see the rushes (films had to be developed in those days, then cut and edited).

The rushes were superb and the editors were pretty openmouthed. The camera never wavered, rock-steady, filming out through the Perspex hood as the world twisted and turned around us. And always the next red Gnat in perfect formation, so close one would think to lean out and touch it.

The feature was screened as a "special" to considerable public and professional acclaim.

That autumn I went back to Broadcasting House and lodged my application for the post of assistant diplomatic correspondent, still yearning to go back abroad. There were boards and interviews. I was twenty-eight and the job normally required someone two decades older.

I met Chris Serpell, the middle-aged diplomatic correspondent, whose deputy the job was all about. He seemed formal and distant, staid, and in all things more like one of the Foreign Office mandarins with whom he consorted daily than a journalist.

But amazingly they gave me the job, effective from the next February. Foolishly, I was elated, for I had no idea what I had stepped into.

There are times in life when you discover what is really going on, but too late. When you can say, "If I had known then what I know now, I would have acted completely differently." Had I known the full level of incompetence of the Commonwealth Relations Office (CRO) and its sister the Foreign Office, and the level of slavishness the BBC foreign news mini-empire at Broadcasting House would dedicate to both ministries, I would have resigned at once, or never applied for the job in the first place. But awareness came later, too late.

A TASTE OF AFRICA

That spring of 1967, I joined the foreign news team, full of hopes that I would soon be sent abroad again to cover foreign news stories. What I did not know was that my presence on that team was absolutely undesired.

My new boss, foreign news editor Arthur Hutchinson, had been extremely upset that he had not been seated on the interview board that had given me the post. Had he been, I would never have got it, because he had a protégé of his own that he wished to bring on. As Tom Maltby explained to me months later, from the first my card was marked.

There is a permanent question in office politics: Does your face fit? This one emphatically did not. All that was needed was an excuse, and this I liberally provided.

To start with, my tasks included attending the regular morning briefings at the Foreign Office and the Commonwealth Relations Office. These two ministries in the heart of Whitehall covered all British foreign affairs, the second one obviously concerning itself with the residue of the fast-dissolving empire and its successor, the Commonwealth.

It seemed to me the other diplomatic and Commonwealth correspondents had really "gone native" inasmuch as they were as close to
mandarins in attitude and posture as the senior civil servants, languid
and disdainful, who briefed them. I never recall a penetrating question
or a hint of disagreement with what we were being told. The "received
wisdom" was duly and obediently noted and thence reported to the public. But by midspring, a single issue was dominating all others: the Middle East. Gamal Abdel Nasser of Egypt was steadily preparing for war
with Israel.

If the briefings at the two ministries, seated by the grave Chris
Serpell, were boring, the growing crisis in the Middle East was absorb-
ing much of the world's attention. Nasser was no friend of Britain, nor
vice versa. In 1956, we had invaded Egypt via Suez in collusion with
the French and the Israelis. It had been a disaster and still rankled in
Britain on the Center-Right.

Yet in the Foreign Office, the anti-Semitism was unmissable. I
found this odd. On most issues, the senior mandarins reflected a lofty
disdain of foreigners, yet made one exception, a preference for Arabs
and Islam. This was mirrored in the left-wing media.

In his young manhood, as an impecunious provincial furrier, my
father had been treated with great kindness by the fur houses of the
East End of London, all run by Jews, many who had fled Hitler. My
own views therefore were the other way.

By the time Nasser closed the Straits of Tiran to Israeli and Israel-
bound sea traffic, it had become hard to see how war was avoidable.
I wanted to go out there on assignment, but was pinned to London. In
frustration, I took my summer leave.

It was on leave that I watched the Six-Day War via the media. It
was a war that shattered an awful lot of misconceptions and frustrated

many prejudices. In early June, Israel took on four surrounding Arab armies and three air forces and crushed them all. The air forces of Egypt, Jordan, and Syria were destroyed on the ground before they even flew. With unchallenged control of the air above them, the Israeli ground forces raced across Sinai to the Suez Canal, roared east to take the holy city of Jerusalem and almost all land up to the Jordan River, and in the north stormed Syria's Golan Heights.

In Britain, the Left had been practically salivating at the imminent destruction of the Jewish state and could only watch in slack-jawed amazement. Most of the British people just cheered. The hero of the hour across two continents, Europe and the United States, became the Israeli defense minister, a one-eyed veteran called Moshe Dayan.

There were three pools of influence in the UK that were not so enthused: the left-wing newspapers, the BBC, and the Foreign Office. In those environs, I was much in a minority when I returned from leave in mid-June. What nobody was paying any attention to at all was a brewing crisis in Nigeria that pitted the federal dictatorship and its own region of eastern Nigeria.

It was on July 6, forty days after the Eastern Region had declared unilateral secession from the federal state, that Nigeria invaded to end the insurrection. That day I was called into the office of Mr. Hutchinson's deputy (he was on leave) and asked to go to Nigeria to cover the extremely short-lived campaign.

I protested that I knew nothing of Africa, could not care less, and did not want the assignment. It was pointed out that everyone else was either still "wrapping up" in the Middle East or on leave. I capitulated. There was a day of "jabs" from the resident medical officer and a minutely detailed briefing on what had led to the revolt, what I would find, and what would happen next. This came from a man from the

BBC World Service West Africa of Bush House, the official voice of Britain. I recall it even now.

The issues, I was told, were quite simple. The east was the home-land overwhelmingly of the Ibo people who, on the spurious basis of some riots a year earlier and led by a self-serving rogue called Ojukwu, had declared secession from the very fine republic of Nigeria, the jewel in the crown of the British Commonwealth in Africa. Their collective character was long-term troublesome and their claims had no merit.

Even so, they had been unwillingly goaded into secession by the military governor of the region, a certain Colonel Emeka Ojukwu, and had unwisely agreed to follow him. The Nigerian head of state, the marvelous Colonel Yakubu Gowon, had no choice but to use the fed-eral army to reconquer the east, which was styling itself as the Repub-lic of Biafra.

The rebel army was a rabble of cooks and bottle washers who would be no match for the British-trained Nigerian army. This force would soon march into the rebel enclave, sweeping all before it, topple the upstart colonel, and "restore order."

I was not wanted in Lagos, the capital four hundred miles west of Biafra, constantly referred to only as the "rebel enclave." Events out of Lagos would be covered by our veteran West Africa expert Angus Mc-Dermid. My job was to fly to Paris and thence to Douala in Cameroon, the republic east of Nigeria. Then over the border into eastern Nigeria and, as best as I could, cross-country to the regional capital Enugu.

It was not wanted that I actually file any report, as communications were cut off from all sides. I would report to the British deputy high commissioner there and stick close to him. As the Nigerian army swept south, he and his retinue would retreat south to the coast, where we would all be taken off the shore by an arranged vessel and returned to Cameroon. Once I had reestablished phone contact from the best hotel, I was to file an "upsummer"—a complete report on the short-lived revolt.

The operation would take between ten and fourteen days. Then I should fly home. Job done. So I flew to Paris and thence Douala.

I found traveling companions in the form of Sandy Gall of Independent TV News, his cameraman, and sound recordists, and we agreed to travel together all the way. The two assignments were rather different.

Sandy had a TV team, I did not. He had to spend one week covering a range of stories as they presented themselves, file nothing, ship no film, just return after one week with whatever he had got. I had to stay until the end.

We arrived in Douala, checked into the Cocotiers Hotel, chartered a small plane, and flew to Mamfe, the Cameroon-Nigeria border town. From there, a local taxi and a lot of persuasion took us across the border into the "rebel enclave." After an exhausting drive, we arrived at Enugu and checked into the Progress Hotel, the principal hostelry of this pretty small provincial capital.

It must have been the next day, about July 12, that I made contact with the British deputy high commissioner, Jim Parker. He was a real veteran "old Africa hand," steeped in knowledge of the country and the Eastern Region. I recall that I saw him alone. Sandy and his team were out filming what they could get of interest in a town still completely at peace. Jim asked me what I had been told.

I related my briefing to him, almost word for word. He listened, grim-faced, then put his face in his hands. He knew where the briefing had come from; I did not. The author and source for it all was the British high commissioner (ambassador) in Lagos, one Sir David Hunt. I had never even heard of him.

I would meet him eventually, years later and after the war, in the guest suite of a British TV program. He turned out to be about the nastiest piece of work I have ever come across. An intellectual who had missed out on every plum in the diplomatic service, he ended up in West Africa, the trash can of diplomacy, and seethed with resentment; a crashing snob and a racist who hid his unpleasantness behind a veneer of affability, about as convincing as a four-pound note.

The reason Jim Parker had put his head in his hands became plain as he talked. Every word I had been given was complete and utter garbage. But David Hunt had sold it hook, line, and sinker to the Commonwealth Office. Who in turn had passed it to the West Africa Service at Bush House and the Foreign News Department of the BBC at Broadcasting House. No one dreamed of disputing a word of it.

Jim Parker spent the rest of the morning explaining to me what had really happened and what was happening right then. Which was nothing. Starting on July 6, the Nigerian army, composed entirely of Muslim Hausa tribesmen from the north and numbering about 6,000, had captured the northern border town of Nsukka, which was not defended. Just south of the town, they met the first defenders, oil barrels filled with concrete. And stopped.

They could have gone round them, but they were frightened to enter the rain forest, which they believed was full of evil spirits. They remained there for weeks.

In the deep south, a landing party from the Nigerian navy had captured the offshore island of Bonny, which had an oil refinery. But the navy could go no farther into the shallow and treacherous Niger Delta and they had no amphibious units.

"So what is happening?" I asked. My briefing said the Nigerian armed forces should be sweeping across the rebel enclave.

"Nothing," he said cheerfully. "Welcome to Africa. Let's go for lunch."

His houseboy had prepared pickles and salad. After that we went to a press briefing at State House, the residence of the regional governor, now of the newly announced head of state, to meet the demon Ojukwu.

The drive enabled us to see a microcosm of the crowds in the streets, consumed with exhilaration at what they saw as their present and continuing freedom at last. They were waving their new half-a-yellow-sun flags and the youths were queuing at the establishment booths to go and fight.

The populace had not yet learned to loathe the BBC and never learned to hate the British, so they ran grinning up to the car with the Union Jack pennant on the bonnet, waving and laughing.

Colonel Emeka Ojukwu was not quite as painted to me in London. The son of Nigerian multimillionaire and Knight of the Empire Sir Louis Ojukwu, he had been sent to a British-run preparatory school in Lagos, then to Epsom College in Surrey. Then to Oxford, where he gained a master of arts degree in history at Lincoln College.

As an ardent federalist, he had joined the army, because he considered it the only institution that was truly pan-national and devoid of regional jealousies. He had risen by merit to the rank of lieutenant colonel, and after the first of the two coups of the previous year, the one in January, had been appointed military governor of the east. His native Iboland. He had been in office for fifteen months until the declaration of independence. He was thirty-four.

In measured terms and an Oxford drawl he explained that he had resisted the clamor from the people for a separation from Nigeria for as long as he could before having to face a decision he could no longer avoid. He could either resign and leave or he could agree to lead his people along the path they had chosen. He opted for the latter.

He told all the foreign journalists present—about six, apart from

Sandy and me—that we were free to rent cars and wander where we wished. His staff would issue a laissez-passer to all, in case there were problems at the overenthusiastic roadblocks.

Back at the Progress Hotel to change, I discovered there were more than a score of other expatriates, mostly British, in residence. These were businessmen representing large firms and franchises, who had been there for years, engineers from a number of foreign aid projects, and so forth. If I wanted confirmation of anything Jim Parker would tell me, I would find it in this community, also steeped in local knowledge.

I took tea with Jim Parker back at the deputy high commission and he explained to me where and why the London briefing was wrong on every single point.

It was the chastening seminar that confirmed the old adage for foreign correspondents: Never mind what the embassy says—go and ask the old sweats who have been there for years.

END OF CAREER

—————✦◆✦—————

The trouble with Nigeria was that historically it had never been one country, but two. Some say it still is.

A hundred years before the British arrived, a Muslim warlord called Usman dan Fodio had led his Fulani army out of the Sahara, through the Sahel of semidesert and scrub, and into northern Nigeria to wage war on the Hausa Kingdom. His horsemen stopped at the line of the rain forests because their mounts contracted tick-borne diseases and died in the tropical rain. So the Hausa/Fulani settled the whole of the north, almost 60 percent of what would become Nigeria.

About 120 years ago, the British arrived by sea from the south. Sir Frederick Lugard conquered the tribes of the forest and annexed the north. Lady Lugard grandly called the place Nigeria and mapmakers drew a single line around it.

The Muslim north was ruled by sultans and emirs who resisted the British until the white men used their Maxim machine guns to urge a rethink. Missionaries arrived by sea to convert the animists of the rain forests—not to Islam but to Christianity. So, two countries, and for fifty years the British ruled them as two countries.

Northern Nigeria continued on its sleepy way, with nominal rule by the British but real rule by the emirs and sultans, with British agreement. There was no middle class, education and technology were shunned, and the common people were slavishly obedient to their liege lords. This extreme deference was extended to the British civil servants, who loved it.

But in the Christianized south, the two main ethnic groups, the Yoruba of the west and Ibos of the east, became avid for education and technical mastery, which they learned from the British. One of the two, the Ibos, passionate for knowledge, consumed education with both hands, and became the effective motor of the country. And they spread throughout Nigeria, north and south.

In the north, southerners had to live in closed ghettos, but they enabled the British to run the place with a minimum of white faces. The Ibos especially were the drivers, mechanics, switchboard operators, masters of machinery, office staff, and junior civil servants. They were also entrepreneurial; they became the traders, shopkeepers, bankers, and money changers.

And they made themselves unpopular. I once heard a British civil servant, in London but originally from northern Nigeria, refer to the Ibos as "the Jews of Africa," and it was not meant as a compliment. By the fifties, there were over a million Ibos resident in the north. That was when the trouble began.

London decided that Nigeria had to be independent within a decade, and that it had to be a united Nigeria. Having run the place for so long on the basis of a schooled but controlled mutual antagonism between north and south, that was a tall order. Even taller was the decree that it had to become a democracy, a concept wholly alien to the feudal north.

The emirs and sultans opposed democracy firmly until it was pointed out that, as they had the numerical majority, they could form a single political party, win the coming election, and rule the whole country. Then they agreed, but only on that condition. A party was formed, the election was held, and of course the Northern People's Congress won. The army had also been intensively northernized, with the infantry entirely Hausa and the southerners taking the "technical" commissions. Independence was accorded on October 1, 1960, under a northern-dominated federal government.

All this I learned from the old sweats visiting the Progress Hotel, from Deputy High Commissioner Jim Parker, and from books, as the first four weeks of this eventless pseudo-war drifted by. I was still bound by my instruction not to file anything but to wait for the coming Federal Army conquest of the "rebel enclave."

Trouble really began in January 1966, with the first of two coups d'état of that year. It was a very odd one, planned and carried out not by generals as usual, but by a cabal of radicalized, educated, and left-wing junior officers. These were the days when a portrait poster of Che Guevara was on every student's bedroom wall.

It was later accused of being an Ibo coup. Actually, the junior officer plotters were multi-ethnic, but six Ibo officers among them were the most prominent, because they had attended courses in England, where they had become radicalized. When they returned, everything about northern feudal rule posing as democracy offended them. So did institutionalized corruption, the scourge of Africa.

They struck fast and accurately. It was a virtually bloodless coup, but the dozen victims were the national leadership. In one night, the federal prime minister, the prime ministers of the North and Western regions, and several other ministers were assassinated. But the coup plotters did not take over. The army woke up, mobilized, and arrested them all. But, that done, the government was gone. An army regime was the only alternative. It took over as the plotters were led off to jail. The chief of general staff, General Ironsi, took over. By chance (and it was chance), he was also an Ibo, but a traditional, by-the-book stickler. It did not save him. The north seethed with quiet rage.

Ironsi appointed a military governor to each of the federal republic's four regions. A Fulani to the north, a Yoruba to the west, a midwesterner to the midwest, and Ojukwu to the east.

In July, the north struck back, and this time it was spectacularly bloody. Hausa soldiers raced through barracks across the country, killing their colleagues of southern ethnicity. Hundreds died that way, but that was just the start.

Northern mobs, with local encouragement, swept into the ghettos and put thousands to the sword. The survivors fled south in waves. The total death toll will never be known; Biafran propaganda later said 30,000 Ibos alone died up there. The British government pooh-poohed it all as several hundred.

This was the "storm in a teacup" that had been mentioned to me in the London briefing as the frivolous reason for the east's secession. The expatriates briefing me in Enugu were not racially bigoted, but they had watched it all happen and concluded it was by any standards a major program. But the east did not secede from the federal union. The killings were in July and August 1966. Secession was in late May 1967. It took ten months of blithering incompetence by Lagos to achieve it.

General Ironsi had been assassinated and every Ibo officer and technician had fled east. A group of Hausa/Fulani officers formed the new government, but on British advice they appointed a harmless Middle Belt junior colonel as the new head of state. Colonel Yakubu Gowon was totally unknown, an "office wallah" and a token mission school–educated Christian from a Muslim-majority part of the country. Ethnically, he was a Tiv and had done a course at Sandhurst, England. He was friendly, agreeable, and polite, but not very bright. He was a puppet leader; the real power behind the throne was Colonel Murtala Mohammed, who would later topple him.

After August 1966, relations between the pretty traumatized Ibos of the east and the federal government in Lagos deteriorated. In London the mandarins of the Commonwealth Office and later the Foreign Office quickly showed a passionate favoritism toward the federal regime, stoked by the resident high commissioner. British governments do not habitually show such adoration of military dictatorships, but this was an exception that stunned even Jim Parker.

Sir David Hunt quite liked Africans, so long as they showed him respectful deference. Colonel Gowon apparently did. When the high commissioner entered his office at Dodan Barracks, he would leap to his feet, slap on his cap, and throw up a quivering salute. Just once, as the crisis became deeper and deeper, David Hunt came east to visit Ojukwu in Enugu, and quickly developed a passionate loathing for the Ibo leader.

Emeka Ojukwu did indeed rise as his visitor entered the room, but in the manner of one welcoming a guest to his country home. He did not throw up a salute. It quickly became plain he was the sort of African, meaning black man, that the former Greek don Hunt could not stand. Emeka was a British public schoolboy, an MA of Oxford, once a first-class wing three-quarter for the college rugby team, and almost a Blue, an award earned for competition at the highest level. His voice was a relaxed drawl. He showed no deference. Jim Parker, who told me this, was standing a few feet away. Hunt and Ojukwu detested each other on sight, something that was made clear in my London briefing.

Early in his time as governor of the Eastern Region, Ojukwu tried, against all the prevailing wisdom elsewhere, to reinstitute a form of democracy. He formed three bodies to advise him; one was the Constituent Assembly, mainly the professional class, doctors, lawyers, graduates. Second was the Council of Chiefs and Elders, vital in an African society, where age and experience at clan level are revered. Third, surprising to Western eyes, was the Market Mammies Association.

Jim Parker explained to me that Ibo society is almost a matriarchy. In contrast to women in the north, Ibo women are hugely important and influential. The market was the core of every village and city zone. The mammies ran them and knew everything there was to know about the mood on the streets. These were the forces urging Ojukwu to pull eastern Nigeria out of the federal republic.

The public mood was not aggression but fear. Radio broadcasts out of the north threatened that the Hausa were preparing to come south and "finish the job." Most Ibos believed these threats, the more so as neither federal nor northern government would close them down.

But the real secession point was eventually compensation. Ojukwu had about 1.8 million refugees, all penniless. They had fled, leaving everything behind. At the one single meeting that might have saved the day, at Aburi, in Ghana, Gowon had conceded a withholding of federal oil taxes as an income stream to cope with the crisis. After Aburi, Gowon returned to Lagos and, under pressure, reneged on the lot.

British official sources in Lagos and London briefed the British media that Ojukwu had been grossly unfair to Gowon. He had turned up fully briefed and was simply smarter. That sort of behavior, journalists were told, was obviously unacceptable. After that, the path slid downhill to May 30 and formal secession, and on July 6 to war.

And yet there was no war. My first four weeks in Enugu were very solitary. Sandy Gall and his team had flown out via Cameroon after their single week. I had been assigned a cameraman from another agency, Comtel. He just happened to be there on another assignment. In dumb amazement, we both sat with other expatriates around the hotel radio listening to the BBC news broadcast out of London but emanating from Lagos. It was quite extraordinary.

In Lagos, a discredited former politician named Anthony Enahoro had been charged to set up the Ministry of Information, meaning propaganda. Each day, he issued the weirdest claims.

According to his morning bulletins, the rebel situation was dire and becoming ever worse. There were anti-Ojukwu riots, brutally put down; the Nigerian army was advancing on all fronts and even now at the outskirts of Enugu.

(We expats were on loungers around the pool, the others staring at me pityingly.)

The reason was simple. Out of Lagos, Angus McDermid, 300 miles from the Niger River, was reporting all this as BBC-endorsed fact. Every journalist will know that he may have to report what a dictatorship is saying, but must make plain early on that it is the government talking, not him. This is the "attribution"—the words "according to the Nigerian government."

To be really fair, add the words "no independent confirmation could be achieved." And early on, in the first paragraph. Failing that, the listener will gain the impression that the allegations are all true and endorsed by the mighty BBC. The broadcasts out of Lagos that first month had attribution, if at all, in the fourth or even fifth paragraph. It sounded like the BBC itself talking. Sitting and listening to it as the expats around me roared with derisive laughter made me frustrated as hell. It was not the bias, it was the sloppiness that Reuters would not have tolerated for a minute. Then at last I got a message from London.

It released me from my instruction not to file out of Enugu. The ten-day war was three weeks old and nothing had happened. I was asked for a "matcher" to the dailies out of Lagos.

In journalistic parlance, a matcher is both confirmation and endorsement. I was supposed to file that everything being said was absolutely true.

The only "riots" were actually queues of Biafran youth trying to join up. The entire Nigerian army was stuck behind a roadblock on the border. I could not report "in voice," but at least a telex connection had been established for written messages. So I sent one.

All right, I agree it was probably intemperate. Deep in the obedient editorial bowels of the Broadcasting House newsroom, it did not go down well. What I had actually done was point a Colt .45 at the forehead of my reporting career with the BBC and pull the trigger.

It was not out of mischief but naïveté. I was trained by Reuters. I had never covered a controversial story in my two years with the BBC. I did not realize that when broadcasting for the state, a foreign correspondent must never report what London does not want to hear.

And that is what I had done. I had told them that my briefing had been garbage and the reports out of Lagos were tripe. Then something very peculiar happened. Tiny Biafra invaded Nigeria.

Ojukwu or one of his staff had noticed that Lagos had transferred the entire Nigerian army across the Niger River way up on the northern border. There was a huge bridge at Onitsha crossing to an arrow-straight road to Lagos. The bridge was intact, the road undefended.

The sheer amateurishness was breathtaking. So the Biafrans put together a column of Land Rovers and trucks, scraped together their meager supply of rifles and Bren guns, and rolled over it, heading west at a steady cruise. I went with them.

There was no opposition. A platoon of Nigerians at the western end of the bridge took one look and ran. The column rolled on across the Mid-Western Region to its capital at Benin City. This, too, was abandoned, and that included the British deputy high commissioner (there was one for each federal state), who hightailed it into the bush. That was how the news got out; someone in the radio room alerted Lagos, which spun straight into panic.

It was the success that was the undoing. The Biafrans could not believe their own speed of progress. Instead of refueling and pressing on for the Carter Bridge, and access to Lagos, they paused for two days.

The next day of motoring brought us over the next border into Western Region, land of the Yoruba, with whom the Biafrans had no quarrel. In several village doorways, there were hands waving. The jeep I was in reached the small town of Ore. There had clearly been a clash. Several dozen Nigerian soldiers lay dead round the village square. Wild pigs had been feeding on the soft parts of their faces. Without cheeks or lips, the dead heads stared up in insane greeting. Then I noticed the shoulder-flash insignia. They were Colonel Gowon's personal Praetorian Guard.

As my colleague from Comtel filmed the scene, I remarked to my escorting officer that if they were using the elite of the elite as a stopgap panic measure, the road must be open and undefended. He nodded, but a second panic was setting in. The sheer nerve was receding like an ebbing tide.

Later, much later, it was reported that the British High Commission in Lagos was preparing to shred documents, and Gowon's personal aircraft was at Lagos International Airport with propellers turning and a flight plan for the north. It was really that close.

It all went wrong, of course, and as usual the flaw was betrayal. Ojukwu had appointed a certain Colonel Banjo to lead the mission but, arriving in Benin, Banjo had contacted Lagos by High Commission radio and tried to cut a deal—for himself. He was later tried and shot for it, but too late.

The column began to retreat, back to and over the Onitsha Bridge. Then engineers blew it up. It remained uncrossable until the end of the war two years later.

Back in Enugu, I noticed the tone of messages out of London had changed again. The early ones begged for every detail of the invasion across the Niger. Once it was known that it had failed, I was peremptorily ordered back to London. So I packed and said good-bye to (by now) General Ojukwu, and an army jeep was assigned to take me to the Cameroon crossing point on the eastern border.

Thence with a local mammy wagon to Mamfe and another bus south to Douala. Finally in the Cocotiers Hotel, I would get a phone connection to London. The instructions were the same. No reports, thank you, just get the next flight home.

I did so, walked into Broadcasting House, to be met with an urgent instruction to talk to no one but to report at once to Arthur Hutchinson. It was a brief interview and to the point. According to him, my reporting must have been biased, and I was summarily fired.

But the BBC does not actually fire people; it sends them to a form of internal Siberia, hoping they will resign, serve out their three-month notice, and leave quietly. I was out of the Foreign News team and reduced back to home reporter. I should report to that department's head,

Tom Maltby. I would never travel abroad for the BBC again and the charge was biased reporting.

That is a serious charge, but no one could explain why a seasoned foreign correspondent, sent to cover an obscure African war, would lose his mind to the political ambitions of an African tribe he had never heard of. However, the decision was final and there was no appeal.

There was no point in appealing to Sir Hugh Carleton Greene; he was struggling with his own resignation dilemma in the face of the departure of far bigger bananas than I after the imposition of Lord Hill on the whole corporation.

So I wandered along the third-floor corridors until I came to the office of Tom Maltby.

FAREWELL, AUNTIE

Tom Maltby was a very decent man and kindly. He had been in the Navy during the war and seen combat but never made a fuss about it. He knew exactly what had happened to my BBC career and why. I tried to explain anyway.

I had reported out of Nigeria only what I had seen or, if reported speech, with immediate attribution. Where was the bias? He explained that was missing the entire point.

What I had done, he explained as to an erring nephew, was contradict the High Commission in Lagos; Sir Joseph John Saville Garner, the senior mandarin at the Commonwealth Office (and thus the British government); the BBC World Service; and Mr. Hutchinson.

But they were all besotted by the original flawed analysis, I protested. Nevertheless, it is the only analysis that is acceptable, he pointed out. Then he added the argument that prevented me from resigning straightaway.

"It is about duration," he said, "if this ten-day or two-week war goes on for, say, six months, they will surely have to reconsider."

It made sense and he could be right. If the Biafran insurrection did indeed collapse rapidly, the analysis of the mandarins would have been proved right, if somewhat delayed; and my own voiced predictions that this was no storm in a teacup would have been shown to be mistaken.

To avoid the strained atmosphere of my mooning about in the reporters' room, he suggested I be transferred to the Parliamentary Desk down at the House of Commons. The political correspondent, Peter Hardiman Scott, had a vacancy for an assistant. So in October 1967, that is where I went.

It was a small and friendly office that over the five months I was there taught me much about the way the country is actually run. It also wiped away an awful lot of benign illusions about the merits of MPs and peers. I was able to avoid the vipers' nest going on up at Broadcasting House as rival coteries vied for power and influence. Then, in February 1968, something happened to change my mind.

In the interim, the Nigerian Civil War had not ended nor improved. It had got worse. The Lagos government had instituted a call-up and hugely increased the size of its army. This was being quietly equipped with torrents of British weaponry, shipped out covertly by the Wilson government, which was assuring one and all that it was neutral.

But the Biafrans had not collapsed. On the contrary. Before secession, Ojukwu had moved the entire financial reserves of the Eastern Region beyond the reach of Lagos and was increasing the size and equipment of his own army on the international black market. Biafra had also set up a representation office in London and engaged the services of an agency to handle media communications.

It had also secured the agreement of Spain to use its colony on Fernando Po island as a staging base and the agreement of Portugal to use offshore São Tomé island for the same purpose. It was no longer cut off. In February Biafra organized a mass-media visit. Just about everyone accepted, with the notable exception of the BBC, which was still filing Nigerian propaganda out of Lagos.

I found the decision so weird that I went to visit Arthur Hutchinson to ask why and to volunteer to return with the rest of the invited British media group to see what was going on. Existing reports indicated that military action was slowly increasing, the Federal forces had made a few gains, but that casualties, mainly among civilians, were increasing.

It was another short interview. I was told bluntly that I was going nowhere, and as for another BBC man going, he told me verbatim: "You have to understand, we are not covering this war."

This struck me as bizarre. Every day, the horrors of Vietnam were copiously reported, but that was an American mess. Nigeria was a very British one, apparently to remain clothed in secrecy.

The all-media group duly flew out, stayed a week, and returned. I sought out a few whom I knew and asked them about their experiences. It was clear the Biafra War did not even seem to be achieving a quick resolution and was indeed getting worse. So I decided to take a week of owing leave and go independently.

I thought it wise not to tell anyone, including the Biafran office in Kensington. I just took some of my savings and flew to Lisbon. From what I had learned, the covert arms flights were leaving from there, and the shipper was a sort of aviation mercenary called Hank Wharton, an American and an amusing rogue, whom I traced to his hotel in the Portuguese capital.

He was very laid-back when I explained that I could not pay him, but said he had a four-prop Constellation leaving in the morning and I could hitch a ride. There were no seats in the clapped-out old airliner, so I perched on a crate of mortars in the back.

It was a long, droning flight, to which I would become much accustomed, the only diversions being trips up to the flight deck to talk with the crew and seek yet another cup of coffee.

Wharton had absolutely no overfly rights, because the members of the Organization of African Unity, all military or civilian dictatorships, sided with Lagos. So we flew out at sea, with the Atlantic through the right-hand portholes and the smudge of the African coast to the left.

There was a refueling stop at Portuguese Guinea, also gripped by an independence war. Coming in to land, low and slow over the jungle, some bright spark from Amilcar Cabral's nationalist fighters fired up at the Constellation. The bullet came through the floor, missed the crate of mortars by two inches, went between my parted thighs and out through the ceiling. Welcome to Africa.

On the tarmac, the crew examined the holes, pronounced that there was no harm done and we would refuel and fly on. It got a bit drafty in the back after that. In the middle of the night, with no lights showing, we drifted into the old Port Harcourt, eastern Nigeria's only airfield. I was immediately arrested.

I explained to a highly educated major who had been an accountant until he enlisted what I was doing there and why. He contacted Enugu and was told to put me in a jeep for the capital. Once there, I was taken to state house to see General Ojukwu, who greeted me with huge amusement. When I explained I had come alone to see for myself, he mused that he had played host to a score of British journalists, so one more would make no difference. He assigned to me a jeep with an army driver, a billet in the old Progress Hotel, and said I could go anywhere and see anything I wanted. He would put me on a Wharton plane on Friday for London.

Within three days, it was clear this war was not going to end anytime soon. The popular mood was that Nigeria would realize the futility of continuing the fighting with the close-down of its revenue-producing oilfields, all now inside Biafra, and respond to Ojukwu's standing proposal of a cease-fire and a second peace conference.

He had offered to share the oil and was quietly negotiating with Shell-BP, the main concessionaire. France under de Gaulle, never slow to exploit a British disadvantage, was making covert gestures of support, and weapons were arriving in a steady stream.

For the record, there were no starving children visible at that time. They would appear later, and the ghastly images of them, splashed across the world's media, would transform everything.

On the Friday, I left for London, confident that I would fly from Lisbon to the UK on the Sunday, ready to reappear at work on the Monday, the end of my leave. Then things went wrong. The first stage was to São Tomé island, and there Hank Wharton's plane broke down. I could not contact London to say I would be back late; I just had to kick my heels until we flew on Monday. I was in London on Wednesday morning. A call to a friend inside the BBC indicated all hell was let loose.

When I reached my flat, it had been broken into. It was a pretty hammy job. The lock was only a Yale, which could have been opened with a credit card or artist's palette knife. The two goons had smashed in a door panel to reach the lock from inside. My neighbors told me there had been two of them, from the BBC, who said they had been "worried" about me, the inference being that I might have committed self-harm under the pressure of career stress.

But my body would have been pretty obvious. These guys had gone through everything. I knew I had left no traces of where I had been. But it was pretty clear that, once again, the party was over.

I packed a suitcase, left a note abandoning the lease with a friendly neighbor destined for the landlord, and decamped to spend two days and nights on the sofa of a friend.

When a reporter is told by his employer to publish something he knows to be a pack of lies, there are only three things he can do. The first is to look to his security, his salary, his pension pot, and do what he is told.

The second is to sit in the corner, blubbing his heart out at the unfairness of it all. The third is to raise a rigid middle finger at the lot of them and walk out. I sat down and wrote a long letter of resignation. It was to Tom Maltby.

I thanked him for his consideration toward me, but informed him that in my view the Nigerian Civil War was going to be a major story with considerable duration and many casualties. In view of the BBC's policy of non-coverage (except from a Lagos hotel), I was going to cover the story myself as a freelance.

I signed off and posted the letter late on Friday, aware it would not be opened and read until Monday morning. On the Friday-night plane, I was back in Lisbon, confronting a bewildered Hank Wharton and asking for another hitch to the war zone. By Sunday night, I was in Port Harcourt, under arrest again, and on Monday morning, about the time Tom Maltby was opening his mail, I was shown into the office of an even more bewildered Emeka Ojukwu.

The practice of embedding war reporters into military units was unknown back then, so the question of paying my way arose. I said I wanted to stay, but had no funds and no employer behind me.

Ojukwu offered me half a tin-roofed Nissen hut, food from state house kitchens, a Volkswagen Beetle, and a petrol allowance. Plus access to the communications company he had engaged to get news dispatches from Biafra to Geneva and thence to the world. After that, I could go anywhere, see anything, and report anything.

I made plain I would not report what his own propaganda bureau wanted, but only what I saw with my own eyes or learned from reliable sources. But what I wrote would be fair.

"That's all I want," he said. "Fair. After that the story will tell itself."

So our deal was struck. I was a freelance with no clients. All I had was a story that deserved to be told and the opposition of a British establishment that seemed determined no one should hear about it.

And somewhere, deep in the bush, the children began to wither and die, but no one knew.

Biafra had been in lockdown since the start of the secession ten months earlier. That meant all borders were closed and the blockade included food. The native Ibos grew their own cassava and yams in ample quantities. Pounded cassava root and pounded yams made the staple diet and never ran out. But both are totally carbohydrate.

It is a fact that an adult needs one gram of pure protein per day to stay healthy. A growing child needs five.

The native population had always raised a few chickens and some small pigs for their eggs and meat. Other than these, there was no protein source and, unperceived, the hens and pigs had been consumed.

The traditional protein supplement had always been fish; not river-caught fish but enormous quantities of Norwegian-imported dried cod called stockfish. These rock-hard sticks of cod went into the family stew pot, became rehydrated, and served as the family protein ration. For nine months, no stockfish had entered the surrounded and block-aded enclave. The meat/milk sources were gone. The national diet was now almost 100 percent starch.

In the deep bush, mothers noticed their babies' limbs were wither-ing to sticks. Heads with glazed eyes lolled on weakened neck mus-cles. Bellies swelled to great drums but full only of air. Thinking their children were hungry, the mothers of the bush fed their offspring more carbohydrates. It would not be until May that they would come out to show their babies to the missionaries, who would know what they were looking at.

My first two months were almost idle. There was little movement on any of the fronts. I had some savings left and decided to take up a long-standing offer from a friend to be his guest on a visit to Israel. So I did.

LIVING HISTORY

Israel in the spring of 1968 was still infused with a spirit of bemused euphoria deriving from its smashing victory of the Six-Day War.

The size of its territory had virtually doubled, more so if one includes the barren wilderness of the Sinai Peninsula, long since conceded back to Egypt. The old, confused borders left over from the 1948 war had been swept away. The Nablus Salient was gone. The city of Jerusalem had been conquered, and the holy places, forbidden to Jews by the Mandelbaum Gate, were open for worship.

Diggers were still revealing foot after foot of the long-buried Wailing Wall, the last remaining section of the old Temple of Solomon. There was a countrywide mood of slightly intoxicated optimism.

But the country that had always contained some Palestinian Arabs had now absorbed half a million more, and the problems of the future were still too far ahead to contemplate, had anyone wished, which they did not.

While some have deemed this mood to be conqueror's arrogance, I choose to accept it as the euphoria of a Dr. Pangloss and his belief that "all's for the best in the best of all possible worlds." There seemed no problem, including that of a negotiated and lasting peace, that could not be surmounted. Seen from forty-five years later, it was the product not of gloating but of a slightly touching naïveté.

During my stay I determined to see as much as possible of the land, and with the help of my London-based friend, had set up a few points of contact. Starting at the Dan Hotel, Tel Aviv, I headed south out of town for Beersheva and the Negev Desert. There was a man living in almost complete isolation in the Negev writing his memoirs who had agreed to give me a few moments of his valuable time.

There is only one way to see the real Israel, and that is to travel everywhere by the Egged buses, so I took one from the Tel Aviv terminal to Beersheva and changed for the connection to Eilat. They may not be fast and they stop everywhere, but they are cheap and my funds were meager.

Out of Beersheva, we passed the nuclear research facility at Dimona, birthplace of Israel's nuclear weapons array and mockingly referred to as a "jeans factory." Then it was the desert.

During National Service, the Hastings in which I had hitched a lift from Lyneham to Malta had refueled at the RAF air base of El Adem in Libya. Otherwise, I had never seen a real desert, let alone motored through one. Later I would see many more, but they are all the same. They just seem to go on and on, a wasteland of dun brown sand and gravel. Only the Bedouin choose to live in them.

After hours of bumping along, we came around the curve of a hill, and far ahead and below was a brilliant patch of green, like a pool table dumped in the middle of nowhere. The green was the irrigated crops of the moshav, or collection of smallholdings, I had come to visit. The bus stopped at the gate, I descended, it broke wind noisily, and headed on to Eilat.

Inside the compound, I was pointed toward a residence that was little more than a Quonset hut standing alone. Outside was a single giant Israeli paratrooper, apparently the only security. He examined my passport, turned, and knocked. A middle-aged housekeeper answered, also looked at the passport, and beckoned me in. "Twenty minutes," she snapped in English, evidently housekeeper and dragon-guardian. She knocked on a study door and showed me in. Behind a desk cluttered with papers, a tiny man beneath a snow-white candy-floss cloud of hair rose and smiled. I was meeting David Ben-Gurion, once one of many, but now regarded by many as the founding father of Israel.

He explained in perfect English that I created a perfect excuse to break from his labors at his memoirs. We sat in opposing chairs and he looked expectant. I wondered how many interviews to journalists he had given; thousands, probably, many famous, and now to a complete unknown.

I calculated that old men can often recall with total clarity what they did in their youth, while having completely forgotten whom they had dinner with last week. I know the feeling too well. It seemed to me he must have been badgered many times for details of the Six-Day War, even though it was Levi Eshkol who was premier at the time.

"When you landed on the shore of Israel for the first time in 1906, sir, what was it like back then?"

He stared for several seconds, then came alive, as if jolted by an electric charge. Then he started to talk, eyes closed, recalling those very first early days. He was not a statesman back then, he was a penniless immigrant from a poor Jewish shtetl in Russian Poland.

He and his companions had berthed at the Arab port of Jaffa, but they were not welcome and could get no lodgings, so they trekked north and camped among the sand dunes. They spoke Russian and Yiddish, not modern Hebrew, which had not yet been standardized.

They were camped in a range of low sandhills and it was spring. The Hebrew word for "hill" is *tel*, and for "spring" *aviv*.

It took six days on a donkey to travel from the coast of this Turkish province to Jerusalem, a journey he made with a petition to the Ottoman governor for land. He was there ten years later, when the Ottoman Empire fell. He saw General Allenby of the conquering British Army enter Jerusalem.

He told me how the general had abandoned his horse and entered on foot, in deference to the holiest shrine of three religions. Somewhere out to the east, Lawrence, at the head of the Arab Revolt, was moving toward his own treasure: Damascus.

Over the years, he had seen it all: both world wars; the Mandate between them; the rise of Zionism; the utterance of the Balfour Declaration; the creation on a Franco-British map of Lebanon, Syria, Jordan, and Iraq. He had seen dictators and monarchs come and go, rise and fall, as the Jews pursued their single goal of, one day, a nation of their own. He had not only seen it all, he had been at the epicenter. He had met the generals and the giants, Roosevelt and Churchill.

Several times, the dragon popped her head around the door to object that it was time for his nap, but he waved her away. What struck me was his tolerance. He had fought all his life for his dream yet seemed to hate no one, not even Haj Amin al-Husseini, the Grand Mufti of Jerusalem, who so admired Adolf Hitler and wanted every Jew on earth dead. He had huge forbearance for the Palestinian Arabs, whose language he spoke perfectly. The only people he had no time for were the fanatics of the Irgun and the Stern Gang. At their mention, he sneered and shook his white-clouded head.

The British, for so long the unwilling army of occupation, he liked, even though he had helped form the Haganah, the Palmach, and the Mossad to outwit and outmaneuver them.

I could have filled ten notebooks, but I just sat and listened to an old man who was sixty years of living history and who had seen it all. Finally tired, he indicated that he needed his sleep. I went to fetch the dragon, who glared at me and escorted him to his sleeping quarters. At the door, he turned and said, "Good-bye, young man. I hope you have been interested. And stay lucky."

I had been indeed. Fascinated. I was shown out and walked to the gate. It was dusk. An Egged bus came by. I waved, and it stopped and took me on to Eilat as darkness fell. David Ben-Gurion died six years later, at the age of eighty-seven. He was one of the greatest men I had ever met.

EILAT

As recently as 1945, what is now the huge port and vacation resort of Eilat hardly existed. It was a motley collection of shacks with orange-crate furniture, clinging to the water's edge opposite the bigger Jordanian port of Aqaba, captured by Lawrence in 1917.

The early settlers and pioneers must have been tough as boots. There was nothing there, but they began to build and to plant. Among the earliest to arrive were Dr. and Mrs. Fay Morris from Manchester. He had flown with the RAF in the war, qualified as a doctor, and emigrated with his young wife. By 1968, both were pillars of the community, but lived modestly in a house they had built themselves.

The previous summer, the Israelis had swept across Sinai as General Israel Tal and his elderly British tanks pushed Nasser's forces back to the Suez Canal. That three-day conquest, although fought along the northern rim of Sinai, brought the entire triangular peninsula under Israeli control. And that included the Sinai Bedouin, to whom Dr. Morris had been appointed official medical officer. The Egyptians, who had always treated the Bedouin contemptuously, had never accorded them a doctor.

Because Sinai is girt on the west by the Suez Canal, which runs down to become the Red Sea, and on the east by the Gulf of Eilat and the Gulf of Aqaba, which also run down to become the Red Sea, and along the north by the Mediterranean, it is virtually an island. And the Bedouin seldom cross water.

From their desert wilderness, the Bedouin have watched the Romans, the Phoenicians, the Greeks, and the armies of Islam cross and recross their land, in conquest or in defeat. Later came the Crusaders, Napoleon's legions, Allenby's British Tommies, and the Israelis.

The Bedouin have witnessed them throughout the centuries. The marching and the fighting were mainly along the northern rim, up by the Mediterranean. The hinterland was always theirs. And their policy was always the same: to withdraw into their deserts of sand and rocks, to not interfere, to not take sides, to watch, and to survive. After July 1967, the Israelis were the first people to treat them decently.

Army engineers built a freshwater pipe from Eilat through El Arish and right across to Suez. They installed taps and troughs every couple of miles. And the water was free, in a land where water is life.

At first, the Bedouin thought there must be a trap, but the taps were unguarded, and slowly they began to come by night, refill their camels, their bellies, and their goatskin bags. Then first contact with Arabic-speaking officers was made. They were offered medication for their many ailments and infections. That was where Dr. Morris came in. He set up clinics at specific oases, and slowly his patients appeared.

Many of the sufferers were female and the miseries were mainly gynecological. It was out of the question for him to examine a Bedu woman, not because he was Jewish, but because he was male. So an army nurse would go into the tent, shout through the flap what she had found, and he would shout back the treatment.

The Bedouin replied in kind. You never see the Bedouin unless they allow you to, but they see everything. Each time a group of Egyptian commandos landed on the Sinai shore, the nearest Israeli army post would be alerted. Duly ambushed, the Egyptians would be disarmed and sent back, but never killed. It was almost a formality.

Through Dr. Morris's offices, I was allowed to accompany an Israeli army group in a command car on a two-day tour of Sinai. It was wild and bleak, a mighty ocean of football-sized boulders that would break most suspensions, interspersed with patches not of fine sand but of red-hot gravel. At two oases, we took coffee with Bedouin, while the women crouched out of sight inside the camel-hair tents.

Today it is so different. Right down the eastern coast is a chain of scuba-diving holiday resorts, from Taba Heights to Ras Mohammed. There are tourist visits to the ancient monastery of Saint Catherine, right in the center of the desert, marking the spot where Moses is believed to have been given the tablets with the Ten Commandments. Back in 1968, the monks had hardly seen an outsider for years.

Finally back in Eilat, I repaired to the beach bar of Rafi Nelson for a very cooling dip in the gulf and a long, cold beer. Among those at the bar was one Yitzhak "Ike" Ahronowitz, who spoke perfect English because he had studied in America. He had also been captain of the *Exodus*, the refugee ship turned back from the Palestinian coast by the British Royal Navy in 1947. He was still only in his mid-forties.

I had been too young to recall 1947, but I knew it had been a powerfully emotional incident and had generated Leon Uris's explicitly anti-British novel and the film that followed in 1960, which I had seen. I asked him if he shared Mr. Uris's feelings. He thought it over.

"Well, your navy officers were obeying their orders. And they were bastard orders." He grinned and raised his beer in mock toast. "So you were bastards, but at least you were polite bastards."

A few days later, I wished good-bye to the Morrises and took a bus north to Jerusalem.

JERUSALEM

————◆◆◆————

I will defy anyone to visit Jerusalem for the first time and not be fascinated by the antiquity of that maze of ancient streets and shrines revered by the world's three greatest religions.

Since the departure of the British and the inconclusive outcome of the 1948 post-independence war, the Old Quarter of East Jerusalem had been closed to the Jews while available to Muslims and Christians. Now it was open to all.

I played the tourist, staying at a humble boardinghouse, wandering the streets and alleys where fifty generations of worshippers and warriors had been before me. From the Via Dolorosa to the hill of Golgotha, from the Dome of the Rock to the Mosque of Al Aqsa, to the Wailing Wall and all that was left of the Temple of Solomon after the total sacking by the Romans, I just wandered and gawped. After three days, I was invited to take tea at the King David Hotel.

I had heard of it. Once the headquarters both of the British Mandate government and the army HQ, the King David Hotel was one of the more modern landmarks of the city, and though the damage of the bombing of 1946 was largely repaired, the scars were still visible. My reading before arriving had taught me the bare outlines.

On July 22, 1946, agents of the ultra-Zionist Irgun organization had eluded the pretty sketchy security measures and driven a van into the underground stores-delivery area. From the van, milk churns packed with 350 kilograms of explosives had been unloaded and scattered round the basement and nightclub.

When they went off, ninety-one were killed and forty-six injured, mostly civilians. If the Army HQ at one end of the building was the target, the bombers placed the device at the other end, hence the civilian casualties.

Twenty-eight British died, including thirteen soldiers, but they were well outnumbered by forty-one Arabs and seventeen Palestinian Jews. I mention this only because of what happened to me later that week.

For years, controversy raged as to whether a telephoned warning had ever been made, or, if made, received, and if received, disregarded. But the bombing was denounced by David Ben-Gurion and the Haganah, yearning for both the British Mandate to end and independence to arrive. In their view, the British were going to leave anyway, as soon as the newly born United Nations in New York made up its mind.

Mr. Ben-Gurion had just told me in Sde Boker, his desert retreat, that the real struggle would come after independence, when the Arabs launched themselves at the new Israeli state to snuff it out. To that end, the Mossad LeAliyah Bet, the purchasing agency outside the country, and Haganah inside the Mandate were trying to smuggle in both fighters and weapons under the noses of the British, who might choose to look the other way or not. Thus the King David Hotel bombing, which poisoned relations, was regarded by the calmer heads as completely counterproductive.

I was taking tea with friends on the upper terrace when I was invited over to be introduced to someone. I found myself facing the black eye patch of General Moshe Dayan, defense minister and architect of Israeli tactics for the Six-Day War. We talked for half an hour.

I had always presumed he lost that eye to a bullet, but he explained to me how it had happened. Before the Second World War, he had been on patrol with the British Zionist Orde Wingate, who designed and taught the principle of guerrilla warfare in that part of the world.

Wingate was a strange one, a Christian with an encyclopedic knowledge of the Old Testament and a conviction that God Himself had given the Holy Land to the Jews. Hence the Zionism. His skills in guerrilla warfare were such that Churchill later plucked him from the Middle East to form and lead the Chindits behind the Japanese lines in Burma.

On that patrol, Moshe Dayan had been staring at an Arab position through field glasses when a stray bullet hit the other end of the lens. It was the eyepiece being rammed back into the socket that blinded him.

I had one last interview set up via my contacts. I wanted to talk to Ezer Weizman, the founder of the Israeli Air Force and another revered figure after the IAF's performance during the war of 1967. By then he was transport minister, and I turned up as agreed the next day at the ministry.

He came bursting out, late, in a tearing hurry and having completely forgotten about our interview. The only way of achieving it was to do it on the drive back to Tel Aviv, but he did not intend to drive; he wanted to fly and the airfield was only minutes away.

"Do you mind flying?" he asked. I knew he had once flown British Hurricanes with the RAF in Egypt during the Second World War, so I mentioned that I also had my RAF wings. He stared, then grinned.

"Right, you can be my copilot," he said, and barked an order at the driver. His ministry attendant looked horrified.

I presumed he would be flying in a multiseat staff aircraft, but his chosen transport was a very small high-wing monoplane of the Cessna/Piper variety, although Israeli-made. We were strapped in, he did the preflight checks, and we took off. Almost immediately, the rising thermals from the Judean Desert caught us and the airplane began to rock and twist in the up-currents.

The interview would have to be conducted through face masks to be heard above the roar of the engine. He climbed to about 5,000 feet and set course for Sde Dov, the military airport outside Tel Aviv. So I asked him how he had established the now-mighty IAF.

He explained that as independence approached back in 1947, he had been charged to find and buy some serviceable fighter planes. The Mossad LeAliyah Bet traced a few to Yugoslavia, then recently liberated from German occupation and under the rule of the former guerrilla Marshal Tito.

Tito may have been a Communist, but it did not matter. He needed the foreign currency and the Haganah was anti-imperialist. The deal was done. There were four of them, abandoned by the Germans, still in maker's grease, stored in their original crates. An Israeli team went north to assemble them. He and his three other pilots followed. Rather strangely, they were four young Jewish fliers at the controls of four Messerschmitt Bf 109s in full Nazi insignia.

Thus they flew south, refueled secretly in Turkey, and arrived over Tel Aviv on the day of independence and of the launch of the Arab war to snuff out Israel. They arrived, virtually flying on vapor, to be told that a squadron of Egyptian Air Force fighters was coming north over Ashkelon. There was no time to land and refuel. They turned south, to find King Farouk's British-built Hurricanes coming toward them.

Thus the first dogfight over Israel was between Egyptians in Hurricanes and Jews in Messerschmitts.

Up to this point, Ezer Weizman had been gesticulating copiously, but now he took both hands off the control column and raised them, fingers spread, to demonstrate how he had led the attack, with Benny Katz from South Africa as his wingman.

The monoplane promptly flipped over, and the Judean Desert went to the top of the windscreen. He didn't seem to mind. As we began to dive upside down, I thought it wise to drop my notepad and pencil and grab the joystick. When she was back on an even keel and heading for the coast, I suggested he resume control. But he just shrugged and went on, with more copious hand gestures, explaining how they had scattered the Hurricanes, which turned back to Egypt, and landed at what is now Ben-Gurion Airport but was then a grass strip.

He took over again as we came to land, shut the engine down, jumped out, gave me a cheery wave, and shot off in his ministerial car. The ground crew let me examine his personal black Spitfire, a superb model, then I took an Egged bus from the main gate of the air base back to downtown Tel Aviv.

CONFESSION

My last night in Tel Aviv on that visit was spent at a pub down an alley running down the side of the Dan Hotel toward the sea. It was owned and run by a very feisty lady, a Romanian redhead, also called Freddie.

There was a crowd around the bar that I was invited to join, including, I think, Moshe Dayan's daughter Yael and her husband, a former tank commander called Dov Zion. In deference to my ignorance of Hebrew, they very politely switched to English, and the conversation moved to where I had been and what I had seen. That included the King David Hotel.

Every one of them had been involved in some way in the independence struggle twenty years earlier, and half at least had been in the Haganah or the Palmach. As the British had then been the occupiers, I expected some hostility, but there was none.

There were anecdotes about smuggling consignments of small arms under melon cargoes past British roadblocks, and all of them were at pains to tell me that the British were divided into two types, so far as they were concerned.

The other-rank soldiers, many of them Paras, had nothing against Jews at all, having often been brought up with them in the streets of London, Birmingham, and Manchester. The soldiers had been fighting the Germans for four years before being posted to Palestine; some had seen the horrors of the concentration camps, and all just wanted to go back home to their wives and families.

They spoke neither Arabic nor Hebrew, and the Palestinians certainly spoke no English. So if there was any conversation, it was between the Diaspora Jews and the Tommies. It was friendly enough. Among the former guerrillas around the bar were several who narrated how consignments of Haganah weapons went past the roadblocks on a nudge and a wink, the melons undisturbed.

The anti-Semitic attitude came hot and strong from the Foreign Office, the civil servants and senior officer corps who rarely disguised their preference for the Arabs. I had heard it said before that more desert sand flows through the British Foreign Office than Lawrence ever saw.

But what really surprised me was that the Israelis' real dislike was not for the British but for their own extremists, the Irgun and the Stern Gang. I could not detect one with a good word to say for them. The collective attitude seemed to be that the back-shooting of British Tommies by the extremists simply made the real job, preparing for the survival war of 1948, even harder.

But at the back of the group was one who stared at me constantly until it became quite uncomfortable. Finally, as drinks were being replenished, I felt a tug at my sleeve and it was the staring one.

"I must have a word with you," he said. Close up, I realized he was not hostile but pleading.

"Not here," he said, and drew me away to the far corner of the bar.

"I have to speak to you. I have waited twenty years. I have a confession to make."

Normally when a journalist hears that someone wants to make a confession, his heart sinks. It is usually about some shoplifting years ago or a failure to report a spaceship landing in the garden last night. One looks around for an escape route. In this case, there was none.

"Why me?" I asked.

"Because you are British," he said, "and you are a Gentile."

I could not see the connection, but I nodded anyway. I would just have to listen to what he had to say. He took a deep breath.

"I was in the Irgun back then. I drove the truck into the King David Hotel."

There was silence between us. The murmur around the bar was a distant backdrop. He was still staring at me, small, wiry, intense, with black, unblinking eyes. Still pleading. I did not know what to say.

"That's it?"

"No, not all. I want you to believe me. I walked out of the basement and went to a café, a French one, right opposite. I used the public phone. I rang the King David exchange and asked to be put through to military HQ. I spoke to a junior officer. I told him there was a bomb."

"And?"

"He did not believe me. He said it was impossible. Then he put the phone down. Twenty minutes later, it went off. But I tried. Please believe me, I really tried."

Whether there would have been time to evacuate that enormous hotel in twenty minutes was a very moot point.

"All right," I said. "I believe you."

"Thank you."

"One question from me," I said. "Why do you not tell them over there?" I nodded toward the warriors around the bar.

"They would kill me," he said. He might have been right, too.

I left Israel the next day. Back to London, to Ashford, to see my folks. Then back to the rain forests. Back to the killing fields of Africa.

OF MICE AND MOLES

Most of the British media have an ongoing problem with the various organs of the British intelligence community, typified by a seeming inability to work out which is which.

Basically there are three main organs. The least mentioned is, ironically, the biggest. This is GCHQ, or Government Communications Headquarters, situated in a vast doughnut-shaped complex outside the country town of Cheltenham. Its task is mainly SIGINT, or signals intelligence.

Basically, it listens. It intercepts and eavesdrops on Britain's enemies and opponents, and sometimes even her friends, on a worldwide basis. In a quixotic throwback to the days of empire, it has outstations in various parts of the world, something even the American National Security Agency, immensely bigger and more generously funded, finds very useful. As a result, there is a constant sharing and interflow of "product" between the two.

It is this unceasing information swap, the invisible but crucial collaboration between the two countries' information gathering and security agencies, that constitutes the much-mocked "special relationship" and that includes a mutual trust and fellowship between the Special Forces as well. It has nothing whatever to do with notional, and often passing, friendships between politicians.

Alongside GCHQ is the Security Service, or MI5. Long ago, its mailing address was PO Box 500, London, so it is sometimes mockingly referred to as Box 500. Its task is in-country security against foreign espionage, foreign and domestic terrorism, and homegrown treachery. It maintains just a few postings overseas to liaise with other, friendly security agencies.

The one regarded as the more glamorous agency is the Secret Intelligence Service, usually referred to by a title it renounced years ago: MI6. There is often confusion between the Secret Service and the Security Service, let alone the swapping of their numbers and thus their functions. But everyone remotely concerned is universally described by those on the outside with another misnomer, that of "spy."

The true spy is almost certainly a foreigner employed deep inside the clandestine fabric of his own country who is prepared to abstract his country's covert information and hand it over to his real employers. The go-between is called an "asset," and the full-time employee who runs him is his "handler."

There is the relatively new nomenclature of "spook," but I never, ever heard the word *spy* used within that world. Only the papers and TV ever use it, usually wrongly.

That apart, MI5 is based at Thames House, on the north bank of the River Thames in London, a few hundred yards from Parliament, and the SIS at Vauxhall Cross on the South Bank almost a mile upstream, after moving from the shabby old Century House in the Elephant and Castle district.

The task of SIS is foreign information gathering and its presence is worldwide, with a "station" somewhere in almost all British embassies and sometimes consulates. Basically, it seeks to discover and forewarn. Politicians are wont to sneer when in opposition but drool with pleasure when, in office, they are taken to a quiet room to have explained to them what is really going on rather than what they thought was going on.

Politicians congenitally loathe to be taken by surprise, which is where the forewarning comes in, but forewarning depends on knowing what the bad people are planning, intending, or have in mind. As that is rarely given away, it has to be discovered clandestinely. Hence the espionage.

This broadly devolves into three categories: electronic intelligence, or ELINT, the scouring of the surface of the world with look-down cameras, mounted either in satellites, drones, or warplanes; signals intelligence, SIGINT, intercepting everything the bad people say to each other, even when they think they have absolute privacy; and HUMINT, or human intelligence gathering.

Britain has never been able to compete with the vast budgets of the United States, and has no space program, but it brings to the table a worthwhile contribution in HUMINT. Infiltrating an agent into the heart of a tricky situation can produce more product than all the "gizmos" could ever see or hear. It is the specialty of the SIS.

As for the terms, those inside the SIS called it "the Office"; those outside use the phrase "the Firm"; and the staffers of the firm are the "friends." Not to be confused with the CIA, which is "the Agency" or "the Company," and its staff, who are "the Cousins."

Considering the sixty million–plus population of the UK and the size of its gross national product, it has always had a smaller SIS than almost any other developed nation in the world, and thus cheaper. The

British taxpayer is far from shortchanged. There is a quixotic reason for this.

Unlike all other agencies, the Firm has always been able to rely on a widespread ad hoc army of volunteers prepared to help out if asked nicely. They come from a vast array of professions, something that causes them to travel a bit. They may agree while on a foreign visit for business purposes to pick up a package, deliver a letter to a hole in a tree, make a payment, or just keep their eyes and ears open and undergo a cheerful debriefing when they get home. It appears a bit weird, but it seems to work.

This is because the best "cover" in the world is no cover at all, but the truth. Thus, if Mr. Farnsbarns really is going to a trade fair to sell his paper clips, he might just slip into a phone booth, remove a letter from the pages of the telephone directory, and bring it home in an invisible slit in a specially prepared briefcase. That is where the economics come in; it is not done for money but just to help "the old country." Very few nations can match that.

There are times in your life when you meet someone and in short order decide he is a thoroughly decent fellow and you can trust him. If you are ever deceived in this later, it is like a hot dagger.

In late 1968, on a brief home visit from Biafra to firm up some correspondent contracts with various London papers, I met a member of the Firm called Ronnie. He sought me out rather than the reverse, and made no bones about what he was, and we hit it off.

He was an Orientalist with good Mandarin Chinese, but to his bewilderment had been made head of the Africa desk. He admitted he knew little about Africa and less about what was really going on inside Biafra. I think we spent about twenty hours over several days while I explained how bad things were, as it became plain the children were now dying of starvation like flies. Had I not trusted his word, I would never have agreed to what came next.

The CRO had amalgamated with the Foreign Office to become the FCO. Both the former secretary of state for the CRO and his deputy, the minister of state, had resigned, one after the other. The former, a deeply devout Scottish Presbyterian, George Thomson, despite the official reason given, simply could not in all conscience continue to preside over a policy he found disgusting and immoral. His deputy, George Thomas, was a religious Welsh Methodist and shared precisely the same opinion.

(The latter went on to become speaker of the House of Commons and retired as Lord Tonypandy, a thoroughly honorable and respected politician, not least for his stand over Biafra.)

But the FCO was in the hands of the appalling Michael Stewart, a complete creature of his Civil Service mandarins. They, headed by Lord Greenhill, had absorbed, lock, stock, and barrel, the policy of the CRO, itself based on the flawed appraisal of Sir David Hunt, still *en poste* as British high commissioner in Lagos and pushing the pro-Nigeria, crush-Biafra policy line with every dispatch.

But there was a debate beginning after fifteen months of the Nigeria-Biafra war, and made more intense by the torrent of hideous pictures showing Biafran babies reduced to barely alive skeletons.

The public marches of protest were starting, notable figures were protesting; the debate might be at a very high level and in complete secrecy, but the FCO was fighting a rearguard action for the minds of the vacillating Harold Wilson government.

Technically, the SIS comes under the FCO but is entitled to disagree in certain circumstances, specifically if it has factual information rather than mere opinion. Ronnie's problem was he had no specific eyes-on information from the heart of Biafra to offset the assurances coming through from Lagos to the effect that the horrors were grossly exaggerated and the war would in any case be over in very short order—the song that had now been sung for fifteen months of a two-week war.

I did what I did, not in order to do down the Biafrans—far from it. I did it to try to influence the Whitehall argument that continued intermittently for the next fifteen months until the final crushing of Biafra, with a million dead children.

The argument was between: "Prime Minister, this cannot be allowed to go on. The human cost is simply too high. We should reconsider our policy. We should use all our influence to urge a cease-fire, a peace conference, and a political solution," and "Prime Minister, I can assure you the media reports are as usual sensationalist and grossly exaggerated. We have information the rebel regime is very close to collapse. The sooner it does, the sooner we can get columns of relief food into the rebel territory. Meanwhile, we urge you to stick with the hitherto-agreed policy and even increase the support for the federal government."

Neither Ronnie nor I could know in October 1968 how long there was to go or how many more to die. But the argument for a cease-fire lost, for two reasons: the vanity factor and the cowardice factor.

It is said that if a tigress sees her cubs endangered, she will fight with deranged passion to defend them. But her dedication pales into submission compared with the fury with which senior civil servants and most notably of the Foreign Office will defend the fiction that they cannot have made a mistake.

The cowardice applied as usual to the politicians, Wilson and Stewart. Basically, it was: "Prime Minister, if you concede to the 'reconsider' argument you would have to admit that for fifteen months your government has made a mistake. How then do you reply to the media question: How can you explain to the public the quarter million children dead so far?" At that point, the response from Wilson and Stewart was, "Very well, do what you feel you must. But hurry."

So the military, advisory, diplomatic, and propaganda help to the Lagos dictatorship quietly increased. Ronnie convinced me that the Firm might be able to win the argument if it could rebut the charge of media exaggeration with eyes-on evidence that the situation was as reported or worse.

But to do that, he needed an asset deep inside the Biafran enclave, what he termed "someone in on the ground." When I left for the return to the rain forest, he had one.

On my return, the job was threefold. To report through the various newspapers and magazines that had accepted me as a stringer (local correspondent on a non-staff basis) the military war as it crawled on its way. To use the same outlets to portray the humanitarian situation, the disaster among the children dying of kwashiorkor (protein deficiency), and the church-based efforts to keep them alive with an air bridge of illicit mercy flights bringing in relief food donated by literally the whole world.

In this, there were at least a dozen other journalists, sometimes twenty, who came and went; there were delegations of parliamentarians, senators, and emissaries from various concerned groups, who simply felt they had to see and report back.

In Europe and North America, the issue, based on the reports and the still and moving pictures, became massive, linking Left and Right, young and old, in marches and protests. There were times when Harold Wilson appeared almost under siege, and twice, I learned later, the "reconsider" policy was almost adopted. Had the opposition Conservative Party leaned its weight, the change of policy might have gone through and the dying of the children would have ended, but Edward Heath, the Tory leader, shared with the FCO his European Union obsession, and he was their man.

The third task was to keep Ronnie informed of things that could not, for various reasons, emerge in the media. Just once, after nine months, things became sticky, when a rumor spread that I was working for London. Had the suspicion developed, my situation might have become thoroughly tiresome. I discovered the source was the ex-Legionnaire German mercenary Rolf Steiner, with whom I had never been on the best of terms.

There was nothing for it but to have a word in the right ear. Two nights later, yelling and screaming, not a happy camper, with his hands roped behind him, Steiner was bundled onto a plane for Libreville and never returned.

A MEDIA EXPLOSION

It should never be forgotten that the Nigeria-Biafra War fell into two quite different periods, and the transition from one to the other lasted no more than a fortnight.

For the first year, from July 1967 to June 1968, it was just an ordinary African war, plodding its incompetent way across the landscape. The Nigerians, with their standing army of 8,000 infantry in the summer of '67, had presumed they would sweep through the secessionist province as of right. The Biafrans believed that Lagos would wage war for a few months and then, realizing it was hopeless, give up. Neither happened.

After the short-lived debacle of the Biafran invasion of the Mid-West across the Niger, Nigeria introduced compulsory conscription, forcing into uniform tens of thousands of unwilling young men. This huge expansion required weapons from rifles to artillery and armored cars, and staggering quantities of ammunition to replace what had largely been fired into the treetops, as well as training. That was where the British Establishment came in. Behind a mendacious screen of "neutrality," the Wilson government poured in the equipment without which the war could not have proceeded. That was what the Biafrans had not foreseen.

The Whitehall-sourced propaganda stumbled from lie to lie, but for the first year the media paid little attention, because eastern Nigeria was obscure, far away, and of minimal reader interest. The first lie was that London would only "fulfill existing contracts," but these were soon swamped by the expansion of the Nigerian Federal Army, and shipload after shipload were needed.

Payment was not the problem; there were always the oil royalties, and Nigeria's credit was good. It came down to the licenses. Impelled by urgings from the High Commission in Lagos, these were granted without demur.

Another early lie was that no weapons at all were being shipped from Britain to fuel the war. The key word was *from*, not *by*. In fact, the supplies were coming from British stocks at the immense NATO weapons park outside Brussels, and thus technically from Belgium. They were then replaced by shipments from Britain to Belgium.

Slowly, both the enlargement and the supplies had their effect. The Nigerian Federal Army crawled across the territory, village by village and town by town. The capital Enugu was taken, to be replaced by the town of Umuahia. Port Harcourt fell and its airport was lost. With Enugu Airport also gone, a new one was created at Uli from a stretch of road two miles long. This became the only entry and exit point, with clapped-out old cargo planes coming in from the offshore islands of Fernando Po and São Tomé.

The transformation started deceptively in May 1968, when the missionaries noticed worried mothers from the deep bush bringing emaciated children for examination.

The missionaries were a network across the country, mainly the fathers of the Holy Ghost and the nuns of the Holy Rosary, both from Dublin. These ran the churches with, attached to them, a school and a dispensary. There were some Protestant missionaries, but the great majority were Catholics. The Ibos were overwhelmingly Catholic, and Islam had never penetrated south of the savannah land.

The priests and nuns knew exactly what they were looking at: kwashiorkor. The total shutoff of protein-rich foodstuffs was finally having its effect. No one had foreseen this, because no one had thought the war would last that long. Without the Wilson government's intervention, it would not have. But the appearance of kwashiorkor transformed an incompetent bush war into a massive humanitarian tragedy, the like of which neither Africa, Europe, nor North America had ever seen. But they were about to.

The priests appealed in Ireland for funds, and a few suitcases of medications came in. But no one took any notice. The media visit of February, which the BBC had ostracized, had been and gone before the signs were evident. I had arrived back after Israel sometime in May. In June, two British newspapers sent a team of one reporter and one photographer each. They were the *Daily Express* and the now-defunct *Daily Sketch*.

Due to the action of Stewart Steven, the foreign editor, I had been retained by the *Daily Express*, so my job was to escort Walter Partington and David Cairns. The visit started with the usual formalities: a briefing on the military situation and then a visit to a couple of fronts where some combat was going on.

Walter, who had arrived with a half case of whiskey and several cartons of priceless cigarettes, declined to move from his allotted bungalow, where he sat consuming his supplies and sharing with no one. David Cairns and I went off to the fronts with army escorts. When we

Back in Biafra children were starving. This photo was taken by David Cairns in June 1968, one of the first seen in English newspapers. The effect was dramatic.

By June 1968 I was back in Biafra. I travelled by boat (*top left*) with Walter Partington, in front, and David Cairns of the *Daily Express*, who took this picture. I am in the back behind Bruce Loudon, a stringer for the *Daily Telegraph*. David took many photos of the escalating war, among them this one of me looking on while an elderly Ibo draws in the dirt (*top right*), and this picture of an unexploded British-made shell, supplied to the Nigerians. So much for denials from London. In September 1968 the *Nigerian Observer* even went so far as to report that I had joined the Biafran army (*right*).

THE NIGERIAN

OBSERVER

Vol. 1. No. 104.   THURSDAY, SEPTEMBER 26,

BBC MAN JOINS REBELS

MR. Frederick Forsythe former BBC correspondent and commentator on Nigerian affairs who was based in Lagos for many months has now joined the rebel

REB DE NO

As more photographs appeared in the British press of the famine in Biafra (*left and below*), the real state of affairs was becoming apparent. A protest rally was held at Speaker's Corner in August 1968 calling the BBC and the Wilson government to account (*bottom*).

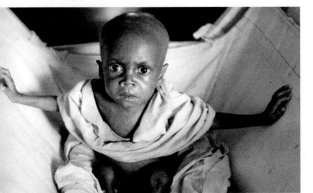

Family matters.

My parents (*left*), a constant
source of support and
encouragement, at their
cottage in Willesborough,
near Ashford.

Carrie, Stuart and me at home in
Ireland in 1979 (*above*). Shane came
along the same year (*left*).

They soon grew up: here we are
bagging game in South Africa,
and later scuba-diving in the
Gulf of Oman.

Sandy and I collect my gong,
awarded for charity work,
October 1997 (*right*).

The Day of the Jackal was written on my portable typewriter in thirty-five days in January 1970 (*left*), published the next year and two years later made into a film directed by Fred Zinnemann, starring the relatively unknown Edward Fox (*middle left*). It was the back jacket of the German edition (*below*) that blew my cover when I was doing research for *The Dogs of War*.

Next came *The Odessa File* (*bottom left*): I used the story of the true-life Nazi war criminal Eduard Roschmann (*bottom right*) the release of the film in 1974 led to his arrest by the Argentinian police. He escape and died in Paraguay three years later.

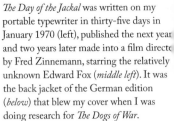

FREDERICK FORSYTH,

geboren 1938, war — be er seine Welterfolge De SCHAKAL und DIE AK ODESSA schrieb — Journ list. Er arbeitete für Reuter Paris, Brüssel, Mailand. der Bundesrepublik, DDR und der Tschechosl wakel, war Fernsehreport der BBC, schrieb 1969 d „Biafra-Story". Die Romar DER SCHAKAL und D AKTE ODESSA wurden e folgreich verfilmt.

Der Schakal Niemand weiß, wer er in Wirklichkeit ist, der Kille aus London, der den perfekten Mord beherrscht wie de Ingenieur eine komplizierte Maschine. Die Kunst des Tötens un ein astronomisches Dollarhonorar scheinen der einzige Antrie für seinen gefährlichen Job zu sein. So auch diesmal, da ihn die OAS für das Attentat auf den französischen Staatspräsidenten engagiert hat, für den bestbewachten Staatsmann der westliche

Welt den zweiten Killer. Diese Geschichte ist zwar ein Roman, aber er basiert au historischen Vorfällen. De Gaulles Preisgabe des französischer Algerien, der Kampf der OAS gegen den „Verrat" des Präsidenten, der Untergang ihres Anführers Argoud im Jahre 1963, das Scheitern vergangener Polizeiarbeit werden sorgfältig recherchiert. Alle Details der Polizeiarbeit werden sorgfältig blendend erfundene Handlung nahtlos eingepaßt. Bei brillanter Erzähltechnik läßt er den Leser alles wissen und atemlos miterleben und hält ihn trotzdem bis zur letzten Seite im Ungewissen.

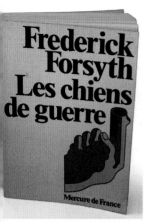

The French edition of *The Dogs of War* (*left*) was used as a handbook by French mercenaries when they attacked the Comoro Islands. They succeeded in taking them over!

Michael Caine starred in the film of my 1984 novel, *The Fourth Protocol*. We had some convivial times together (*below*).

Research is important: in 2009 I went to Guinea-Bissau to research cocaine trafficking for The Cobra (*bottom*).

Back to the beginning. In a Spitfire, flying high over the Weald, just like they did in 1940.

got back, Walter was a bit too indulged to be able to write copy, so I wrote and transmitted all his dispatches myself, but in his name.

(Rather amusingly, when he got home he filed the lot for the International Reporter of the Year award—and won.)

Then we found the starving children at a Catholic mission house. David Cairns and his colleague from the *Sketch* took hundreds of pictures, stored the rolls in light-proof capsules, and took them home. Back then, we could transmit words by telex, but not photos.

I never saw the editions of the *Express* and *Sketch* that appeared the following week, but the effect was dramatic. Today, we have all seen pictures of starving children from Africa and Asia, but in 1968 no one in the West had ever seen anything like it.

This was the catalyst the situation required. It changed everything, turning a low-intensity, low-interest African war into the greatest humanitarian cause of the decade.

Back in Britain, later Europe, and then the United States, ordinary citizens just expressed their horror, protested, and donated. Out of this was created the most extraordinary mercy mission the world had ever seen, a nightly air bridge from the offshore islands to the ultra-basic Uli airstrip in the heart of the rain forest.

From Denmark, a Protestant minister, Vigo Mollerup, recruited airline pilots from all the Scandinavian airlines to give up their vacations to fly freight planes carrying baby milk concentrates through the night to Uli. That was called Nord Church Air. What they carried was contributed by the World Council of Churches (Protestant) and Caritas (the international Rome-based Catholic charity). The Pope ordered Monsignor Carlo Bayer, a Silesian, to raid the funds of Caritas and mount the Catholic contribution.

Also in the mix was the ICRC (International Committee of the

Red Cross) under the Swiss Karl Jaggi. And what was really extraordinary was that the whole thing was illegal. By law, those lifesaving planes were invading Nigerian airspace against the wishes of the Lagos-based military junta, which acquired MiG fighters and pilots from the Communist bloc to try to shoot them down. That was why the relief planes had to fly at night and land in darkness. It had never happened before, and it has never happened since.

By late autumn, the air bridge, collectively called Joint Church Aid, or mockingly Jesus Christ Airlines, was up and running, or rather flying, and it continued to the end. The three main agencies, WCC, Caritas, and ICRC, all put an estimate of children who died at about a million and a similar figure on those saved from death.

By the end, the network of feeding centers sprawled across the still-defiant enclave, where the children lay waiting for death or a bowl of protein-rich milk, served an estimated transient population of half a million. The burial parties would often put a hundred children from one center into their mass grave in a single day.

And the media came, in hundreds, with their reporters and their cameras, along with hundreds of volunteers who just wanted to help in whatever way they could. Many had to be refused passage—there were just too many.

And the British government of Harold Wilson and the Foreign Office? It stuck doggedly to the old discredited policy, doubling up the supplies, advice, and propaganda aid to the Nigerian junta. The press office of the FCO stooped to quote incredible levels of mendacity to fulfill its brief.

One canard that had seriously been proposed to the attendant press in London was that there were really no starving children in the "rebel enclave" save for a group kept deliberately as living skeletons for display purposes. Whenever a mission of visiting VIPs was touring the villages, these emaciated wretches would be trucked ahead of them so that they were always there to greet the visitors. It was an ex–public school product with an old-school tie and a degree who offered that little gem to the media.

On another occasion, the war hero Group Captain Leonard Cheshire VC was asked to go to visit, be shown around Nigeria only, and return to peddle the official line. He duly went to Nigeria, but then refused not to go to Biafra. What he saw on the second visit so shocked him that he came back and denounced the official policy. He was immediately smeared as a gullible fool.

It was pretty standard to smear every journalist who expressed disgust at what was going on as either a mercenary, arms dealer, or Ojukwu propagandist, even though a million pictures are rather hard to dispute.

No massive humanitarian tragedy, save those inflicted by nature herself, is possible without two kinds of contributors. Hitler could never have carried out the holocaust that he did if he had relied only on the uniformed sadists of the SS. Behind them had to stand another army of organizers, administrators, and bureaucrats—the enablers.

Someone had to constantly supply the uniforms and the boots, the guns and the ammunition, the wages, the rations, and the barbed wire. Someone had to oversee the supply of instruments of torture and of gas pellets. Someone who never pulled a trigger or turned on a gas chamber. But these people enabled it to happen. It is the difference between the doer and the desk doer.

Starting with Sir David Hunt's biased and flawed analysis, which was adopted by the Commonwealth Relations Office, taken over and intensified by the Foreign Office, and cravenly endorsed by Harold Wilson and Michael Stewart, what happened could not have happened without the wholesale and covert contribution of the Wilson government. I remain convinced of it to this day.

Nor was it necessary to protect some vital British interest, and what interest merits a million dead children? Britain could have used its huge influence with Lagos to militate for a cease-fire, a peace conference, and a political solution. It chose not to, despite repeated opportunities, pursuing Hunt's conviction that Biafra must be crushed no matter the cost, but without ever explaining why.

That is why I believe that this coterie of vain mandarins and cowardly politicians stained the honor of my country forever, and I will never forgive them.

A USEFUL CERTIFICATE

———◆◆◆———

The plan was to march many miles through the Nigerian lines to blow up a bridge that formed a major supply route to one of their most advanced salients into Ibo territory.

To be frank, there were no "lines" in the sense of fortified trenches across the landscape. The media liked to draw lines on maps by linking Nigerian advance points, villages they had reached and where there was a Nigerian army presence. But in that rain forest, there were myriad narrow tracks known only to guides from the nearby villages, along which it was possible to march through the "lines" and into the bush hinterland behind them. To reach the target bridge, such was the plan.

The mission was to comprise three mercenaries and twenty of the best-trained Biafran "commandos," along with a couple of local guides who knew the tracks in the bush. I elected to go along, suspecting a good journalistic story.

On the first night, we were halfway there. We camped because even the guides would not march at night. It was not just dark in the forest; it was pitch-black. So we camped and built a small fire. After a pretty basic dinner, the group settled down to sleep, as ever consumed by mosquitoes and amazed at how noisy the jungle is at night.

There was Taffy, the South African with the Welsh name; Johnny, the Rhodesian with a South African name; Armand, a Parisian with a Corsican name; and me, an Englishman with a Scottish name. And the Biafrans, who were all Ibos. Out of the darkness Taffy suddenly spoke.

"I'm prepared to bet I am the only person around this campfire who can prove he's sane."

We all lay there slowly working out that the only way you can prove you are sane is if you have a certificate to say so. And the only way you can be issued such a certificate is on release from a lunatic asylum.

I lay there thinking: I am miles from bloody anywhere. If I disappear tonight, no one will ever know what happened to me, or even ask. I could simply vanish. So I am lying next to a giant who is armed to the teeth and joking that he is half mad. I stayed awake.

There are moments when the question "What the hell am I doing here?" simply will not go away. The next day, Johnny, the explosives wizard, blew the bridge and we marched back through the bush into the Biafran heartland. I made a point of marching behind Taffy in case he had forgotten about his certificate.

MR. SISSONS, I PRESUME

The plan was to motor by Land Rover to the last known Biafran position, then march on to a point far down the road from Aba to Owerri,
and mount an ambush. I agreed to go along, even though this would be
an all-Biafran affair with no white mercenaries involved.

I was always quite chary of going with an all-Ibo patrol, because if
things went seriously pear-shaped, they could simply vaporize into
their native rain forest, whereas I would be lost within ten yards and
quite likely to walk into a Nigerian army unit mistaking one for the
other. The faces were the same, the uniforms similar, and the forest
bewildering.

But everything went smoothly. We knew Aba had fallen and was a
new Nigerian strongpoint. Owerri was still being contested. The road
might carry Nigerian convoys of troops and supplies; hence the night
ambush. It never occurred to me that some fool on the Nigerian side
might send up a party of visiting journalists.

So the commando officer picked his spot on a grassy bank above the
road and we settled down to wait. After an hour, there was the low

rumble of engines coming up from the south, then the wash of dimmed headlights.

We were invisible in the long grass and under the trees, but the road, with no tree cover, was visible by moon and stars. The lead Nigerian Land Rover stopped several bullets and drove itself straight into the rain ditch, blocking the road for the convoy and preventing escape forward. The lorries behind panicked, stopped, and began to shed the dim forms of the men inside them. The Biafrans kept firing and the Nigerians started shouting and screaming.

Then, above the noise, I heard a single voice shouting in perfectly accented English: "I've been hit, oh, my God, I've been hit." That was the first indication there were any Europeans down on the road.

Peering into the gloom, I discerned the shouting figure on the road and the voice made plain it was a fellow countryman. Next to me, a Biafran soldier also spotted the target and raised his FAL rifle to complete the job. Journalistic rivalry may occasionally become tense, but never that bad. I reached out, eased his barrel upward, and his shot went off through the treetops. He turned and I could see the whites of his eyes glaring at me. Then the ambush commander blew his whistle—the signal to shimmy backward off the bank, into the forest, and run like hell.

The Englishman on the road had taken a bullet in the thigh. Months later, I learned that he was Independent Television News star Peter Sissons, who was evacuated and flown home, and made a full recovery.

Years later, at a fancy-dress charity ball of all things, and being somewhat in my cups, I let it slip. He and his wife were there. Peter took the news with appropriate dignity, but his wife gave me a big wet kiss.

WORTH A LARGE ONE

A dozen years after the Biafra War, I found myself in a London bar with a long-term veteran of the SAS regiment. Out of the blue, he remarked, "You owe me a large one."

If someone like that tells you he is owed a drink, do not argue. Just go to the bar and buy him a double. So I did. When he had taken a deep draft, I asked him why.

"Because," he said, "I once had your head in the crosshairs of my scope sight, and I didn't pull the trigger."

I reckoned that merited an entire bottle. It also confirmed something I had long suspected. The Special Air Service specializes (among many other things) in deep penetration into target territory, information gathering, and withdrawal unseen. Rumors had long persisted that part of London's extensive help to Lagos had been the presence of our Special Forces. Political denial had always been a bit too shrill.

There was certainly no such presence until 1968. My only time west of the Niger had been as a BBC correspondent with the Biafran invasion across the Onitsha Bridge the previous year. After my return in 1968, I had always been inside the Biafran enclave. The only time my contentedly sipping bar friend could have seen me was through a screen of trees deep inside Biafra.

So much for official denials.

BITS OF METAL

Of all the bits of metal that have been thrown in my direction, the nastiest are mortars. This is because they are silent. The only thing you hear from a falling mortar shell is a soft, feathery whisper just before it impacts. Usually not even long enough to dive for cover.

If the ground it falls on is soft or swampy, as sometimes happened in Biafra, the bomb might embed itself at the moment of impact, spending much of its explosive force and its sheets of shrapnel in the surrounding mud.

But if it falls on hard ground, it detonates with an earsplitting crack. That is not the problem; the real problem is that the casing transforms into many hundreds of fragments of razor-sharp metal that spray outward from knee-high to well over the head, and in a 360-degree circle from the explosion. Anyone caught in that hail of shrapnel will probably be torn apart and killed, or at least crippled.

That is why I came to loathe them—the silence. The Nigerians, unlike the Biafrans, had artillery with shells constantly resupplied by London, despite the lies. But they were comfortingly inaccurate as gunners, and an incoming shell makes an audible whoosh like a subway train entering a station. Just enough time to go facedown in the dirt and hope the blast will go over your back.

Machine guns are not funny, but the Nigerians simply put the gun on full automatic, using the entire magazine in one blast, usually aiming high and taking the tops off innumerable innocent trees. Time enough to hit the dirt or dive into the friendly rain ditch and get below ground level.

When it came to rifles, the Nigerians used the NATO-issue SLR, or self-loading rifle. These, too, they put onto the automatic fire setting and went through the magazine in seconds. When you saw the branches above your head start to shred, if you hit the dirt, you would probably stay alive. That apart, the half-trained (if that) compulsory recruits had trouble hitting a barn door at ten paces. Literally hundreds of millions of bullets went through the treetops.

The Biafrans had far more limited supplies, coming in by planeload rather than shipload, but the mercenaries trying to teach ammo-conservancy had an impossible task. In Africa, "spray the landscape" seems to be the only infantry tactic.

Among the Biafrans, the two most feared weapons were the Saladin armored car and the Ferret scout car, both London-supplied. The Saladin had one cannon, which the crew did not know how to use, and each had a heavy machine gun, which was really nasty. But you could hear them coming, too, the growl of the Ferret and the whine of the Saladin usually giving you time to get out of the way. Unfortunately, if the Biafrans heard the Saladin whine coming their way, they would just run for it, and down went another defended village.

At a certain point, Nigeria acquired an air arm; Ilyushin twin-jet bombers and MiG-17 jet fighters, both flown by mercenaries, Egyptians or East Germans. The Biafrans had no anti-air forces, though that did not stop them wasting ammunition by blazing upward whenever they saw one. The Nigerians had no pilots at all, because the only ones they had ever had were Ibos. So the Ilyushins and MiGs could fly low, pick their targets, and bomb or strafe them. But they never changed the course of the war. I was only once caught by a MiG.

I happened to be on a long, straight laterite road with grass fields on either side, so no tree cover. The MiG appeared to my right, visible through the driver's-side window of my Volkswagen Beetle (Nigeria then drove on the left of the road). I had seen him, but he had also seen me and he was flying in the same direction at about 3,000 feet.

Through the windscreen, I watched him drop the port wing and haul the fighter through 180 degrees, diving to level out just above the road. I slammed on the brakes, bailed out, and went into the rain ditch just as he opened up.

He came down the road with his cannon, ripping small fountains out of the laterite surface, roared overhead, and was gone, making only one pass. He could not have been much good. Despite plowing up the road, he missed the Beetle completely. When he was a dot on the horizon heading for the Niger and home, I was able to start up the VW and crawl through the potholes and thus get back to my bungalow in Umuahia town.

But the one who came nearest to sending me to a new and apparently better place was the mortarman outside Onitsha. I had been visiting the front line south of the riverside city by the bridgehead, but it meant a long hike back across a bare and exposed hillside to where I had parked my car, deep in a grove of trees. I was a third of the way across the flank of the hill when someone across the river must have seen me, presumably with field glasses. It must have been the white face that irritated him, because he really let fly.

I heard that soft whisper and went flat. It was a ranging shot and landed more than a hundred yards away. No damage, but also no cover. I looked around for a friendly rain ditch and spotted one twenty yards to one side. I made it just in time as the second one landed.

Rain ditches make good cover, but the locals tend to use them as latrines. In the rainy season, the waste matter is washed away, but this was during the dry months, so a rain ditch is not recommended for a crawling holiday. Still, it was better than getting shredded. I lay and counted the seconds. Seven. Then the third landed. Closer, but above my head.

I jumped out and began to jog, counting the seconds and hoping my new friend was going to be short on imagination.

He was. At six seconds, I went back into the ditch, and at seven the next one came down. This was not a 60mm party planner, but an 81mm "company" mortar. Very nasty.

I hoped he was watching the fall of his shot, then dropping his next effort down the tube. Travel time for the bomb, exactly seven seconds. I have never liked jogging and this jog least of all. Up-run-dive-bang. Then I made it to the point where the hillside curved away from the river. Two more runs and I would be out of sight.

Hoping he could see me, I turned and gave him a rigid middle finger. Then I was out of sight. There were three more, but they became wider and wider, until I could reach my car and drive home. And that is why I hate mortars.

OF MORE MICE—AND MERCS

For the Biafrans, the experience of foreign white mercenaries was extremely patchy. Both sides used them, but the idea that they were invincible game changers, a reputation deriving from the Congolese wars a few years earlier, proved to be a myth.

For the Biafrans, the first intervention came from France, then ruled by Charles de Gaulle. His principal "fixer" in Africa, Jacques Foccart, responsible for a wide range of skulduggery in the ex-French empire and elsewhere, arranged for about forty mainly French "mercs" to be recruited by ex-Legion icon Roger Faulckes and sent down to show how warfare should be done. They cost Biafra a fortune in its scarce hard-currency reserves.

They duly arrived and were assigned to the Calabar sector, where Nigerian and Biafran troopers were locked in a struggle for the riverine city. On their way there, driving without forward scouts, they ran into an ambush and lost several men. Retreating in disarray, their next stop was the airport, where they demanded to go back home. General Ojukwu, in disgust, just let them go.

But seven opted to stay and were joined by three non-French who came later. They were a mixed bunch. Two were deluded fantasists, two had a taste for killing, and one enjoyed cruelty. Some of the French group stayed because they were wanted in France for various offenses. Finally, there were ex-soldiers from national armies who had simply failed to adapt to civilian life.

There were also three mercenary pilots who flew in Biafra's short-lived air force until they were shot down or crashed their aircraft and left. Three of the land-based mercs died in combat.

Giorgio Noriatto, whom I never met, was an Italian, and the first to die. He was killed fighting in the Imo River area as the Nigerians advanced out of the creeks toward Aba.

"Tiny Bill" Billois was a French giant, known for obvious reasons as "Petit Bill," weighing in at around 350 pounds. He survived, but died later in a light aircraft crash in France years after the war. Always at his side was his cousin Michel, who was so self-effacing he was hardly noticed, and that included when he left.

Mark Goossens was a former Belgian paratrooper, another huge man. He died with a bullet through the liver during a forlorn attempt to recapture Onitsha city.

The third to die was a Britisher, Steve Neeley, whom I found thoroughly unpleasant. He drove around with a bone-white skull on the bonnet of his Land Rover. It was the head of a dead Nigerian, which he had boiled fleshless and mounted with steel wires above the radiator cap.

He disappeared in the Abakaliki sector and it was later rumored one of his own men might have done the job. They attested he was dead, but the body was never found.

The other five were Rolf Steiner, who had been appointed their commander and called himself colonel. He was ex–Deutsches Jungvolk (a sort of Hitler Youth), ex–Foreign Legion, invalided out of Dien Bien Phu, Vietnam, just in time, and one of the Faulckes group who elected to stay on. He postured and paraded around in his confiscated American limousine, his staff car, but I never recall him going into combat. He spoke only French and German, so I did a fair amount of interpreting. That made him a good source of information, but I never took to him. Then there was Taffy Williams, already mentioned.

The only three I could like were, Alec, a Scot, who survived, returned to the UK, married, and qualified as a truck driver; the Rhodesian, Johnny Erasmus, the explosives king, ex-Rhodesian army; and Armand, from Paris, who had been amicably advised by the police chief to leave the city for a while until "things blew over." He was the one who quietly donated his salary to the missionaries to buy food for the children.

And finally there was the mythical Major Atkinson, in the form of this writer. One day in the autumn of 1968, I turned up at a Biafran advance headquarters, intending to go up to the front line to see if there was a journalistic story worth covering. Seeing me in the usual pale safari jacket, the brigade commander objected.

His case was perfectly sound. It was well known that the Nigerian army was quite paranoid about white mercenaries and had never heard of a war correspondent. To show up in a leaf-green forest environment with a white face and a pale jacket was asking for trouble. If anyone were to glimpse me through the trees, the entire zone would be drenched in automatic fire. If nothing else, it would be unfair on the Biafran soldiers who might be close by.

He insisted I change into a camouflage jacket and ordered one of his staff officers to lend me his spare. It happened to have the half-a-yellow-sun emblem of Biafra on each sleeve and a major's crowns on each shoulder. In order not to waste the day, I put it on and went into the front.

That apart, I had taken to carrying a French automatic in a holster at the waist. This was because I'd had described to me in detail what the Hausa soldiers would do to any white mercenary who was taken alive. So my borrowed pistol had one slug in it—for me, if worse ever came to worst.

On the way back, I ran into a group of British press, also being refused access to the front line and not happy about it. One of them recognized me, and that was that. On their return to London, the Foreign Office press desk seized upon it with alacrity. Too late to protest that I always changed out of the "camo" jacket when not at the front, and that the pistol remained locked in the glove compartment of the Volkswagen.

As for the real mercenaries, I think they are all dead now, though when this book comes out, I may be in for a couple of surprises!

MEMORIES

———◦———

There is nothing noble about war. The adjective may apply to those who have to fight in them in defense of cause or country. But war itself is cruel and brutal. Things happen in it that coarsen the senses and scar the memory. And the most vicious of all conflicts is the civil war.

Of the thousand memories I bore back from the two years I spent trying to convey the realities of Biafra to the readers of Britain, Europe, and the United States, the most abiding is that of the dying children.

They died in the villages, by the roadsides, and, alongside those who survived on the relief food, in the feeding centers. These were established almost wholly around the missions—churches, schools, dispensaries, and a field the size of a football pitch, where they lay in the grass, on rush mats, or in the laps of their mothers, who held them close, watching them wither and slip away, and wondering why.

As the effects of kwashiorkor intensified, the children's curly dark-brown hair diminished to a ginger fuzz. Their eyes lost focus but appeared immense in their wizened faces. The weakness from departed muscle made them listless until, unable to move at all, they passed away and a figure in a cassock came to intone a last blessing and take them to the pit.

The bellies ballooned, but only with air; the lower limbs were drenched with feces; the heads lolled on vanished muscles. And always the low moan as they cried in pain. And one image above all, on the grass field outside the window of my hut.

I was tapping away at my typewriter with the window wide open. It was late summer 1969 and the air was balmy. I almost missed the low sound above the clatter of the keys. Then I heard it and went to the window.

She was standing on the grass outside, a scrap of a girl of seven or eight, stick thin, in a flimsy cotton shift stained with dirt. In her left hand she held the hand of her baby brother, stark naked, with listless eyes, a bulbous belly. She stared up at me and I down at her.

She raised her right hand to her mouth and made the universal sign that means "I am hungry, please give me food." Then she held her hand up toward the window and her lips moved with no sound. I looked down at the tiny pink-palmed hand, but I had no food.

My food came twice daily from the cooking compound behind the cluster of Nissen huts where the few visiting whites lived. But that night I would dine with Kurt Jaggi of the Red Cross—good, nutritious food imported from Switzerland. But not for three hours. The kitchens were closed and locked, and there was no way either child could take solid food. Until dinner I would exist on king-size cigarettes. But you cannot eat cigarettes; there is no nutriment in a Bic lighter.

Foolishly, I tried to explain. I'm sorry, really sorry, but I have no food. I had no Ibo, she no English, but it did not matter. She understood. Slowly her outstretched arm sank back to her side. She did not spit, she did not shout. She just nodded in silent understanding. The white man in the window would do nothing for her or her brother.

In a long life, I have never seen such resignation, such towering dignity, as in that wasted form as she turned away, all last hope gone. Together the two little forms walked away across the field to the tree line. In the forest she would find a shady tree, sit at its foot, and wait to die. And she would hold on to her kid brother, like a good sister, all the way.

I watched them until the trees took them, then sat at my table, put my head on my hands, and cried until the dispatch was damp.

That was the last time I wept for the children of Biafra. Since then, others have written documentaries about what happened in those last eighteen months of the thirty months of the "ten-day war" predicted out of Lagos. But no investigative writer has ever undertaken to expose *why* it happened and who exactly enabled it to happen. For the Whitehall establishment, the subject is closed. It is taboo.

FLIGHT OUT

It was two nights before Christmas 1969, and clear that the last embattled enclave of the Biafran revolt was finally crumbling. The Ibos were simply exhausted to the point that their soldiers could hardly stand. In the manner of Africans when all hope is lost, they simply "went for bush." Meaning, they just vaporized into the rain forest and returned, without weapon or uniform, to their native villages.

The Nigerian army could have taken the remnant of the enclave that night, but they continued their snaillike progress for another fortnight until the formal surrender on January 15. I had no way of knowing it would be that slow and found myself at Uli airstrip to see Emeka Ojukwu leave for years of exile.

His supporter President Houphouët-Boigny of the Ivory Coast had sent his personal jet for him, but that was a very crowded flight, with no room for hitchhikers. Also on the airstrip that night was another plane, wholly unexpected and unheralded.

It was a very old and pretty clapped-out Douglas DC-4, a four-propeller job that seemed to have an awful lot of air miles under its belt.

The pilot and, as it turned out, owner was a South African whom I had met, surrounded by Irish nuns. His story was bizarre.

His name was Jan van der Merwe and he had never met Ojukwu. But he had seen him on television and been impressed. Without any invitation and at considerable risk, he had flown in from Libreville, Gabon, to see if he needed a flight out to safety.

I was surprised that an Afrikaner, almost certainly a keen supporter of apartheid, should decide to take such a risk to help a failed black man whom he had never met. But I had noticed Ojukwu sometimes had that effect on people.

Van der Merwe's offer was politely rejected on the grounds that the Biafra leader already had transport, but the nuns had ideas of their own. They were in charge of two or three lorry loads of children and babies so emaciated that if they did not get professional care without delay, they would also surely die. So the South African agreed reluctantly to take them on board instead. The nuns began to carry them one by one up the gangway to the dark interior of the freighter. There were no beds or seats, so they laid them on the floor and came back down for more.

Eventually, on what had once been the busiest nocturnal airport in Africa, there were three planes left: the Douglas and two official jets from the Ivory Coast and the Red Cross. I later described all this, just the way it was, in the first few pages of my novel *The Dogs of War*.

I gratefully accepted a king-size filter from Jan and asked if he had a copilot. He had not; he had flown alone. Up on the flight deck, the right-hand seat was free. It was mine if I wanted it. I did.

The Nigerians had been kind enough to put a price on my head, rumored at 5,000 naira: not a fortune but more than enough for a poor Hausa soldier to claim it eagerly. And the terms were dead or alive, so survival seemed unlikely. The third-from-last plane out was a better bet than trying to hide among the missionaries. My knowledge of the Creed was a bit shaky.

When the loading was finished, Jan and I climbed to the flight deck, and, one by one, he started the engines. It was pitch-dark and the airport lights were off when we taxied out to the far end, turned around, and faced down the runway. After a pause, waiting for runway lights that never came on, Jan just pushed the four throttles open and we took off in darkness, apart from the low glimmer of the stars. There were Nigerian jets up there somewhere, and had they seen us, it would have been "game over."

The first problem began out over the Niger Delta. Jan wanted to get clear of the landmass before turning for Gabon, so he took the shortest route to the sea, due south. The last of the mangroves of the delta were dropping behind us when the port outer failed. It coughed several times and cut out. Jan closed down the fuel lines to it and the moon came out. We could see the propeller blades rigid and motionless in the moonlight. He carefully turned east for Gabon. We were hugely over-loaded and flying on three.

I rose, walked back, and looked through the door from the flight deck to the hold. The babies lay in their blankets wall to wall, while the nuns tried to minister to them by dimmed torches, surviving somehow amid the stench of vomit and diarrhea. I closed the door and returned to the right-hand seat. Over the Gulf of Guinea, the starboard outer began to cough and splutter. If it packed in, we were all dead. Jan coaxed and nursed it to stay turning.

He began to sing hymns—in Afrikaans, of course. I just sat in the right-hand seat, staring out at the moon on the water, coming closer and closer as we dropped toward it. Far away on the forward horizon was a dim line of lights. Libreville airport.

The French colonists had built their airport right on the sea. The DC-4, wheels dangling, came over the sand dunes with a few feet to spare. As the tarmac appeared, the spluttering engine gave up the ghost and stopped. The old crate dropped with a noisy clunk onto the runway and ran to a stop.

Red Cross ambulances appeared for the Biafran children, and the Catholic Church for the nuns. Jan Van Der Merwe and I sat on the flight deck wondering why we were still alive. He was muttering the old Dutch prayers of thanksgiving; I listened to the ticking of the engine blocks cooling in the tropical night.

We adjourned to the airport crew room and I met an officer from the officers' mess of the Foreign Legion. I said good-bye and thank you to Jan and went across to the mess for food and a bath as a guest of the Legion, simply because they were avid for news. A bit of influence was brought to bear and I secured a free flight back to Paris on the morning Air Afrique plane. From there, my last remaining funds got me home to Kent via Beauvais and Lydd. Thence a hitchhike to my parents' retirement cottage at Willesborough, outside Ashford. They were quite surprised to see me, but at least we had Christmas together.

They were elderly, so New Year's Eve was quiet and I returned to London on New Year's Day. My situation was pretty dire.

I had no flat, but a mate let me doss on the sofa. I had no savings left, but my father loaned me a few hundred pounds to get by. I certainly had no job and no prospects of ever getting one for a long time.

In my absence, I had been comprehensively smeared from the usual official quarters. I was not the only one. The late Winston Churchill, grandson of the war leader, had also visited Biafra representing the *Times*, had written of his horror at what he had seen, and had been denounced as a professional publicist for "the rebels." And there were others. From the pro-Establishment organs of the media, the gloating was unrestrained.

The situation was so miserable that I decided to do something that even then seen as crazy by all I knew. I thought I might get myself out of this mess by writing a novel.

As a recourse, it was lunatic. I did not know how to write a novel, let alone secure its publication. I knew nothing of publishing or the finances of book writing. I thought you could take a manuscript to a publisher and, if he liked it, he would buy it for a single sum like a pound of butter. I had no agent and knew nothing of royalties, or the years-long delay before they actually arrived.

But I did have a story—or I thought I did. I cast my mind back to the Paris years and my conviction back then that the OAS was not going to succeed in assassinating Charles de Gaulle with their own volunteers being hunted high and low by the far more professional counterintelligence forces that Paris could bring to bear. Unless they brought in a professional from outside.

On January 2, 1970, I sat down at the kitchen table in my borrowed flat with my trusty old portable typewriter, with its bullet scar across the tin cover, rolled in the first sheet of paper, and began to type.

Charles de Gaulle was still alive, in retirement at Colombey-les-deux-Églises. He died on November 9 that year. I was told later that no one had ever postulated the murder of a living statesman since Geoffrey Household's *Rogue Male*, about an attempt to kill Adolf Hitler. But that gunman never went through with it.

I was also told no one had ever had an entire novel with an anonymous hero, or featured real politicians and police officers in a fictional manhunt. And no one had attempted such an obsession for technical accuracy. In other words, it was all madness. Still, when you have nothing else to do and nowhere else to go, you might as well get on with it.

I wrote for thirty-five days, from when my friend went off to work until her return after dark; that is to say, all through January, seven days a week, and the first two weeks of February. Then I typed the last line of the last page.

I rolled the first page back into the machine and stared at it. I had called it THE JACKAL. That seemed a bit bare and might be taken for a nature documentary set in Africa. So in front of the title, I typed THE DAY OF. If I say so myself, not a single word has been changed since.

I was still very broke, but I had a manuscript. The remaining problem was that I had not a clue what to do with it.

AN UNWANTED MANUSCRIPT

For the whole of the spring and summer of 1970, I hawked the manuscript of *The Day of the Jackal* around the publishing houses of London, choosing my targets from *Willings Press Guide.* It actually went to four; three rejected it outright and I withdrew it from the fourth. But along the road, at least I learned what was wrong—apart from the fact that it might be a rotten novel.

The unsolicited manuscript is the bane of the publisher's life. They arrive by the trolleyload: typed (in those days), handwritten, illegible, ungrammatical, unreasonable. There used to be a tradition in which on Monday mornings they were distributed among the junior readers for first assessment.

The junior reader was often a student or very recent arrival in-house and a long way down the pecking order. His or her job was to read it and provide a brief synopsis with a judgment, and that was what would go up to the next level of assessment. But no one high up the food chain would dream of reading anything other than an established author or possibly a very famous person who had put pen to paper.

The horror stories were the legends of publishing. Most authors, hailed as mega–best sellers, had had their first manuscript rejected over and over again; and it still goes on, because no one has the faintest idea who will be the next Ken Follett or John Grisham or J. K. Rowling.

Among authors, the nightmare stories that go the rounds concern the yearlong struggle to find anyone to publish their masterpiece. Among publishers, the horror takes are about those who turned down Harry Potter because who cares about a schoolboy wizard with a wand? And usually it is only the first chapter that is read anyway.

The Day of the Jackal had a major problem here because the first chapter is ridiculous. It purported to outline plans for the killing of a former French president who was very much alive, and everyone knew it. So the junior readers' judgments probably said, "We know the climax already, the plan fails." Manuscript returned.

Two of my rejections were simple printed forms. One was kind enough to write a letter. I wish I had retained and framed it, but I threw it away. It said the very idea would have "no reader interest." Then I had yet another lucky break.

I was at a party and was introduced just socially to someone called Harold Harris. I had no idea who he was. Toward the end of the party, someone mentioned that he was the editorial director of Hutchinson, a major publisher.

I had already decided my solution might be to write a three-page synopsis of the plot, pointing out that the point of the story was not the death of de Gaulle, which clearly did not happen, but the manhunt as the assassin came closer and closer, eluding the huge machine ranged against him.

The following day, a Friday in September, I am afraid I ambushed Mr. Harris quite blatantly. I turned up at Hutchinson's office in Great

Portland Street and faced the usual screen of secretaries in place to keep unwanted wannabes away from the Presence behind the big door.

But I explained we were close friends and my call was social. I was allowed in. Harold Harris was puzzled until I pointed out we had met socially the previous evening. His perfect manners caused him not to summon the burly commissionaire, but to ask what he could do for me. I replied: I have a manuscript of a novel.

His eyes glazed over in horror, but I had got this far, so I plunged on.

"I know you have no time, so I will not take it up, Mr. Harris. Well, maybe five minutes, tops."

With this, I advanced to his desk and placed the brief synopsis upon it.

"All I ask is that you glance at this and, if you think it is worthless, then chuck me out."

Looking as if root canal surgery would be more welcome, he started to read. He finished the three pages and started again. He read it three times.

"Where is the manuscript now?" he asked.

I told him with which publisher it had lain for eight weeks. He stared pointedly at the ceiling.

"It is quite out of the question for a publisher to read a manuscript while a copy resides with another publisher," he told me.

Asking him not to move, which he had no intention of doing, I was out of the office and down the stairs. I could not afford taxis, but I hailed one anyway and drove to the other publisher. It was the lunch hour. I could raise only the hall porter with my demand for my manuscript back, and he found a junior secretary on her sandwich break who retrieved my paper parcel from the reject pile and gave it back to me with a pitying smile. I returned to Great Portland Street and handed it over.

He read the whole thing over the weekend and rang on Monday morning.

"If you can be here at four this afternoon, with your agent, we can discuss a contract," he said.

I had no agent, but I was there anyway. With my ignorance of publishing, royalties, and contracts, he could have skinned me alive. But he was an old-fashioned gentleman and gave me a fair document with an advance of five hundred pounds. Then he said:

"I am toying with the idea of offering you a three-novel contract. Do you have any other ideas?"

The thing about journalists is that they lie well. It comes from practice. It is also why they have great empathy with, or antagonism for, politicians and senior civil servants. Common territory.

"Mr. Harris, I am brimming with ideas," I told him.

"Two synopses, one page each. By Friday noon," he suggested.

Back on the street, I had a major problem. The story about the Jackal was supposed to be a one-off, something to tide me through a bad patch. I had not the slightest intention of becoming a novelist. So I tried to analyze the story that had been accepted and to recall what I knew about from personal experience and could use as background. I came up with two conclusions.

The Day of the Jackal was a manhunt story, and I knew a lot about Germany. While in East Berlin, I had heard about a mysterious organization of former Nazis who helped, protected, and warned each other in order never to have to face West German judicial hunters and answer for their crimes. It was called ODESSA, but I had thought it was part of the relentless East German propaganda against the Bonn government.

Perhaps not. Ten years earlier, the Israeli Mossad had hunted down Adolf Eichmann, living under a pseudonym outside Buenos Aires. Perhaps another hunt-down of a disappeared mass murderer?

And I knew about Africa and white mercenaries hired to fight in jungle wars. Perhaps a return to the rain forests, not to another civil war but to a mercenary-led coup d'état?

I wrote both down, as required, on a single sheet of A4 paper and presented them to Harold Harris that Friday. He skimmed through them and decided without a second's hesitation.

"Nazis first, mercenaries second. And I want the first manuscript by December next year."

I did not know at the time that he was Jewish, lapsed but from an Orthodox parentage. Nor that in April 1945 he had been a young German-speaking officer in British Army Intelligence. Nor that he had been summoned across Schleswig-Holstein to interrogate a mysterious but suspicious prisoner. He had not yet arrived in his jeep when the prisoner bit on a cyanide capsule and killed himself. That man was Heinrich Himmler.

I had one last problem before signing the three-novel contract. Apart from the coming five hundred pounds, I was still broke.

"There will be living costs and research and traveling and lodgings," I said. "Could I have something to tide me through?"

He scrawled something on a sheet of paper and gave it to me.

"Take this to accounts," he said. "Good luck and stay in touch. Oh, and get an agent. I recommend Diana Baring."

The piece of paper I clutched was quite an act of faith. It was an authority to draw six thousand pounds against future royalties. In 1970, that was rather a lot of money.

Back on the street again, I started to think. Who the hell knows about Nazis? Then I recalled a book called *The Scourge of the Swastika*, which I had read years earlier. It was by Lord Russell of Liverpool, who had been a senior British prosecutor at the Nuremberg trials during the forties. I would have to track him down and see if he could help.

Before then, I had yet another lucky break. I had met a man called John Mallinson, who prided himself on being an agent, albeit without clients. I did not look him up, but coincidentally we met again at the flat of a friend. I told him what had happened in Great Portland Street. He became quite excited.

"What about the film rights?" he asked. I had not a clue. He scoured the Hutchinson contract. "They're still yours. Appoint me as your film agent and I'll find a buyer."

By November, he had done exactly that. The film deal was done with Romulus Films of Park Lane, headed by John Woolf. But his right-hand man in all things was John Rosenberg, and it was with him that we dealt. The offer was £17,500 plus a small percentage of net profits, or £20,000 outright sale in perpetuity.

Most people are good at some things and useless at others. I am pathetic at money. I had never seen £20,000, so I took it. I have no idea how many millions the film has made over the years. I can only excuse myself with the thought that I had no idea the book would sell over a hundred copies or the film would ever be made. Even the way it was made was a fluke.

That winter, the Hollywood giant Fred Zinnemann flew over to discuss a project with John Woolf. It was to film a successful play called *Abelard and Heloise*. There had always been a problem. The film could not be made while the play was onstage anywhere. That December, it closed in England and was not staging anywhere else.

The day before Zinnemann arrived, it was decided the play would reopen in a British provincial city. The Hollywood director's trip was fruitless after all. Desperately embarrassed, John Woolf was apologizing in his office, knowing his guest had to face a rainy London weekend with nothing to read. Frantically, he reached for something John Rosenberg had placed on his desk.

"We have just bought this," he said. Mr. Zinnemann took it and left. He was back on Monday. "This is my next movie," he told a delighted Romulus Films.

I knew none of all this until later. As I look back, it was not really *The Day of the Jackal*, the one-off to clear my debts, that changed my life. It was Harold Harris and his three-novel contract. It just occurred to me that if I could make a good living dashing off this nonsense, why get my head blown off in an African rain ditch?

But the more immediate problem was trying to find Lord Russell of Liverpool to ask him about underground Nazis. And I had the problem of what to call them. I needed two titles. In German, ODESSA stood for Organization of Former Members of the SS. As far as the world was concerned, Odessa was a city in Ukraine or a town in Texas. Well, here was a third one. *The Odessa File*.

For the mercenaries I recalled a quote from Shakespeare. "Cry 'Havoc,' and let slip the dogs of war." I had heard someone had used *Cry Havoc*, but not *The Dogs of War*. So I filched it from the Bard.

THE ODESSA

Lord Russell of Liverpool had retired to a small cottage at Dinard, a town on the French coast facing the Atlantic, and that was where I found him. I had no introduction, so I just turned up and knocked. When I explained what I needed, he was helpfulness itself.

Though he was a mine of information about the war and the Nuremberg trials, these had been twenty years earlier. I sought details about secret pro-Nazi elements still in existence in 1971. He referred me to the wellspring of Nazi-hunting, the Vienna-based researcher Simon Wiesenthal. With a letter of introduction, I headed south to Austria.

Like David Ben-Gurion, Simon Wiesenthal began by conceding he could spare me twenty minutes of his time, but when I explained what I sought, he became so enthusiastic that we spent days poring over his records. The germ of my idea was not for a Nazi fugitive who had fled to South America, but one who had changed his name and disappeared right in the heart of Germany, with help from equally covert friends. The response of Herr Wiesenthal was that the right choice might be difficult, not because there were so few but that there were thousands of them.

It seemed there were two mutual-help brotherhoods still very much active in the Germany of 1971. There was the *Kameradschaft*, or Comradeship, and the ODESSA, which was in no way fictional.

"What I seek," I explained, "is to invent a mass murderer of the Nazi era who, like so many, had stripped off his uniform at the very end, adopted another persona, and disappeared into postwar German society, returning to office, influence, and respectability under another name. Like a concentration camp commander."

He beamed and gestured to a shelf of files behind his desk.

"Why invent one? I have a dozen real ones."

We pored through the files and settled on Eduard Roschmann, former camp commander at Riga, Latvia, and known as the Butcher of Riga. He had been a real monster, but one among many.

And I learned of that amazing day in the spring of 1945 when a single US Army jeep, driving north through Bavaria with just four soldiers on board, had seen plumes of smoke rising from the courtyard of a medieval castle.

Driving unchallenged over the drawbridge, they had discovered a dozen SS men in overalls tending a bonfire. They arrested the lot and hosed out the fire. Experts came up from General Patton's headquarters to discover that what was being burned was the entire SS personnel archive. Only 2 or 3 percent had been consumed by the flames. The rest was now lodged under American care in West Berlin. That included the entire file on Captain (Hauptsturmführer) Eduard Roschmann of Riga, an Austrian-born fanatic now high on the wanted list. Slowly, my story was coming together, but there was less and less to invent; it was beyond fiction, but it was all true.

The real irony was that I could say anything I wanted about this monster. Wherever he was, he was hardly likely to come out of hiding to sue.

Finally, Simon Wiesenthal pointed me back north to Germany with a huge volume of information and even more warnings. I thought his conviction that West German officialdom was comprehensively penetrated by a generation steeped in either participation in, or sympathy for, what had happened between 1933 and 1945 might be just paranoia, but it was nothing of the sort. It all came down to the issue of "which generation."

A fanatical Nazi aged twenty-five at the end of the war would have been born around 1920. He would have been steeped in Nazi education from age thirteen onward and almost certainly a member of the Hitler Youth from that age. He could well have been a mass murderer by twenty-five.

By the time of my research, he would have been fifty-one or -two; that is, at the prime of life and a high-ranker in any of a hundred official positions. Nor would I receive obstruction only from wanted criminals. Behind them was the even larger army of guilty desk-doers, the bureaucrats without whose organizational flair the Holocaust could never have happened.

This was the generation that now ran Germany, blossoming in its economic miracle. After 1949, the founding under Allied aegis of the new Federal Republic of (West) Germany, the chancellor was the undeniably anti-Nazi Konrad Adenauer. But he had a terrible quandary to resolve.

Nazi Party members were so pandemic that had he banned them all, the country would have been ungovernable. So he cut his Faustian pact. Delving into the past when considering appointment or promotions was neither practical nor desirable. According to Simon Wiesenthal, every branch of the public function was impregnated with bureaucrats who had never pulled a trigger but had helped those who did. Research, he said, was not a question of open hostility but of closed doors. Police officers who volunteered to join the Nazi-hunting commissions quite simply terminated their own careers. They became outcasts. And he turned out to be right.

He also pointed me toward clandestine groups who still really believed in the coming of the Fourth Reich one day and whose meetings I could attend with my fluent German. So I did. The more I delved into the murk of pre-1945 Nazism and its post-1945 admirers, the more I came to the view that in all the history of the human race there has never been a creed so foul. It had not a single redeeming feature, appealing only to the nastiest corners of the human soul.

But it was all hidden, back then. The participant generation never spoke of it and the young generation was profoundly ignorant and indeed deeply puzzled by foreign hostility when they met it.

Despite their professed loathing of fascism and Nazism, the Communists of the East, behind the Iron Curtain, offered no help or cooperation whatsoever.

Thus, all investigation of all the crimes committed east of the Iron Curtain during the Nazi time was allocated to different state attorney offices spread across West Germany. Riga came under the state attorneyship of Hamburg. I started there and met a blank wall of closed doors. I was puzzled. Surely they were lawyers? I rang Simon Wiesenthal. He roared with laughter.

"Yes, of course they are lawyers. But whose lawyers?"

I realized many must have been or still were in the Comradeship. But slowly I made contact with either younger men, untainted because they were too young, or anti-Nazis who had lived through it and survived unsullied. They talked, but quietly, furtively, in darkened beer bars, once convinced I was just a British investigative reporter. And slowly the story came together that in 1972 appeared under the title *The Odessa File*.

Starting in Hamburg, I drifted back south again until I returned to Austria, from which my villain Roschmann had come. In an antique shop, I found an old Jew who had been in Riga under Roschmann and had survived, even the death march west as the Russians advanced. His wife assured me her husband had never spoken of it and never would. But she was wrong.

The old man was courtesy itself and offered me tea. We sat as I explained the plotline of the story I had in mind. I do not know why, but he began to correct me. It was not like that, he said, it was like this. Darkness fell. As his wide-eyed wife brought relay after relay of tea, he talked for twenty hours. In the book, the testimony of Salomon Tauber is recounted to me, detail by detail, by candlelight in a Viennese antique shop. I just moved Herr Tauber to Hamburg.

For a hero, I needed a young investigator of the new generation to inherit the diary of the dead Tauber and do something about it. So I invented Peter Miller, and his investigative trail almost exactly matches my own during that summer of 1971.

I returned to the UK in June for the launch of *The Day of the Jackal*. It was a very quiet affair. No one had heard of the title or the author. It had not been reviewed. Hutchinson had begun with an audacious five thousand copies, raised to eight thousand as the book buyers of the major stores slowly increased their orders. The PR lady for the launch was Cindy Winkleman, now the mother of the British TV star Claudia.

Then I went back to Germany to tie up the last details. I wrote *The Odessa File* that autumn and presented it to Harold Harris, as promised, before Christmas. Slowly, *Jackal* was climbing the charts, and the second novel had a better media reception. Hollywood succumbed to the wiles of my new agent, Diana Baring, and bought the film rights.

The movie, when it came out in 1974, starring Jon Voight as Peter Miller and Maximilian Schell as the villainous Roschmann, led eventually to the quixotic twist in this tale.

In 1975, in a fleapit cinema on the coast south of Buenos Aires, an Argentinian was watching the Spanish-language version when it occurred to him that Eduard Roschmann, who had reverted to his real name, so convinced was he of his safety, was living down the street. So he denounced him.

Argentina was in one of its brief windows of democratic government under President Isabel Perón, widow of the old tyrant Juan Perón, and, seeking to do the right thing, had Roschmann arrested. West Germany slapped in a request for extradition.

Before the legal formalities had been completed between the West German embassy and the Ministry of Justice, Roschmann—on bail, thanks to a local magistrate—lost his nerve. He ran north for the sanctuary of the pro-Nazi dictator Alfred Stroessner of Paraguay. He reached the border and waited for the ferry across the Paraguay River to safety.

Right in the middle of the river, he had a massive heart attack. Witnesses said he was dead before he hit the floor, or in this case the deck. What followed must have come from a very flaky comedy show.

On the Paraguayan bank, the terminal master refused to accept the body on the grounds it belonged to Argentina. The captain insisted the dead man had paid full fare for his crossing and the cadaver belonged to Paraguay. The ferry schedule insisted the boat depart, so the body went back to Argentina, still lying on the foredeck.

It went back and forth four times, becoming ever more smelly under the tropical sun. Then two detectives arrived from Vienna to identify it. Thanks to the American jeep in Bavaria in 1945, they had fingerprints and dental records from the Roschmann file in the SS personnel archives. They asked for the body to be unloaded at last and the Paraguayans conceded.

Proof positive was established and the clincher was the two missing toes, amputated when Roschmann fled the British through the border snows in 1947. With the ferry refusing to have the corpse back, the Paraguayans buried it in a gravel bank just back from the water's edge.

So today the bones of the Butcher of Riga lie in an unmarked grave in a gravel bank beside the Paraguay River. It took a bit of time but eventually, thanks to the movie, job done.

DOGS OF WAR

———————

Just as my years in France had convinced me the OAS was not going to succeed in toppling Charles de Gaulle, my years in Africa taught me something else.

This was that in the immediate aftermath of the colonial era, there were several independent republics on the continent so small, so chaotic, so badly governed and defended that they could be toppled and taken over by a small group of professional soldiers with the right weaponry and a few dozen loyal levies. Thinking to write my third novel and set it in Africa, I notionally selected three.

Top of the list was Equatorial Guinea, an island republic off the coast of Nigeria. It had once been Spain's only African colony, linked to an enclave on the mainland called Rio Muni. For a while, under Spain, it had been a stopover for Biafra-bound food flights by the International Red Cross. Independence came in 1968 and it plunged into chaos and terror.

The ruler was Francisco Macías Nguema, a Fang from Rio Muni. He was probably mad and certainly savagely cruel. He transferred his government to the island, then called Fernando Po, now renamed Bioko. He had a small army of Fangs, which terrorized the indigenous Bubi people. His cruelties soon became legendary. But behind the screen of terror, he was immensely weak.

His bodyguard/army was hung with weapons, but he was so paranoid that they had no bullets because he could not trust them. Had he fallen, no one would have come to his aid. His fellow Fangs were hundreds of miles away, the Bubi loathed him, and the very few diplomats and aid workers left despised him.

He lived in the barracks of the former Spanish gendarmerie, converted into his fortress, on top of the national armory and the national treasury, which he had confiscated. If that one building fell, so would the republic.

Researching all this was no problem. There was no need for me to risk going there, so I did not. But I was able to talk to a score of former inhabitants, mainly Spanish, who gleefully explained how he could be toppled by a small attacking force. One remarked, "To knock off a bank is merely crude. To knock off an entire republic has a certain style."

With control of a republic comes membership to the United Nations, international loans, arrest-free diplomatic passports, and various other Christmas treats. There was even an exiled rival in Madrid who could be installed on the presidential throne as a puppet successor.

There need only be five rules. Strike hard, strike fast, and strike by night. Come unexpected and come by sea. Parenthetically, the eventual book was imitated twice. In 1975, the French mercenary Bob Denard attacked and took over the Comoro Islands, at the top of the Mozambique Channel.

He was acting with the knowledge, assistance, and on behalf of the French government. Amusingly, as his French mercenaries came up the beach in the predawn darkness, they all carried a paperback edition of *Les Chiens de Guerre* (*The Dogs of War* in French), so that they could constantly find out what they were supposed to do next. Denard succeeded because he came by sea.

In 1981, South African mercenary Mike Hoare tried the same trick on the Seychelles, but failed because he came by air.

For my own story, I soon had all in place—the men, the ship, the target—but lacked vital knowledge. The weapons. Where in Europe could a clandestine mercenary operation secure its weapons? The cover story would be a plausible private-sector operation involving deep-sea diving for oil exploration and upon invitation.

But the African levies to be picked up en route, one of the subplots, would need submachine carbines and plenty of ammunition. The half dozen mercs would need a heavy machine gun, RPGs (then called bazookas), grenades, 60mm mortar flares, and explosive charges. All that would also require practice and rehearsal time, hence the long, slow cruise on a small merchantman out at sea.

But where to get all this stuff? Back then I could not call on informational help from the authorities. To find out, I would have to penetrate the world of the black market arms dealers and see it from the inside, and I was not prepared to attempt a thriller without such vital areas explained.

My contacts advised me that the heart of the black market arms world was in Hamburg and its kingpin was a certain Otto X, who posed as a respectable businessman—but then they all do. So to Hamburg I went with another advance from Hutchinson, which was very happy with the sales of the first two.

I thought it unwise to use my own name, so I took that of the pilot who flew me out of Biafra and declared I was Frederik van der Merwe, a South African. I even had papers to prove it, prepared by the forger who had taught me about false passports in *The Day of the Jackal*. Mr. van der Merwe was the youthful assistant of a South African multimillionaire wishing to assist Jonas Savimbi in the Angolan civil war. And thus I managed to get into the inner councils of Herr Otto X.

There I learned about End User Certificates, the documents purporting to come from a reputable sovereign government entitled to purchase defense equipment for its legitimate purposes. For a fee, Otto X could obtain false ones on the right-headed paper and signed by a "purchased" African diplomat assigned to an embassy somewhere in Europe. It was all going swimmingly, until something happened that I had not foreseen.

One morning, Herr Otto X was in his limousine when it stopped at a red light next to a bookshop that was launching the German version of *Der Schakal* (*The Day of the Jackal*) that same day. There was a display in the window, but one copy had fallen over and on the rear cover was a picture of the author.

Herr Otto X found himself staring at Meneer van der Merwe and suffered a complete sense-of-humor failure. Fortunately I had an unknown and unsuspected friend at court. I was in my hotel room opposite the main station when the phone rang. There were no introductions. A voice spoke, clearly British, with the clipped tones of education.

"Freddie, get out of Hamburg now. And I mean now. They are coming for you."

Like my father in 1938, I did a runner. I grabbed my passport and a fistful of money, left the luggage, and went down the stairs, past the receptionist and across the Station Square. I did not bother with the ticket office, but went straight for the trains. One was just beginning to move, its doors closed but with one window wide open.

I went through it on a forward roll and landed on the lap of a plump German businessman, who also lacked the gift of humor. I was still apologizing when the conductor appeared to check tickets. No ticket.

I explained I had just had time to catch the train, which was gathering speed through the suburbs, and asked to pay in cash.

"Where are you going?" he asked.

"Well, where are *you* going?" I replied.

"Amsterdam," he said.

"What a coincidence. A single to Amsterdam, in economy."

"You are in first," he said, "you'll have to move." So I got my ticket, apologized again, and went to find a harder seat.

My father's younger brother was living and working for a British company in Scheveningen at the time. He managed to get me a passage on a merchantman out of Flushing for England.

Back in my London flat, I gathered my research papers around me, sat down, and wrote *The Dogs of War*, presenting the manuscript to Harold Harris just before the deadline.

I wondered about the voice on the phone that had saved my bacon in Hamburg. The only explanation that made sense was that also in the circle around Herr Otto X was another infiltrator from a body I knew only as the Firm, checking on behalf of my government on possible arms sales to the IRA. But I never found out who he was, and so far as I know, never met him.

The spring of 1973 was restful. I had completed my three-novel contract, had no ideas for a fourth, and was just beginning to see some serious money coming in. Then I dropped by at John Mallinson's flat for a drink, and someone else, on her way home from a modeling assignment, also came by. She was an auburn-haired girl whose legs seemed to go on forever. We married in Gibraltar that August.

And a letter came from David Deutsch, the producer appointed by

John Woolf to make the film of *Jackal*. It had filmed in London and was then shooting all the French scenes in Paris. Would I like to come over for a visit and meet the star, Edward Fox? Of course I would.

I knew the face because, months earlier during preproduction, Fred Zinnemann had asked me to his office for a consultation. With his Old World Viennese courtesy, he explained there was a problem with the casting.

The Hollywood studio that would distribute the movie wanted a known star. Michael Caine had been interested, ditto Roger Moore. Charlton Heston had begged for it. But Zinnemann wanted a man who, though an excellent actor, was still little known enough to vanish in the crowd, as the Jackal was supposed to do.

In his Mount Street office, the director solemnly placed six photos before me, all postcard size. They were all of handsome young men, blond, staring at the camera.

"Which, for you, is the Jackal?" he asked. I scanned them all and placed my finger on the bottom right-hand photo.

"That one."

"I am so glad. I have just signed him. His name is Edward Fox."

The other five were male models. Edward had already gained his spurs as Lord Trimingham in Joseph Losey's *The Go-Between*. But internationally, he was still relatively unknown. *The Day of the Jackal* was going to change that.

AN UNUSUAL DINNER

Fred Zinnemann was a brilliant director, but it was as if he were two men. Off the set, he was Old World courtesy personified, but on the set he was a miniature dictator. Perhaps he had to be to get the films made; there are some very large egos in filmmaking.

He was staying at the Hotel Warwick in the rue de Berri, just off the Champs-Elysées, with Edward Fox very much under his wing and control. He did not really want his new young star going off into town at night, lest he be late for the early starts that were necessary to get out to the studio and into makeup.

I arrived at the hotel on time and he introduced me to Edward. Dinner was friendly, but slightly formal, and ended rather early for the City of Lights. I suspected Edward might have been up for a more adventurous evening.

As we were crossing the lobby toward the door and out of earshot of Mr. Zinnemann, I asked if he had actually ever met a contract hit man. He said he had not.

"Would you like to?" I asked.

"Well, as I am supposed to be playing one, it might be interesting," he said.

I told him that at eight the next evening, there would be a taxi parked across the street with me in it. He should just cross the road and jump in.

It was quite a long shot, but I was lucky. I hoped Armand would be in town, and when I contacted his doting sister, she said he was indeed, and she would tell him to call me at my hotel. He rang just before midnight and I told him what I had in mind. He seemed amused, but would not come to the Eighth Arrondissement, setting up a "meet" in the heart of the red light district at a café-bar I had never heard of.

Of the six mercenaries who had stayed on in Biafra after the bulk of the French-supplied contingent ran into an ambush and then to the airport to evacuate themselves, as I said, I really liked only three: Alec the Scot, Johnny the Rhodesian, and Armand.

Armand was lanky and swarthy, with the black hair and eyes of his Corsican ancestors. He spoke rarely, but observed the world with an ironic half grin.

He had gone to Biafra only because the chief of the Brigade Criminelle of the Paris police had advised him in the friendliest way that he should leave Paris for a while to avoid an embarrassing arrest. There were no hard feelings, the spirit being that we all have to make a living.

So he had joined the group being organized by Jacques Foccart, the French government's Mr. Dirty Tricks for Africa, to be led by ex-Legion legend Roger Faulckes. When the French contingent ran for home after a week, Armand stayed on, and indeed to the end.

I discovered that he had actually sought out the Irish missionaries and monthly handed over his pay to buy more food for the children. He also told me, when I learned of it, that he would be immensely displeased if word got out. One did not lightly displease Armand, so I kept quiet.

Armand had never really been a gangster in Paris because he never joined a gang. But he occasionally acted as settler of accounts between the gangs of the Paris underworld. The city police had no objection to the place being cleaned up a bit, which was why they mostly left him alone.

On one occasion, Madame Claude, proprietress of the corps of the best call girls in Europe, felt she was being followed, possibly with intent to kidnap. She, too, consulted the chief of detectives, who recommended she engage Armand to look after her.

A week later, her driver again noticed the lights of the stalker car in his mirror. Armand, sitting beside him, asked him to pull over and stop. The car behind did the same. Armand got out and strolled back to have a word. There was a brief conversation through the side window of the car behind. It hung a U-turn in the middle of the boulevard and drove off. That was the end of that.

Although he was much younger than her, Madame Claude developed a huge crush on him, made more so by his polite disinclination to take advantage. So she offered him the choice of her school of extremely pricey ladies—on the house, so to speak. But he preferred, as he put it, to roll his own, so he left her employ.

The bistro he had stipulated was down a side street, and as the taxi entered it, we noted that both pavements were lined with streetwalkers. We got out, and as I paid the driver we received a chorus of the usual salutations.

"Alors, blondie, je t'emmène? Tu veux monter, non?"

Edward, who had been to Harrow, of course did not understand a word, but the sense was clear enough. It was a warm night, their dresses were minimal, and their bosoms jacked up to resemble party balloons. I settled up with the taxi and ushered him inside.

There was a bar, then a bead curtain, and the dining area behind it. We penetrated the curtain and joined Armand at the table in the far corner, where he was toying with a *citron pressé* (he did not drink alcohol).

Introductions made, we had a civilized dinner. Armand spoke no English and Edward schoolboy French, which is to say very little indeed. I interpreted. With his innate manners, Edward asked no really embarrassing questions, so there were no tense moments, until the end.

And that was not the fault of any of us. Word had spread to the bar area and thence to the street that there was a film star dining inside. The French are film crazy, and the idea of a real film star a few yards away was to the streetwalkers as a large fly to a salmon. They invaded the dining area, shoving their figures at us both until they realized that only Edward was in films. Then they were making him some very bawdy suggestions.

The future Jackal was pink as a traffic light, the underworld executioner was laughing his head off, and I was trying to get the headwaiter so that I could settle up and escape. Then Armand was gone, out the back via the kitchens, and I have not seen him since. The bar owner summoned a cab by phone and I was able to deliver Edward back to the Warwick and Fred Zinnemann pretty much intact.

Forty years later, at a garden lunch party at my home, I told the anecdote to a merry audience to explain how we met. Edward was there with his wife, Joanna David, who had never heard it. I ended by saying that in forty years I had never told him what it was the girls were saying to him. He leaned across the table.

"No," he said, "you never did. What was it?"

"They were offering you freebies. Whatever you wanted. On the house. And in their world, that is a very serious compliment indeed."

He thought it over.

"I don't suppose there is any point in going back?"

As we are both well into our seventies, I very much doubt it.

PERFECT JOY

———— ◆◈◆ ————

If you were to ask ten people for their definition of perfect joy, you might well get ten definitions or a few less than that. Pretty high on the list would be that moment when a father gazes down at his newborn child, the tiny face puckered in outrage at having been expelled from a safe, warm womb into a world of troubles. Of these, it knows nothing and from them must be protected, which is where the lovelorn father comes in.

There will be other choices, including palm-fringed lagoons or a hole in one while winning the U.S. Open. Reject all of these, for I know what is perfect joy, because I have seen it.

The call, when it came in summer 1973, was as always terribly diffident. Could we possibly get together for a chat? Of course we could. They did not want me to come to Century House in case someone saw me. And a lunch booth in a restaurant, however expensive and discreet, can always be bugged by a waiter working for the other side.

So it was a safe house, in reality an apartment in a block, scanned daily and certainly before every use. It was so discreet that I have forgotten where it was, save only it was in Mayfair, London. There were three of them and they were not from the Africa Desk, but concerned with operations in East Germany, so I did not know them. But they knew me, or at least the contents of my file.

"There is no question of trying to pass for a German, so no refresher course. Just a question of a British tourist slipping inside and bringing something out."

I still reckoned the voice on the phone that got me out of Hamburg just in time was that of a Friend, someone from the Firm, and one good turn deserves another. Besides, it all seemed so simple.

There was an asset, a Russian colonel, working for us deep inside East Germany, and he had a package that we needed brought out. No, not in East Berlin, but based outside Dresden. He could not get farther than a meet in Dresden. It began to be not quite so simple. Dresden was a long way in.

The proposed plan had been minutely studied long before the meeting at the safe house and appeared to have the fewest flaws. It would have to be by car, because the package, which in deference to Alfred Hitchcock I always called the McGuffin, would have to be concealed far from prying hands and eyes on the way out. Besides, there was another package for the asset that had to go in. So, a swap. One in and one out.

They knew I had a car, at that time a Triumph Vitesse drophead convertible. Could they borrow it for a day or so? Of course.

I had to leave the Triumph outside my apartment with the keys under the floor mat. I never saw who took it or returned it. No need to. It just vanished and reappeared, but slightly different.

The battery in the Vitesse was in the engine bay. It sat on a tray beside the left-hand engine wall. Two metal clips prevented it from moving and a thick rubber pad prevented vibrations. The pad had been removed, slit open, and a cavity created.

To get at the cavity, one had to use a spanner to release the positive and negative leads, then undo the two retaining clips. Lift the battery out and place it to one side. Peel the rubber pad open. And inside was the fat wad of papers destined for the asset and the cavity in which his reports (whatever they were, I would never know) would ride out of the workers' paradise.

I spent a day by the curbside in the warm summer sun practicing until I had it all down to less than thirty seconds. And there was more.

The "cover" was a visit to the Albertinum Museum, East Germany's cultural jewel, amazingly untouched by the Anglo-American bombing of February 1945, which had flattened most of the city. Greco-Roman treasures were my new enthusiasm, and there were books to study as if for an exam. Finally, it seemed I was ready to roll.

It was a long drive across France and West Germany to the East German border, but under the Four-Power Agreement, my British passport entitled me onto the autobahn running across East Germany to the enclave of West Berlin. Once there, I avoided all contacts I had made during my time ten years earlier.

But there was a travel agency permitted by the East German authorities to be the conduit for visas for genuine Western tourists whom the Politburo was keen to entice into East Germany for the foreign currency they brought.

My handler, Philip (a pseudonym, of course), certainly did not wish to be photographed sitting beside me in the passenger seat when the Triumph entered East Germany, so he had flown into Tempelhof, the airport that serviced West Berlin only. He waited in a different hotel until the visa came through and my passport returned. The agency took its fee and gave me my passport back. Philip secured the final OK from London, meaning the asset was ready, and I was cleared to roll through Checkpoint Charlie the following morning.

There were several conditions for the visa. A minimum sum in deutschmarks had to be changed into worthless East marks, and this was duly done. On the East German autobahn south, there were specific filling stations where I was allowed to refuel. I had no doubt that if the Stasi were not going to tail me all the way, there would be checkpoints along the route at which the dark-blue Triumph with British number plates would be "clocked" and noted.

And there was just one hotel in Dresden where I was expected and where a reservation had been made.

I had not seen Checkpoint Charlie for ten years, but it was much the same. West Germans (but not West Berliners, who were forbidden) and other Europeans queued as usual by the checking sheds while mirrors on wheels were run under the chassis to scan for contraband.

The usual "bonnet up" and "boot open" orders, the usual nervous obedience, the usual tourist attempts to be lighthearted, the usual grim, unsmiling response. The border guard assigned to me looked around the engine bay, but touched nothing. The battery pad had passed its first test.

My small valise had been emptied and searched inside the shed and, that apart, the boot contained nothing, so I was allowed to replace it and slam the lid shut. Then the final curt wave toward East Berlin, the barrier rising, and the roll into Redland.

I had memorized the route through the southern outskirts of East Berlin toward the Dresden autobahn. Of course, there was the second border check—the one to get you out of East Berlin and into rural East Germany. This I recognized: it was the one through which the Magdeburg Stasi had escorted me after the RB-66 incident in the pine forest ten years back. I hoped Captain Holland's leg had mended.

Then it was the open road, south into Saxony province and the city of Dresden, which I had never seen. The hotel was clearly marked on my street map and I was installed by midafternoon.

The car park was underground, and this was before the all-seeing CCTV cameras. There seemed to be no one watching, though I had no doubt my room was bugged, my telephone was tapped, and that it would be searched while I was at dinner. So I left the McGuffin under the battery pad until morning.

There was no point in going out to wander the streets. My brass-buttoned blazer yelled "Englishman" to any drably dressed East German, so I stayed in and studied the two books I had brought with me on the Albertinum Museum and its many ancient treasures. I hoped these would be noted by the hotel staff and that if they reported, which they almost certainly would, it would be to say the Brit was simply obsessed by Roman antiquities.

Not entirely unnaturally, I slept lightly and woke early. The meet was for two o'clock in a certain aisle between display cabinets inside the museum. I breakfasted at eight and checked out at nine, paying cash (no credit cards back then). But I left my valise with the concierge and was assured my car could remain in the garage until I needed it. I was not told what else would happen—that my case would be searched again. Good, there was nothing in it.

At half past nine, I ducked down into the garage, waited until another hotel guest drove out, clipped open the bonnet, removed the McGuffin, slipped it into my blazer pocket, replaced the battery, reconnected it, and closed up. Then it was a leisurely walk with textbooks under the arm to the museum. At five to two, I was in the aisle between the cabinets, engrossed in shards of pottery.

There were others there. Couples, threesomes, the inevitable guided groups of schoolchildren. I had my picture book open, comparing the photographs with the real artifacts behind the glass, occasionally looking out for a single man with a dark-red tie and black stripes. A few seconds after two, he turned into my aisle.

Germans usually do not have Slavic features, but this one did. And the tie. I saw his glance settle upon the one I was wearing: dark blue with white polka dots. No one else remotely like either of us. Then a wandering curator in uniform. Sometimes the simplest way is the best way.

"*Entschuldigung* [excuse me], where is the men's room?"

He was politeness itself and pointed out the sign *Herren* above a door at the end of the gallery. No eye contact with "Chummy" standing ten feet away. He should know the "meet" would be in the toilet. So I wandered away toward it, entered, relieved myself, and was washing my hands when he entered. Apart from us, it was empty and all the stall doors were open. He, too, began to wash his hands. So two noisy streams of water. His turn. In German.

"Excuse me, did we not meet in Potsdam?"

My reply.

"Yes, I was there last April."

Enough. No one else was talking this garbage in Dresden that morning. I nodded to two adjacent stalls. He took one, I took the other. Under the cubicle partition came a fat package of paper. I took mine and slid it the other way.

I defy anyone to resist the small worm of anxiety in the pit of the stomach at that moment. Is Chummy the real Chummy or was the real asset picked up a week ago and broken in the interrogation cellar to reveal all the places and ID codes of the coming "meet"?

Is the place about to be invaded by screaming hordes of goons with drawn pistols, handcuffs, clouts about the head? Even the silence seems menacing. But the biggest fear of all is not that you have run out of tradecraft or luck, but that far away back home, some bastard has betrayed you. "They" knew all along, they were waiting for you, mocking all your precautions. That is why Dante put the traitor in the final circle of hell.

Nothing happened. Chummy left the booth and I heard the outer door slam shut. I have never seen him since. I hope he is all right. There were still eighteen years of the USSR to go, and the KGB had a very nasty procedure for traitors.

I also left the booth, but had another hand wash to kill time. When I left, I bumped into another man coming in, but he was just a visitor. We nodded, passed, and I strolled out, still clutching my textbooks. There were a few more hours to kill until dusk, for I wanted to motor in darkness.

The visa expired at midnight and the way to the West was not via East Berlin but south to the Saale River crossing point, one of the few tourist-approved crossing points. South of Saale, in the town of Bayreuth, Philip would be waiting.

Back at the hotel, I collected my valise with assurances of having had a wonderful time in Dresden and copious compliments on the superb Albertinum Museum. Then down to the car park. But there was a large conference party checking in. Too many people. If I was seen waist-deep in my own engine bay, there might be offers of help, the last thing I needed. I kept the McGuffin in my breast pocket, got into the Triumph, which was already attracting curious glances, and drove out. Darkness was descending. I took the signs pointing to the Geraer Kreuz, the major autobahn junction where the highway turned south to the Bavarian border.

It was pitch-dark when I saw the lay-by in the headlights and, as I had hoped, the road by night was almost empty. I eased to the right, slid up the shallow ramp until the pine trees enveloped me, and stopped. Lights out. Wait, have a cigarette. Relax. Nearly there.

There was a small spanner in the glove compartment. Not enough to arouse suspicion, but vital for the nuts on the battery leads. I got out, opened the bonnet, and used my spanner to ease the first nut, the one on the negative battery lead. There was no need for a torch, the sickle moon was enough. At that moment, the lay-by was flooded with a harsh white light.

Another car had cruised up the ramp behind me, its headlights undipped. I slipped the spanner into my trouser pocket and straightened up. The car behind was a Wartburg saloon, and by its own lights I could see its livery: green and cream, the insignia of the *Volkspolizei*, the People's Police, the VoPos. There were four of them climbing out.

They had clearly by then recognized the Triumph and the number plates as British. The reason they had come off the autobahn made itself plain when one of them faced the woods and unzipped his fly. A comfort break, but that bursting bladder might prove to be their lucky night.

The senior of them was a top NCO, what I took to be the *Unteroffizier*. The other two examined the Triumph curiously while their colleague urinated. The NCO held out his hand.

"*Ausweis, bitte.*" The "please" was good news, still polite. I dropped into Bertie Wooster mode—the hapless, helpless, harmless English tourist, completely lost and very dim. Halting German, awful accent.

The NCO examined the passport page by page by the light of a torch from his pocket. He saw the East German visa.

"Why are you stopped here?"

"It just stopped, Officer. I don't know why. Just motoring along and it starts to cough, then cut out. I had just enough speed to get here before it stopped."

The Germans are probably the best engineers in the world, but they know it and loved to be told it. Even East German engineering was enough for its degrees to be acknowledged in the West. So I laid the flattery on with a trowel.

"I cannot understand engines, Officer. So I do not know what to look for. And I have no torch. You Germans are so brilliant at this . . . I don't suppose you could have a look?"

The senior NCO thought it over. Then he snapped an order at the one who had finished his ablutions and buttoned up his fly. In that crew, he seemed to be the mechanic.

"*Guck mal*," he said, gesturing toward the engine bay. "Have a look."

The urinator took the torch and went into the engine bay. Inside my breast pocket, the fat pack of papers was beginning to feel like a tombstone, which it could turn out to be if I was ordered to empty all pockets.

Then there was a shout of triumph and the engineer straightened up. He was holding up in his right hand the disconnected battery lead, illuminated in the torch beam.

"*Hat sich gelöst*," he shouted. "It just shook itself off."

Then it was all grins of pleasure. Point proved. Germans are better. I was handing around Rothmans, much appreciated. The disconnected lead was replaced and I was bidden to try the starter. It kicked into life at once. Bertie Wooster was beside himself with amazement and gratitude. Bonnet down and locked. Salutes all round. Please, *mein Herr*, on your way.

An hour further on, I did it again and this time was not disturbed.

At half past eleven, I rolled into the arc lights and customs sheds at the Saale River crossing.

And there it was thorough. Boot, engine bay, high-powered flash-lights into every crevice. Upholstery patted for hidden lumps, with mirrors and lights rolled underneath.

Inside the customs shed, pocket and body search. I was the only crosser; I had their undivided attention and I suppose they were bored. Excess cash handed over, passport taken to a back room, muffled sounds of phone calls. Eventually, with expressions of disappointment on their faces, the curt nod. Proceed. Valise back in boot, climb in, start up. Roll.

Back then, the East Germans had a trick. Their border point was a quarter of a mile inside East Germany. After the lifting of what looked like the last pole, there was a long, slow cruise at only ten kilometers per hour down the last stretch. It was bordered on both sides by chain-link fence. Unclimbable. And watchtowers with machine guns. Easy to hear the roared bullhorn command "Halt. Stehenbleiben." Halt, stay where you are.

Finally, at the end, another barrier. Behind it, the West Germans were watching, hidden behind their own lights, field glasses on the approaching car and the East German controls farther back. There were no shouts as front bumper approached the barrier, which finally jerked into action.

Perfect joy? Oh, yes. Perfect joy is the sight of a red-and-white-striped pole rising into the Bavarian night as the rearview mirror fills with the wash of headlights.

I was very late into Bayreuth and found Philip at the only place in town still open for coffee, the railway café. He seemed distraught. He thought he had lost me. I was touched. So I gave him the McGuffin, went to the hotel, and slept like a log.

The next day I filled the tank and drove back across Bavaria, over the Rhine, through France to the Channel port of Calais. Thence the first ferry of the day for Dover and the chance to see once again, standing on the forepeak, the great white cliffs coming through the morning mist.

FRIENDS AND OPPONENTS

———◦◦◦◦———

There are few experiences that appear so harmless, but turn out to be so exhausting, as the round-the-world promotion tour.

At first blush, it sounds varied and interesting. Just twelve cities in twenty-four days with a couple of "rest" weekends in the middle and first-class all the way. Why not? The reason why not is that after six or seven days, the effects of rapidly changing time zones, strange beds, constant airports, and the draining dawn-to-dusk interviews are starting to drag at the nerve ends, exacerbating the inevitable jet lag.

I only did one such, and that was in 1978, to promote the fourth novel, *The Devil's Alternative.* Just Toronto, Vancouver, Hong Kong, Brisbane, Sydney, Auckland, Perth, Johannesburg, Cape Town, Frankfurt, and back to London. It was all new to me and exotic. Years later, just two stopovers stand out—Hong Kong and Mauritius, which was a weekend break between Perth and Jo'burg.

By the time the airliner touched down at the small and crowded Kai Tak Airport in Hong Kong, I was only a third of the way into my journey and still pretty fresh. The Peninsula Hotel had sent a car, and I had to admit I had never, ever been looked after like this.

I had just been bowed into my suite on the tenth floor of the Peninsula when the phone rang. It was "Johnny," the Firm's head of station for the colony and several outstations besides.

"Are you on for dinner tonight?"

"Er, yes."

"Splendid. I'll pick you up. Far end of the front car park, eight o'clock, red car." Then he was gone.

The Peninsula in those days had not one but a fleet of chocolate-colored Rolls-Royces for its guests. At eight I was on the front steps peering through the regiment of Rollers when I saw a flash of a red car right at the back. It turned out to be the most clapped-out Jowett Javelin I had ever seen, with Johnny beaming at the wheel. The Jowett car company has long ago passed into history, and quite rightly, too.

Johnny clearly knew his Hong Kong intimately, but I was lost within seconds of entering the narrow alleys of the Walled City. Finally, even the Javelin could go no farther, so it was parked by the curb and we walked.

The thought occurred to me that if the British taxpayer, accustomed to seeing James Bond in his Aston Martin, could see this rolling scrapyard, he would realize he was not actually being overcharged by Her Majesty's overseas intelligence arm.

Johnny strode knowledgeably down alley after alley until we came to a door studded with heads of big black nails. He knocked. A small panel opened. There was a rapid exchange in Chinese, though whether Mandarin, Hakka, or Cantonese, I could not tell. Then the door creaked open and we were inside. That was when I realized that my host for dinner was an honored guest.

The restaurant was not large, perhaps fifteen tables, and entirely populated by Chinese diners. Not a single "round-eye" in sight. I was not surprised; they could not have found the place.

The serving staff appeared to be two young men, alike enough to be brothers (which they were) and both strapping six-footers with black buzz-cut hair. Out of the kitchen came the proprietor and chef, evidently the father, also over six feet with am iron-gray buzz cut. He greeted Johnny as a friend.

There were no menus. Johnny ordered for both of us, and what he asked for was met with beaming approval. When we were alone, I asked, "They are pretty big for Chinese."

"They are Manchu," said Johnny. "They grow big up there."

"And the language?"

"Mandarin."

The meal was beyond excellent, probably the best I have ever had. I commented on the warmth with which he had been greeted.

"Well, they are colleagues in a way."

"Working for London?"

"Good Lord, no, they are Beijing's intelligence branch down here." I was getting a bit confused.

"I thought they were the enemy."

"Good heavens, no, the Russians are the enemy. The KGB. Beijing can't stand them, so they keep us up to speed on everything the Sovs get up to, and they always know first."

Now the old perceptions were really spinning.

"So we get along with the Chinese, although we are supposed to be on different sides?"

"Absolutely. Except for the Nationalists, the residue of the old Kuomintang. They are a pain in the arse."

"I thought the Nationalists were anti-Beijing."

"They are. That's why they are a pain. They have a colony several bays along the coast. They scrimp and save until they have enough to buy some illegal guns, then they set off in a sampan or two to invade Mainland China."

"What happens to them?"

"Oh, I tip off my friend here"—he nodded toward the kitchen—"and the idiots are intercepted as they land."

"Aren't they executed?"

"Oh, no, we have an arrangement. They just disarm them and send them back. Then they have to scrimp and save for another year to buy some more guns, then it happens again. Look, the People's Liberation Army could take this place before breakfast if they wanted. We are very much guests here.

"A peaceable Hong Kong suits both sides. For Beijing, it is a valuable income stream and a meeting point where we can talk unobserved. Their new man, Deng Xiaoping, is more of a pragmatist than a dogmatist. For us it is a trading center and a listening post. Anything that threatens to disturb that cozy relationship is a menace. That includes the Kuomintang for us and the KGB for them. All we have to do is keep Beijing sweet and the Russkies inside their box."

As he settled up and we were bowed out the door, I realized that I had just learned over superb chow mein that what the Western newspaper-reading public had been told for years was complete bunkum.

The car was untouched, though in many alleys of the world it would have been stripped. But no one had laid a finger on it. They wouldn't dare.

The next day, the RAF unit tucked away behind Kai Tak gave me a ride around the colony in one of their helicopters. I think it was a Skeeter, but anyway it was extremely small, just a Perspex bubble under a noisy fan. The cabin had no doors, so on the steep banks one was held only by the straps to keep from plunging two thousand feet to the ground.

From this vantage point, one could see the Gurkhas patrolling the heather hills of the New Territories, looking for the refugees who came over in a constant stream, seeking a new life away from Communism. But the colony was far too small. So they were picked up, escorted to a camp on Lantau Island (now the new airport), and then sent back.

There was another cozy agreement, so that they were not punished; just told not to do it again and resettled a long way away. That evening I was asked to address the Hong Kong Foreign Correspondents' Club. I did so completely sober, to be congratulated, as the previous guest, comedian Dave Allen, had fallen face-forward into the soup.

The last day, Jardine Matheson asked me to fire the ceremonial Noon Day Gun, and then it was off to Kai Tak for the flight to Brisbane.

After Australia and New Zealand and the same interview questions another hundred times, my flight west from Perth passed right over the island of Mauritius. Hutchinson, my publishers, who were paying for this tour, suggested that as there was nothing for me in Jo'burg until the Monday, I take a rest break on this lovely resort island. I was lodged at the Saint Géran Hotel, still one of my world favorites to this day, thirty-five years later.

While there for only sixty hours, I fell in love—twice. There was a dive shop and a resort course. A few hours of instruction in the pool permitted two real scuba dives over the nearby reefs. And I was smitten by the silence and the beauty of this underwater world. I have been diving ever since.

And there was a game-fishing boat, the *Chico*, which was booked. But one of the pair who had reserved it cried off and the general manager, Paul Jones, who remains a friend to this day, was looking for a stand-in. As a boy in Kent, I had fished for bream and rudd in the Hythe Canal, but this was different—eight hours on the vast and rolling Indian Ocean with lines streamed for marlin, sailfish, kingfish, wahoo, tuna, and bonito.

I forget what we caught, but it was over a dozen, without the marlin or sailfish, and when we tied up at the dock in the late afternoon I was smitten again. I later based the story "The Emperor" on that day at sea. Then it was a car to the airport and the flight to Jo'burg. I was decanted at Heathrow ten days later, feeling like a wrung-out dishcloth.

But since then I have dived the reefs from Lizard Island, Queensland, west to the corals of the Baja Peninsula on the Sea of Cortés; swum with shark and manta ray among the atolls of the Maldives and the Amirantes; hooked marlin, sailfish, and amberjack (always returned to the ocean), and wahoo and kings (for the dinner table).

My only drugs are silence and solitude, and in an increasingly noisy, frantic, and crowded world, on or under the sea is where I find them.

FIVE YEARS IN IRELAND

———— ◆◆◆ ————

There was not the slightest reason why Irish politician Charles Haughey and I would get on, but we did. To his political enemies, he was relentless, and vengeful for any slight or ill turn. When relaxed over a dinner table, I found him an amusing rogue. And he was certainly a rogue.

As a passionate republican, he had little time for the English or anything British, but seemed to make an exception for me, perhaps because he realized I had quickly seen through him.

My wife and I had left the UK for Spain in January 1974 to escape the electoral victory of the Labour Party under Harold Wilson and the tax policies of Dennis Healey, who raised income tax to an eye-watering 83 percent when he came to office as Chancellor of the Exchequer in April. The year in Spain was to avoid the possibility that most of the earnings from the first three novels would disappear, perhaps never to be repeated. But it was never intended that we should settle in Spain. It was the statutory "year of absence."

By Christmas 1974, we were in Dublin (outside mainland UK and therefore outside the tax net), looking for a house to buy, and settled in the village of Enniskerry, County Wicklow, just south of Dublin. Years earlier, when his party, Fianna Fáil, had been in office and he was finance minister, it was Charlie Haughey who had introduced a Finance Act with a little paragraph at the bottom that hardly anyone noticed. It made all creative artists, including writers, exempt from income tax.

I must have been the only immigrant who did not even know that (I may have mentioned that I am not very good with money). When I revealed my ignorance of the law, I was met with local amazement and then approbation. At least I had come because I liked the place.

To make friends in Ireland is the easiest thing in the world, because they are so friendly to start with. Add to that a terrific sense of humor. In the north, the guerrilla campaign of the IRA against the Belfast government and the British armed forces posted there was at its height, but in the south, the Republic of Ireland, all was quiet and immensely sociable. There were tales of Brits who had to leave because they could not take the partygoing, so they took their damaged livers back home.

It was shortly after settling there that my wife and I met Charlie Haughey socially, but through the offices of his longtime girlfriend. It was a relationship that everybody knew about, but nobody mentioned, and the entire media practiced auto-censorship. Those days are long gone.

The lady gave small, intimate dinner parties around the pine table in her basement kitchen, and that was where we could converse with the other Charlie Haughey—shirtsleeved, affable, and humorous. Like Harold King in the Reuters's Paris office, he first tried to intimidate, and if that did not work, relaxed and let the Irish charm come through.

I enormously enjoyed my five years in Ireland and recall with affection the innumerable and uproarious dinner parties. Before going to Spain, in an act of pure madness, I had bought a Rolls-Royce. It was far from new and far from the top of the price range. It was a classic that I had restored at a specialist's in London. Once it was restored, I had it resprayed from black to white. It had the old-style vertical Greek-temple grille with the winged lady flying above the bonnet. This monster was driven all the way to the Costa Blanca and a year later shipped to Ireland. In both a Spanish village and Enniskerry, it was—how shall I put it?—rather noticeable. But I liked it and might have kept it longer but for the trip north to County Antrim to visit my in-laws.

We drove sedately up through Dublin, past the airport at Swords, and on to the IRA hot spot of Dundalk. North of that, the road was largely empty until we reached the border post and the start of County Armagh, the first of the six counties that make up British-owned Northern Ireland.

The Irish border post was hardly manned at all. The barrier pole was up and a hand behind the glass window of a booth beside the road waved us on. At the British control, the pole was down, so we stopped. Out of the undergrowth came a strange Caliban-type figure.

He was in camouflage fatigues, wearing a tam-o'-shanter with a red bobble on top, and clutched a submachine carbine. Apparently one of Her Majesty's soldiers, but not one I had ever seen before. He scampered up to the driver's-side window, peered through, and gesticulated that I should wind it down.

It was electric, and when it hummed downward, he jumped in surprise and addressed me. I could not understand a word he said, but from the accent, which I had heard in Tangier, I knew it must be Glasgow. When I failed to respond to whatever he asked, he became agitated and the barrel of the submachine gun appeared under my nose.

At this point, a quite different figure came out of the bushes: very tall, gangly, and clearly an officer. He, too, approached and spoke, but in a laid-back drawl.

"Awfully sorry, old chap, he's asking to see your papers."

The captain took over and scanned my passport. From his flashes, I realized these were the Cameronians, who had established a fine reputation when based in Germany as the Poison Dwarfs.

The pair reminded me of the White Russian officer commanding Oriental troops outside Magdeburg fifteen years earlier. The captain dismissed the soldier with a stream of the same incomprehensible dialect.

"Are you the writer fellow?" he asked.

"Yes."

"Good show. Nice car."

"Thank you."

"Do you think it is wise to drive it right through Bandit Country?"

I recognized the media term for South Armagh, which I still had to cross.

"Perhaps you should," he drawled. "Anyway, on you go. And take care."

With this encouraging farewell I let in the clutch and the white beast purred forward into County Armagh and its silent and hostile hedges. A week later, it was the same going back to the south—a very quiet drive both outside the car and inside. After that, I sold the Rolls and bought a nice anonymous Austin Montego estate car.

About that time, the Cosgrave government fell and Fianna Fáil came back to office, with Charlie Haughey appointed minister of health under prime minister Jack Lynch, with whom he had feuded until he finally toppled his own premier and took over in 1979.

Hardly had he got the top slot when Ireland received Pope John

Paul II on a state visit. Over the pine kitchen table, Charlie put to me a pretty odd request. He said he needed a monograph to present to the cabinet on security—he was terrified of an attempt being made on the pontiff while he was in Dublin.

I suggested it was out of the question for His Holiness to be in mortal danger in Dublin of all places, and that the British government had a dozen security experts with years of experience. He countered that he would not turn to London, but that the Irish Garda had had no experience with this sort of thing. He needed the techniques that had kept de Gaulle alive. There was nothing for it but to do what he wanted.

I thought back to all that de Gaulle's bodyguards had let slip when chatting with the French media in 1962 and put together a paper stressing the difference between close-up protection against the madman and the hazard of the long-range sniper.

I never knew whether he put this paper to the cabinet as his own work or mine, or as that of some anonymous ace known only to him. Probably the last. Anyway, the three-day visit of the pope went off without a hitch, though I noticed a few snipers from the Irish Army perched on the rooftops, scanning all the windows opposite.

Both our sons were born in Dublin: Stuart in 1977 and Shane in 1979. But in the autumn of 1979, my wife developed an all-consuming fear that something might happen to our two babies.

In the case of Ireland in 1979, such a fear was far from illogical. IRA renegades had already kidnapped the Dutch businessman Tiede Herrema, who was rescued unharmed after a nationwide manhunt, and others had more recently visited the Outwood home of my friend the Canadian tycoon Galen Weston. Neither he nor his wife, Hilary, were in residence but they terrified his personal assistant.

By the early spring, the condition was serious. One friend in Dublin remarked to me: "You're not the most famous man in Ireland, you're not the richest man in Ireland, and you're not the only Brit in Ireland. But you're probably the most famous, richest Brit."

So a kidnap attempt on one of the babies was not a complete fantasy at all. It was time to go, and it was my Irish-born wife who was the more adamant for a departure back to England. It seemed courteous to inform our friend the prime minister. Without explaining why, I asked for an interview at his office in Kildare Street.

He greeted me warmly, but somewhat puzzled. When the door was closed, I explained that we were leaving and why. He was horrified and asked me to stay. I made clear the decision was made.

He could not offer me Irish citizenship. As the firstborn son of a firstborn son of a man from Youghal, County Cork, I had that right, anyway. So he offered to make me a senator of Ireland. Apparently, the Senate is part-elected, but a few seats can be nominated. I thanked him, but declined.

Accepting the reality, he led me out of his office and then down the length of the long hall to the street door, his arm around my shoulders. Doors popped open as openmouthed senior civil servants looked out to see their premier draped round a Britisher, never seen before or since.

A few days later, I had one last call from him. It was to give me his word that not a single IRA man in the country would dare raise his hand against me or my family. The only way he could have known that was if he had given a flat order to the Army Council of the IRA. Not many men could do that.

On April 7, 1980, loaded to the roof and with more luggage on the roof rack, the Montego rolled onto the ferry from Dun Laoghaire to Fishguard.

Margaret Thatcher had won the 1979 election and the maximum

income tax rate had tumbled from 83 percent to 60 percent, which, though high, was acceptable. We arrived in London just in time to see on television the interruption of the World Snooker Championship in the final frame as the SAS stormed the terrorist-occupied Iranian embassy.

Since then, I have lived in Surrey, St. John's Wood, Hertfordshire, and Buckinghamshire. But I have never emigrated and never will.

A NEAT TRICK

————————⋄◆⋄————————

By the summer of 1982, my physical situation had become extremely comfortable—boringly so. I was on the threshold of forty-four, eight years married, the father of two growing boys of three and five, living in a large white house at Tilford, a village in the county of Surrey, and had realized that I could apparently make a comfortable living writing novels. No wonder I was bored.

There is a passage in the John Buchan novel *John McNab,* where the hero is in a similar state and goes to his doctor. This shrewd man, after a complete examination, advises his patient: "As your doctor I can do nothing for you, but as your friend let me offer you advice. Go and steal a horse—in a country where horse stealing is punished by hanging."

I did not feel the need to go that far, but I had to do something more interesting than sitting on the terrace reading the papers and drinking coffee.

It happens that though I do not suffer from acrophobia—the panic-stricken fear of heights—I do not really like them. In an apartment on the thirtieth floor of a skyscraper, I would prefer not to go to the balcony and lean over. In truth, I would prefer to be back inside behind the plate-glass doors.

I had taken off many times and landed each time but never jumped out halfway. Perhaps that was the answer. I asked around for a good parachute club. A friend in the armed forces advised me the best (by which I mean the safest) was the Combined Forces school at Netheravon in Wiltshire. Having been paid for by that ultra-generous philanthropist, the taxpayer, it had state-of-the-art equipment and had never lost a trainee to the forces of gravity.

I was of course a civilian, but the RAF stretched a point and let me in, so on the given date I motored down there. Even that recently, things were far less formal than now. There was no medical, just the signing of that amiable document the "blood chit." It simply said that I accepted that if I were to become a tent peg in the middle of a Wiltshire meadow, it would be entirely my fault and my estate could sue nobody.

The course on which I found myself had thirty to forty volunteers, all drawn from various branches of the army and air force and all in their late teens and early twenties. In other words, they were all young enough to be my offspring. They seemed to have insatiable appetites and were able to consume up to half a dozen big meals a day. They also had terrifying levels of energy.

Perhaps due to my age, a billet was kindly found for me in the officers' mess, which was familiar enough because Netheravon is an air force base. On the first morning, I joined the three-day course in the main hangar.

The CO was Major Gerry O'Hara of the Parachute Regiment but the instructors were Flight Sergeant Chris Lamb of the RAF and Corporal Paul Austin of the Royal Marines, both younger than me and slightly puzzled by my inclusion.

We started with classroom explanations of the forces of gravity, wind drift, and speeds of descent. Then came lectures on the equipment yet to come. We would be using the Aeroconical 'chute; none of your flying wings or stunt 'chutes, which were for real experts. The Aeroconical was a simple dome of parti-colored fabric, and we would not even have to open it. There would be a static line attached inside the aircraft that would open the 'chute automatically as we jumped. The instructors would be in the airplane with us and would affix the static lines for us. Simple enough.

We would be jumping over the airfield from the side door of a de Havilland Dragon Rapide from about three thousand feet, and descent speed would be about fourteen mph. The remainder of the "ground time" was dedicated to coping with the thump of impacting with Mother Earth at that speed and coming to no harm. This involved landing and rolling over at the same time.

The rest of day one and the morning of day two were spent in the hangar, leaping from platforms, landing and rolling, until we could do it without feeling more than minimal impact. All this took place between pauses for the inevitable brews of tea, without which the entire British defense structure would collapse. Lunch breaks involved my going back to the mess for a served lunch with the attending stewards, while the youngsters repaired to their refectory for yet another massive fry-up. I failed to understand where they were putting it all. The trick came at the end of the second morning.

The two instructors told us that the next morning would see the first jump. It was a lie, just in case of any middle-of-the-night disappearances. After lunch, the first of the two Dragon Rapides landed and we were told to draw parachutes. There was also to be a draw for the dubious position of "first out, first stick."

The elderly but still very serviceable biplanes were standing by, with propellers ticking over and side doors open as the draw was made. Due to cramped conditions inside, the "stick" would be sitting on benches down both sides of the interior and would rise to clip on static lines only at the last minute and on command. But the first man out would have to sit in the doorway all the way, clambering to his feet only when tapped on the shoulder by the jumpmaster. Then a hat was passed round.

It was full of small scraps of paper, each with a pupil's name on it. With his eyes closed, Chris Lamb groped inside and came out with a scrap. When unfolded, I was surprised, as the odds were thirty to one, that the name was mine.

Only later, back on the ground with a chance to examine the hat, did I learn they had all got my name on them. The two rogues had calculated that if the old codger did not freeze in the doorway, none of the teenagers would dare do so, either. Freezing up and refusing to jump meant immediate RTU—return to unit.

In reverse order of jump, we piled into the Rapide's fuselage, the "last out" group disappearing toward the tail. I found I had no seat at all. I had to sit in the doorway with legs and feet in the slipstream. We took off and climbed sedately to a point three thousand feet above the airfield. I began to get the "skyscraper balcony" syndrome. The fields were postage stamps, the huge hangars thumbnails. I thought longingly of my home in Tilford.

Paul Austin had a word through the cabin door and the engine noise died. The whirling propellers still seemed about a foot away from my face and I wondered if I would not jump into the blades. It was easy to forget that even with engines throttled back, there was still a fifty mph slipstream out there and gravity would do the rest.

There was a tap on the shoulder and I stood up. A fist with a raised thumb appeared, meaning "static line attached." Then the final tap. Deep breath, lean forward, and kick. Within a second, it was all gone—engine noise, slipstream, airplane. Just silence and the soughing of a gentle breeze, the hemisphere of silk above, the harness tight all around the body, the feet dangling over nothing and the postage stamps very slowly coming closer.

Then it became quite restful. Time for a good look around. Spectacular views over many miles of lovely countryside; surely one was not descending at all. But at fourteen mph, the airfield came up at a rush, then a huge thump as the jump boots hit the turf. Twist, roll, absorb the shock, turf under the backside then the shoulders, roll again, and stand, hauling in the billowing silk before it collapsed in an untidy pile. Then pick it all up and start the long walk back to the hangars.

Willing parachute packers took it all away: collapsed 'chute, shrouds (which are not sheets but nylon lines), and canvas harness. Time for a relaxing cigarette, then the Rapide was landing for the second jump.

I strolled over to the discarded hat and realized that mine was the only name on any of the scraps of paper, then had a few well-chosen words with Chris and Paul. But there had been three no-jumps, so the disgraced ones were being led away to change out of overalls and back into uniform. No second chances.

On the second jump, I had a small problem. The landing was too heavy. A gust of breeze lifted the 'chute, then dropped me from too high up. A low click in the left ankle. On the walk back to the hangars, it began to hurt. I was damned if I was going to miss out on my three-jump certificate, so I hid the limp until we were back in the Rapide for the third time. At least now I had a bench to sit on.

The third landing was a one-footer, then a Tilly (a blue RAF Land Rover) came to meet me. Someone in the group by the hangars with a pair of binoculars had seen the limp. At the medical bay, an RAF doctor cut the boot off with a scalpel. The meat was beginning to overflow the top of the boot and no one was going to try to pull it off for fear of having to cope with a very noisy author.

That exercise cost me a new pair of top-of-the-range jump boots to replace the ones I had borrowed and ruined. Luckily, it was only a sprain and, duly strapped, I was able to hobble along to the celebratory piss-up.

My Jaguar saloon had automatic shift, so the next morning I could drive home one-footed, using just the right one for all the controls.

I got my certificate, signed by Gerry O'Hara, and it was suggested I should graduate to skydiving: coming out at ten thousand feet with a pull-your-own D ring and lots of time to plunge back to Mother Earth at one hundred miles per hour. But on balance, I have preferred to stick to skyscrapers and nice, fast elevators made by Mr. Otis.

But I still have Major O'Hara's piece of paper on the office wall, and fond memories of Netheravon and its cheeky jump instructors.

THE AMAZING MR. MOON

There must be a reason for it, but I have never met a man who has confronted the mighty rage of the oceans in a small boat who does not believe in God.

Man spends most of his time running around in crowded cities convincing himself how important he is in the scheme of things. But there are five places where he can confront the reality of his utter insignificance.

Two of these are the great deserts, of sand and gravel or snow and ice. Lost in these, he is but a speck of dust on a huge sheet of pure barrenness. Then there are the mountains, also clothed in snow and ice, peaks among which he will vanish to invisibility.

The sky is a huge and lonely place, but here at least his lack of importance is short-lived, because when his fuel runs out, gravity alone will end his solitude. But most fearsome of them all is the towering, pitiless might of the enraged ocean. Because it moves.

When, in 1513, Vasco Núñez de Balboa, peering out of the jungle of Darién toward the west, saw a great expanse of blue water, it was calm, sparkling, seemingly friendly. So he called it El Mar Pacifico, the quiet sea, the peaceful sea, the Pacific. He had no idea what the Pacific could do when it is consumed with rage. The Indian Ocean is the same.

As with all oceans, the Pacific can be flat as a lake, or moved only by a gentle swell, blue under the sun, welcoming, gentle, inviting the mariner to share its calm and splendor. Or it can rise in terrifying mountains, lashed by deranged winds, prepared to seize that same mariner, crush his presumptuous craft, swamp him, consume him, and consign him in perpetuity to a cold black grave, where he will never be seen again. That is why men who sail the oceans hope there must, please, be Something even mightier Who will protect them and bring them home to safe haven.

With hindsight, that twenty-twenty vision that we all have but too late, it was unwise of me to disregard the maps and go game fishing off the Mauritian coast in 1985.

We had gone as a family, two parents, two small boys, to the Saint Géran Hotel on the east coast. The weather programs had mentioned a cyclone, but it was well to the north and heading in a straight line east to west, and a hundred miles north of the island. So I decided to go game fishing.

The resident game boat *Chico* chugged out of the lagoon just after dawn, my favorite hour, through the usual cut in the reef and out to sea, heading east. At the helm was Monsieur Moun, whom everyone called Mr. Moon. He was elderly, dark, wrinkled—a Creole who knew his sea and his island and had never been anywhere else nor wanted to.

It was a one-client charter and the wireman was his son, who was sharing the afterdeck with me to tend the four big marlin rods, the lines, and the lures, and who would help swing the catch aboard. The breeze was light, the swell gentle, the sky blue, and the sun hot—a recipe for paradise. We trolled patiently for two hours, always eastward until Mauritius was a dim smudge on the horizon. It was at about noon that the sea calmed even more, down to a flat and slightly oily sheen. Mr. Moon spotted the danger sign; I did not, too busy scanning the four lures astern for a hoped-for strike.

I noticed only when his son began staring at his father, perched cross-legged upon his revolving office stool, adapted to a captain's seat behind the wheel. Then I, too, followed his gaze. Mr. Moon was looking straight toward the north. Along the horizon was a very thin dark line, like a bruise between the sky and water. I realized it might be serious when he uttered a series of orders in Creole to his son, who began to bring in the four lines and the *Chico* swung in a circle and pointed back to the west. The smudge on the horizon, the island of Mauritius, had almost disappeared.

I did not know what had happened to change both the mood of the sea beneath us and on the deck on which I stood. The cyclone had swerved through ninety degrees. It was roaring down from the north.

The *Chico* was not one of those modern techno-wonders with two huge chunks of Japanese technology bolted to the stern, capable of sending a GRP-hulled fishing boat screaming across the sea at twenty knots in choppy water or thirty in flat. It was an elderly workboat of plywood with an internal chugger of an engine. A chugger it might be, but Mr. Moon moved the throttle to full ahead, max power. The chugger did its best and we increased speed to ten knots.

The black line on the horizon widened to an inch and the sea changed from an oily calm, not to a snapping chop (that would come later) but a rolling swell that became ever deeper. At the top of the peaks one could see the horizon smudge, but seemingly no closer. In the troughs, the sea was no longer blue, but valleys of moving green, growing deeper and darker. Indian Ocean cyclones take no prisoners.

Mr. Moon said nothing, and nor did his son. The lad took the rods out of the holders where they usually traveled and stowed them in the small forward cuddy cabin. The *Chico* pounded west as best she could, and with agonizing slowness the smudge became the principal mountain peak of the island. The northern sky darkened and clouds appeared, not white and fluffy, high against the blue, but dark and hunched like a fighter entering the ring.

There was nothing to do but stand and watch. I tried to converse with Mr. Moon in his other native tongue, French, but he was too absorbed to reply. His gaze just flickered from the island to the cyclone, calculating speeds, angles, and engine revs. So I walked back to the stern and joined his son.

It may be thought that a Creole, descendant of the native Africans, cannot go pale. Not true. The lad had a sickly pallor. He was badly frightened and we both knew why. The island came into closer view as the old engine banged and hammered under its casting. It was clear our lives were going to depend on this old mariner. The island became more distinct, but so did the black-clouded fury behind us. Whatever speed it was moving at, it was well above ten knots, and we could go no faster. We rose on swell after swell, seeming almost stopped at the peak, then plunged down into the valley and up again.

Somewhere ahead was the coast of Mauritius and the lagoon from which we had come. Between us was the reef and the gap in the coral through which we had to pass to stay alive. At last we saw it, but then my hopes plunged. It was clear I would probably not see my family again.

For the wind had taken the waves and tormented them into a frenzy of white water. This white wall was slamming into the reef, where it exploded upward thirty feet. But the roaring crosswind from the north was pulling the wall like a curtain across the entry gap in the coral. The gap had vanished.

If we hit the coral, the *Chico* and her three passengers would be torn to pieces. Coral may only be made of trillions of polyps, but it is hard as concrete and fanged with teeth that can cut steel. Few vessels that have ever hit a coral reef have not been torn open. I walked up the deck to stand next to Mr. Moon, hunched upon his stool like a brooding cormorant.

His eyes were darting forward to the mountains of his native land, not behind to the menace from the stern.

He was calculating angles from the mountain peaks behind the wall of foam to the dimly visible roof of the hotel. He was trying to work out where, in the liquid insanity ahead of him, lay the thirty-yard-wide gap where the coral grudgingly offered a free passage to an incoming boat.

I turned to look behind and realized that if he missed it, we were dead. There was no possibility of turning away to find another haven down-coast. None either of turning back to sea. Behind us, the cyclone had caught up.

There was a gigantic wave, a vertical wall of rolling green, twenty, maybe thirty feet high and foaming at the top as the base responded to the shallowing beach beneath, about to break forward and crash down. It was like the Empire State Building on its side, rolling at forty knots.

I never saw the *Chico* hit the foam wall. One second it was in front of us and death behind, then the whiteness enveloped the boat, tumbling onto the afterdeck and frothing onto the scuppers. The whiteness cleared and there was blue sky ahead and above. Jagged shards of coral flashed past, barely six feet from the hull.

The ocean spat the *Chico* like a cork from a champagne bottle into the lagoon and then the Empire State hit the reef with enough force to make thunder seem halfhearted. Observers on the shore later said the spray went up a hundred feet.

The *Chico* slowed, engine back to cruise revs. Along the shoreline were gathered the full clientele of the hotel. I could see my wife with her hands over her face and two small boys jumping in the shallows. We tied up at the dock to meet an ashen-faced activities manager.

The cyclone locked down the island of Mauritius for forty-eight hours, then passed through, as they all do, and a tropical resort island was restored, as they always are. Takeoffs were resumed from La Plaisance airport and we flew home to London.

There is no way to reward a man like Mr. Moon, who wanted no reward at all, but I did my best. I also learned two things that day. If going out to sea, check the weather; and why men who go onto the ocean in small boats believe in God.

BACK TO ZERO—START AGAIN

━━━◆◆◆━━━

It was on a bright, sunny morning in the spring of 1990 that I learned that financially I had been completely and utterly ruined.

In 1988, my first marriage had sadly but amicably ended. In an uncontested settlement, my wife and I had split everything we had into two equal halves. Very shrewdly, my wife had taken the large London apartment in which we lived and a bloc of investment portfolios. The latter she encashed and invested in property, which increased hugely in value.

I had taken the balance entirely in managed funds, all invested in a series of carefully chosen portfolios. In the same year, I acquired a small farm in Hertfordshire and moved there. In 1989, I met the lady who would become my second wife and to whom, twenty-six years later, I am still married.

That spring morning, I was writing the first chapter of what would become *The Deceiver*. There was a knock on the study door. I was irritated because, when writing, I ask only to be left alone with strictly the typewriter and the coffee. Interruptions are confined to the outbreak of fire or some major crisis. But I replied with a curt "What?"

The answer came through the door. So-and-so has collapsed. She named the head of the investment company through which, but not in which, I had invested my life's savings. The man was one whom I had known for thirteen years and whom I thought, wrongly as it turned out, that I could trust.

I misunderstood the word *collapse* and presumed a heart attack or stroke, which seemed odd, because he was only in his forties. She meant his company had collapsed and he had been arrested.

Even when I learned the truth, I was not particularly worried. After all, my investments were nothing other than what had been chosen on his recommendation, and I had insisted on fund managers who were utterly reputable, solid, and above all safe. No spectacular returns, thank you, no matter how inviting the blandishments. It was only when seated with the detectives of the Metropolitan Police City Fraud Squad that the full measure of the swindle was explained to me.

The investments simply were not there. The documents were forged. The savings had been raided, embezzled, and spent trying to prop up the great Wizard of Oz–style facade. And I was not the only one. Other victims were banks, insurance houses, and all the private clients.

Receivers were appointed, but quickly realized the total assets of the collapsed sham would be just enough to cover their own fees. Naturally. The total missing sum from all the victims combined was about £32 million, £20 million to financial institutions and the remainder from private clients.

It was a strange year. The detectives slowly prepared their case for the Crown Prosecution Service, and I was amazed to learn how many victims would refuse to testify. It is the vanity factor. Those who pride themselves on their acumen cannot bear to admit they have been taken.

I had no such inhibitions, having always known I was useless in the management of money. So I became the detectives' favorite guest and they explained how it had all been done.

Actually, I was not simply penniless, but owed an additional million pounds. This was because, seeking to buy the farm, I had suggested I encash some portfolio to buy the place outright. I was persuaded to take out a mortgage instead, as the shrewd management of the million would generate more than a mortgage would cost. It was all bunkum, of course. The necessary portfolios could not be encashed because they were not there. So it was soon clear I was worth zero minus an extra million.

The case ground on at a snail's pace. Eventually, in 1993, it came to court. I was not needed as a witness. Thanks to a brilliant defense lawyer, a useless prosecutor, and a judge who had never tried a criminal case in his life, the charges were reduced to two small technical offenses and the sentence was 180 hours of community service.

The Biafran affair had deprived me of any faith or trust in the senior mandarins of the Civil Service. The trial of 1993 did the same for my belief in the legal system and the judiciary.

Anyway, I had made up my mind that there was only one thing for it. That was, at the age of fifty, to write more novels and make it all back. So I did.

THE PASSING OF HUMPY

There were three of us standing at the stern of the game-fisher *Otter* out of Islamorada, in the Florida Keys, and we were after amberjack, those big, heavy, deep-bodied giants of the mackerel family who fight like hell.

Both my boys were with me; Stuart, the fanatical angler who never took his eyes off the rigs, and the younger Shane, who could get bored when nothing struck. The *Otter* was hove to several miles out into the Gulf Stream, right over a submerged mountaintop called "the 409," because it was 409 feet beneath the water, or simply "the Hump." It was the school summer holidays of 1991.

It was Shane who first saw the tiny, fluttering object off the stern, struggling toward us on exhausted wings, coming from the east. High above the little traveler was a black-backed gull, its orange razor beak eager for a kill. Another joined it and they screamed at the sight of the tiny prey beneath them. One by one we ceased watching the rod tips for the giveaway tremble of a bite far below and watched the struggle.

The little flier was not a seabird at all—there is none that small. It was evidently exhausted and at the end of its strength. It dipped in tiredness toward the tea, fluttered frantically to rise and struggle on for a few more yards. We watched in silence, yearning for it to win. A few more yards and it could fall onto our afterdeck. But tiredness won. It finally sank again and the sea rose to take it.

But it was only a few feet from the transom. Perhaps there was a chance. I grabbed the scoop net from the deck and, above and behind me, watching from his flying bridge, skipper Clyde Upchurch engaged gear and moved back a few feet. I got the mesh beneath the little bird that lay motionless on the swell and hoisted it aboard.

I am no ornithologist, but I was pretty certain it was a finch out of Africa. It should have been emigrating to Europe, but clearly had been blown way off course and out to sea. Disorientated, it must have taken refuge in the rigging of a freighter and thus had crossed the Atlantic, but without food or water seemed weakened.

But there was land behind us, the chain of Florida's islands six miles away, and perhaps the little fellow had sensed this and tried to get there. But it had failed. Above the stern the gulls screamed in outrage over their lost meal and veered away.

Shane took the tiny body in his cupped hands and went back into the cabin. Because of where we were, we named the little stowaway Humpy. And we went on fishing.

Shane prepared a bed of paper tissues and laid what we presumed was the little corpse upon it in a pool of sunlight on the cabin table. Ten minutes later, he gave a yell. The tiny beady eye that had been closed in death was now open. Humpy was still alive. Shane appointed himself nurse in chief.

He formed the flat bed into a nest of soft tissue paper, took some bottled water, and dribbled a few drops onto the beak. It opened and the drops disappeared. Humpy woke up and began to preen. More spring water, more tissues, a slow wipe-off to clear the tacky salt from the plumage. Humpy perked and fluttered.

It was another thirty minutes before he felt able to fly. Shane was catching flies trapped in the cabin windows. I suggested Humpy was a seed eater, as he refused the flies but finally accepted a tiny crumb of bread from the packed lunch. Then he spread his wings and flew.

Not far at first. Just off the table, around the cabin and back to the table. As in pilot training, we called it circuits and bumps. He did about a dozen circuits of the cabin, had a rest, had more drops of water, and then found an open window. Shane yelled in alarm and rushed outside.

Humpy was doing his circuits, all right, but around the moored boat. The afternoon wore on, and it was time to go. The charter was almost over and we had to get back to Islamorada. Then it all went wrong.

With lines retrieved and rods stored, there was no cause to stay. High aloft, Clyde engaged gear and pushed the throttle forward. The *Otter* leaped to the command and Shane screamed. Humpy was somewhere astern and his salvation was racing away to the west. We all turned and yelled, but Clyde could not hear us above the engine roar.

Stuart ran up the ladder to tap him on the shoulder. The *Otter* stopped in the water, but she had surged for at least two hundred yards. We all gazed astern, and there he was. Fluttering above the wake, trying to catch up with the only sanctuary for miles around.

We started shouting encouragement . . . and the gull came back. Humpy so nearly made it. He was ten yards from the stern when the sharp orange beak took him. I noticed a box of lead weights lying open on the deck, seized the largest I could see, and flung it at the gull above us.

A hit would have been impossible, but the gull must have seen some dark object coming toward it, for it uttered another raucous scream. And dropped the little finch in its beak. The crumpled form fell back to the surface of the ocean again. Clyde backed the *Otter* slowly toward the feathery lump on the water. Again I fished it out.

But this time there was no hope. The gull's beak had crushed the life out of Humpy and no more drops of spring water could bring him round. Shane tried all the way back to the marina, and the salt on the finch's wings was washed away again, but this time by the tears of a little boy.

That evening, in a cigar box lined with moss, beneath the casuarina trees of the Cheeca Lodge Hotel, we buried Humpy in the sand of the New World, which he had tried so hard to reach, like so many before him, and very nearly did.

A VERY BURNING QUESTION

—◆◆◆—

It was a very simple query put to me by the Firm in 1992: Do you by any chance know anyone high in the South African government? And the answer was yes.

Because of years patrolling southern Africa, I had a passing acquaintanceship with Pretoria's foreign minister Roelof "Pik" Botha, even though by then I had not seen him for several years.

If the profession of foreign correspondent made a very good cover for a bit of "enhanced tourism" on behalf of the Firm, an established author researching his next novel was even better. It enabled me to go just about anywhere, ask to meet and converse with just about anyone, and pose just about any question. And all to be explained as research for a novel yet to be written—or not, for all anyone could prove.

Back in the seventies, the target had been the Rhodesia of Ian Smith and occasioned several visits to Salisbury, now renamed Harare. Once again my amiable but witless "Bertie Wooster" pose paid dividends. The men at the top were white supremacists, which is to say racial bigots.

There is no greater lure for the bigot than the earnest inquirer who, seeming basically sympathetic and right-wing, asks that the complexities of the situation be explained to him. No white supremacist can resist. As nothing other than a seeker after knowledge, I was favored with many hours of explanation—and classified information—from the likes of Rhodesian foreign and defense minister Peter van der Byl. He was a way-out racist who referred to his domestic staff—all Matabeles because he loathed the Shona—as "my savages."

I do not think any of them suspected, as I listened, nodded, and smiled, that my views were the opposite of their own. But what they revealed was useful back home.

In the eighties, with Rhodesia now Zimbabwe, the target was the South Africa of the National Party, the originator and enforcer of apartheid, which was both brutal and tinged with insanity.

I once found myself closeted with General Hendrik van den Bergh, the head of the Bureau of State Security, the dreaded BOSS, and he insisted on telling me a story to prove not only his legitimacy but his sanctity as well.

"Let me tell you this, Mr. Fosdick"—he always called me Fosdick, forefinger waving, eyes alight—"I was standing once, quite alone, on the High Veldt when a great storm came up. I knew the land was riven with iron ore deposits and lightning strikes would be frequent and dangerous. So I took shelter under a large *mwataba* tree.

"There was an old kaffir standing nearby, also sheltering. And the storm raged with biblical intensity. The thunderbolts poured out of the sky and the thunder was enough to deafen me. The tree was struck and split down the middle, its core a smoking ruin. The old kaffir was struck and at once electrocuted.

"But the storm passed, Mr. Fosdick, and the sky cleared. And I was not touched. And that was when I knew, Mr. Fosdick, that the hand of God was upon me."

I recall thinking that I was alone with the mast of one of the most brutal secret police forces in the world, and he was mad as a frog.

On another occasion, I was invited as dinner guest at the house of professor Carel Boshoff, head of the Afrikaner Broederbond, the Brotherhood, which was the intellectual and ecclesiastical (Dutch Reformed Church) origin and underpinning of the whole concept of apartheid.

Dinner proceeded with the usual courtesies until, over pudding, he asked me what I thought of the Homelands Policy. This was a particularly pernicious idea whereby the indigenous ethnic groups that made up the black majority would be allocated tracts of barren and often unworkable land, and be told that this was their true and original "homeland."

As such, they could then have a token "government" and thus lose their citizenship of the Republic of South Africa (the RSA) and thus any rights they might have had in the first place, which were already few enough. I visited one of the "homelands," Bophuthatswana, the so-called home of the Tswana people. It made the old American Indian reservations look like Shangri-La, although Sol Kerzner built a resort called Sun City on it to bring in a bit of tourist revenue.

Anyway, I was by then heartily tired of expressing views that were the inverse of what I really thought, so I explained exactly what I thought. My half-eaten dessert was removed and I was escorted from the house.

But in the course of all this, I met Pik Botha, the only man among them that I liked. He was practical rather than theoretical, had traveled very widely, and seen the outer world. I suspected that despite his position he was a moderating influence on successive presidents and probably privately despised the extremists around him.

By 1992 it was clear to anyone with eyes that the rule of the National Party and apartheid was finally moving to its close. There would soon have to be elections and they would have to be one man, one vote, which the African National Congress under its recently released and newly elevated chief Nelson Mandela would win. The white president, the last, was F. W. de Klerk, and Pik Botha was his firm ally and partner in reform.

Nevertheless, there was something "our political masters," as the Friends put it, urgently wanted to know, and the "received wisdom" (as they also put it) was that an inquiry via our embassy in Pretoria was not the right channel. Too formal, too undeniable. What was needed was a quiet inquiry in a very private situation.

It was summer in Europe, winter in South Africa, and both parliaments were in recess. Ministers were also taking their holidays. It was known that Pik Botha had two passions: game fishing and big-game hunting. But the winter seas off the Cape of Good Hope were too rough, so it would probably be a game lodge for the foreign minister.

Then it was discovered he would indeed be vacationing for a week on a game lodge in the South African section of the Kalahari Desert.

These lodges are situated in the corners of simply enormous game reserves where the natural fauna—mainly antelope—are protected from their natural predators such as lions, leopards, and crocodiles. So they overbreed. The numbers have to be culled to preserve the life-support system. To defray costs, licenses are issued, and amateur hunters, escorted by professional game wardens, are allowed to track and shoot limited numbers for a fee appropriate to the size of the animal being taken.

Personally, I will take out of circulation either something that is a pest or vermin and has to be culled for the preservation of the rest of the ecosystem or if it will definitely reappear on the dining table. Or, like rabbit and wood pigeon, both. But not for fun and not for a wall trophy. But this would have to be an exception. The question was very important.

Of course, there had to be a cover story, and it was sitting at home doing schoolwork. My two sons would come with me.

Over the years, I had tried to introduce them to as wide a variety of adventurous holidays as possible, so that they could perhaps latch onto what really enthused them.

Thus we had been snorkeling and diving in the tropics, skiing and snowboarding in the Alps and Squaw Valley, flying, riding, and shooting. My older son, Stuart, had decided already; he was a passionate fisherman and has remained so. Shane had no particular preference, but had demonstrated on the estates of friends that he was a crack shot, a natural.

The game reserve where Pik Botha would spend part of his vacation in the Kalahari was discovered and bookings were made for me and the boys for the same week. So we flew to Jo'burg, thence to Krugersdorp, and thence by light aircraft to a dusty strip in the grounds of the shooting lodge.

It was a very convivial week, and Pik Botha was affable when we met again. He was eager to bag himself an eland and spent days tracking them. I thought it wise at least to "purchase" something for Stuart and Shane. On the second day, Stuart bagged his impala and was delighted when the forehead and horns, stripped to whitened bone, were presented for him to hang on his wall.

Shane was lectured lengthily by a warden as to what he should do, listened politely, and then from the back of a stationary truck put a bullet through the heart of a blesbok with a snap shot at 150 paces. The buck was photographed, but the real picture was the warden's face. After that, he became their mascot.

My opportunity came on the penultimate day. A very small party would camp overnight in the wilderness. There were Pik Botha and his "minder" from Pretoria; the two sons of the owner of the ranch; my two lads and me. Plus two game wardens and several African porters.

After a long day tracking, the porters built a fine fire of brushwood, a barbecue and a *braai* provided a meat supper, sleeping bags were unrolled, and we settled down to sleep. The atmosphere was intensely relaxed and I thought the moment was ripe. We were all around the dying fire with the four sleeping boys between the foreign minister and me. So I asked quietly, "Pik, when the rainbow revolution comes and the ANC takes over, what are you going to do with the six atom bombs?"

South Africa had long had atomic bombs, built with Israeli help. Everyone knew this, despite the strict secrecy surrounding them. London also knew there were six and they could be carried by the RSA's British-built Buccaneers.

That was not the problem. Nor was the moderate Nelson Mandela. The problem was that the ANC Party had an ultra-hard-line wing, including several devoted pro-Moscow Communists, and even though the USSR had been disbanded by Mikhail Gorbachev the previous year, neither London nor Washington wanted nuclear bombs under the control of the anti-West extremists. It only took Nelson Mandela to be toppled by an internal coup as so many African leaders had already been and . . .

My question hung in the air for a few seconds, then there was a low chuckle from across the embers and a reply in Pik's Afrikaans-inflected voice.

"Freddie, you can go back home and tell your people we are going to destroy the lot."

So much for an elaborate cover story. The old buzzard knew exactly what I was, who I was asking for, and what they wanted to hear. I tried to share the joke.

But, to be fair, they did. Before the de Klerk government handed over power, they destroyed all six. Three of the casings are on display somewhere, but that is all. Three of the Buccaneers still fly out of Cape Town airport, but only for tourist rides.

FROM MAIKO TO MONKS

Over many travels I have had the chance to attend a variety of religious ceremonies in rites far different from my own Anglican background. These have included Russian Orthodox, Roman Catholic, Jewish, and Muslim, and in some of the finest cathedrals, synagogues, and mosques of those faiths. But my wife, Sandy, has always been fascinated by the Orient and by Buddhism.

In 1995, my Japanese publishers, Kadokawa Shoten, invited me once again to be their guest in Tokyo to promote the latest novel, and Sandy came with me. Going all that way, it made a lot of sense to extend the visit after the publicity work to see more of the real Japan.

So when the usual round of interviews and book signings in Tokyo was over, we took the bullet train west to the former capital of Kyoto. This is a beautiful little city, full of parks, gardens, temples, and shrines, both to Buddhism and Shintoism. But Buddhism could wait; there was another aspect I wanted to explore.

With a guide, we penetrated the small area known as Gion, the home of the geisha culture. Contrary to a common misconception, the geisha is not simply a prostitute, but a highly skilled entertainer dedicated to restoring the exhausted male client with what is best described as relaxation therapy. Bedtime may follow, but it is by no means inevitable.

There are only about 120 true professional geishas left, perhaps because they are multitask-skilled after years of training, which costs about half a million pounds. The training madame will hope to recoup this, fee by fee, when her charge starts to earn professional commissions.

A geisha can sing, dance, recite poetry, flatter, and play the samisen, a sort of medieval lute with strings plucked only by the fingernails. To listen to and understand her client's possible financial woes, she reads all the commercial pages in the daily papers and keeps abreast of current affairs.

The geisha's uniform is the full kimono with obi sash, bouffant jet-black hair (a wig), bright-red lips, and a bone-white (powdered) face. Many clients will not wish any of it to be removed. In Gion, one can see many of these practitioners of the ancient arts, in full regalia, click-clacking along on their wooden sandals, heading for their nightly engagement, eyes cast down in order never to make eye contact with anyone but the client.

Sandy and I were lucky as we were invited to visit a geisha training school, something a *gaijin* (foreigner) rarely manages to do. It took a password to gain entry through the heavily timbered door.

The geisha usually comes from the most deprived rungs of society, from parents so poor they are content to sell their daughter into a world from which she will never emerge. But not just any girl will suit. A skilled madame, running such an academy, will look for exceptional beauty, grace, a clever mind, and a singing voice that, with schooling, will become crystal pure. The parents are paid off and never see their daughter again.

Once a young woman is absorbed into the geisha world, it is virtually impossible for her to leave it, marry, and become a mother, let alone a housewife. Something about her can be instantly recognized and will never leave her.

A husband would immediately know and feel shamed. His colleagues would spot it and may be tempted to become lascivious, or at least mocking. Their wives would become instantly hostile. Conventional suburbia is not for the geisha. It is a closed world with a long, hard road in and no way out.

Some madames run agencies of only skilled geishas; a few run training schools, such as the one we visited. The trainees are called *maiko*, meaning "dancing girl," but they are taught much more than dancing, and that includes knowledge of every detail of the male body and the male psyche, specializing on the erogenous and susceptible points. The only aim is to please the male. The *maiko* paint only the lower lip as a sign of virginity. The client who will one day take that will be charged a huge premium.

Considering we were in a sort of bordello, the polite proprieties were scrupulously observed. Anything else would have been crude, rude, and offensive. Incidentally, when a Japanese girl laughs or giggles, she may not be amused. She may be profoundly embarrassed. Laughter is also a defensive shield.

So we squatted on cushions on the floor and conversed through the interpreter with the madame while her trainees, in their "apprentice" kimonos, served small cups of saké. They are taught to seduce with their eyes alone, eyes made large and docile with skillfully applied makeup, and I have to admit they are extremely disconcerting. Sandy kept shooting me warning glances.

Finally, it was time to go, with copious and mutual bowing. Years later, I know I could never find it again.

There was a visit to a saké factory, where, hidden behind the modern machinery of stainless-steel vats and hissing steam is a small, separate enclave where saké is still made by the old medieval processes involving the transformation of the rice into the purest saké possible, all by hand and therefore immensely slowly and carefully. The product is tiny and dedicated only to the use of the emperor and the royal court. Nevertheless, we were permitted a few cups in tiny ceramic thimbles, and it really was like no other saké I had ever tasted.

But the pinnacle (literally) of our tour was to proceed toward Osaka and then, just short of the teeming city, to divert to the mountaintop monastery shrine of Koyasan. This peak is so hard to get to that the railway line runs out and the last section is accomplished by funicular.

In fact, unable to read the train signs at Osaka station, we missed the fast connection and found ourselves on the slow train with more than thirty stops to our destination. But it proved to be an advantage: throughout the journey the train labored from halt to halt with local peasants getting on and off, clutching baskets of eggs, cages of live chickens and ducks, all the paraphernalia of market day in rural Japan. After recovering from the shock of seeing two *gaijin* sitting in their train, the locals chattered and beamed away, even though we understood not a word, an experience very few tourists achieve on the streets of Tokyo, particularly since only about 15 percent of the Japanese are rural anymore, the huge majority now urbanized.

Koyasan is a monastery of immense age and holiness, featuring the graveyard where the remains of the founder of Shingon Buddhism are laid. It takes paying guests in the form of pilgrims who wish to spend a long weekend living in the style of the old medieval monks.

The first stop was to meet the abbot, who greeted us in broad American. No need for an interpreter this time. He had fought with the

Imperial Japanese Navy in the Second World War, been captured, and imprisoned in California and stayed there until the fifties.

The living accommodations were literally unheated cells, and the diet various cold foods, but nothing hot. The better news was that one could place an order for warm saké, which we did, in quantities that raised a few eyebrows.

There is a small town grouped around the monastery, something that enabled us to wander and see a side of Japan not to be observed in the cities.

At one point, I asked the abbot if his own monks confined themselves to the cold vegetarian food that we were being served.

"Good God, no," he said. "I wouldn't have a congregation at all if I demanded that. No, they just serve you pilgrims, then go around to McDonald's."

It may have been the altitude or the saké or both, but we slept soundly on our futon mats and were up before dawn for the early-morning service in the temple. I'm afraid I made an ass of myself.

Squatting on the heels with the buttocks just off the floor and the knees under the chin was the required posture, which Sandy could manage with ease. Before we met, she had spent twenty years in the film business, ending with over two years as PA to Elizabeth Taylor. To stay sane in a completely crazy world, she had taken up kundalini yoga. This included retaining her British calm while attending the garden funeral of the Taylor family goldfish with complete Judaic rite presided over by a rabbi. As for me, after a few minutes, my old knees were on fire.

I had no choice but to let my backside hit the floor and take the weight, and straighten the knees. But that posed another problem. It is very rude to point the soles of the feet at fellow worshippers, so I had to squirm until the soles were pointing at each other and I was squatting like a frog on a lily pad. At the end, it took four other pilgrims to help me up.

That apart, it was a beautiful service, all in Japanese of course, with copious helpings of joss and incense, bells and chanting. Among the several hundred worshippers, we were the only other *gaijin* present, and therefore objects of some curiosity.

But top of the range in the hilarity stakes was the ritual communal bath. This was absolutely crucial to the worship, the ritual washing of every part of the body. The women went one way, the men the other.

The Japanese regard dunking a dirty body in unmoving water as peculiar. The washing comes first, then the immersion. I was shown where to strip, given a towel to wrap around the waist, and a small booth with a showerhead, soap, and a scrubber. The booth faced away from the open piping-hot water of the pool.

I noted that there were half a dozen middle-aged businessmen in the pool, just disembodied heads on the surface of the water, staring at me. So I faced the wall, dropping the towel, and scrubbed from chin to feet. Finally, I had no choice but to turn around and face the pool.

The six heads were still staring, but not at my face. Two feet further down, and the expressions were of considerable worry. As I turned, the six expressions changed; not to horror but to the most profound relief. Someone had clearly told them something about naked Europeans that was completely untrue.

After that, it was a farewell to the abbot, then the train (the fast one this time) down the mountain to the railhead and the bullet train back to Narita Airport and home.

A VERY UNTIDY COUP

———··❖··———

With hindsight, it was probably a mistake to go researching cocaine shipments through Guinea-Bissau, and I certainly never intended to land in the middle of a coup d'état.

The reason for the visit to this West African hellhole of a place was simple. I had spent months researching a novel, which became *The Cobra* and was based on the enormous criminal world behind the cocaine trade. These quests had taken me through Washington and the DEA, London, Vienna, Hamburg (again!), Rotterdam, and finally to Bogotá and Cartagena in Colombia, source of most of the white powder.

But there was something missing. In South America, I had discovered that much of the cocaine destined for Europe did not take the direct route at all. Ships with very large consignments left the coast of Colombia and Venezuela to steam due east to West Africa and unload their cargoes in the creeks and mangrove swamps of countries where the entire law-and-order infrastructure could be purchased with bribes.

Then the cocaine bales could be broken down to smaller loads and taken north, via the land trains across the Sahara to enter Europe from the south. Foremost among these African transshipment points was Guinea-Bissau.

This is the former Portuguese colony where I had staged through forty years earlier, perched on a crate of mortars, when a bullet came through the floor and went out the ceiling. Since then, it had had twenty more years of independence war and twenty of civil war that had left the capital, Bissau City, pretty much gutted. There was (and for all I know still is) a community of Colombian gangsters who have built themselves seaside palaces and oversee the cocaine operations. As the Michelin Guide used to say, "worth a detour."

The United Kingdom has no embassy there, nor even a consulate. Nor does Guinea-Bissau have representation in London. But I traced a consulate in Paris and was duly issued a tourist visa. The only air passage is from Lisbon (the old colonial connection) to São Tomé island with a stopover at Bissau.

Finally, the honorary British vice consul in Bissau was a very nice Dutchman with a franchise for Japanese off-road SUVs. I had been in e-mail contact with Jan out of London and he kindly agreed to meet me on landing and show me around.

My TAP airliner took off from Lisbon at eight thirty p.m. What I did not know was that hardly had it turned south than, in the Guinean army HQ, a large bomb went off, blowing the chief of staff into several artistic pieces all over the office. That was the start of the coup.

Later revelations showed that those responsible were probably the Colombians. The timer and trigger mechanisms were assuredly too sophisticated for local assembly. But that was not the view of the army, which wanted revenge and suspected President João Bernardo Vieira. It was all tribal; the bulk of the army are Balanta, but the president and his entourage were Papel. There is no love lost. So at 33,000 feet, I sipped my champagne and tried for a couple of hours' shut-eye before landing at two a.m. local time.

On touchdown, the aircrew clearly did not want to hang around and did not even shut down the engines before leaving. Those descending were three or four Guineans and me. I entered passport control quite prepared for the long hassle of luggage search and bribe contributing that are habitual between touchdown and car park.

Then Jan came bustling through, waving his diplomatic passport, and whisked me out in double-quick time. We made the usual introductions, he grabbed my valise, and strode to his SUV. When we were bowling along the high road to the city, I remarked that he seemed to be in something of a hurry.

"Look in the rearview," he said.

The horizon behind us was awash with oncoming headlights.

"That's the army," he said, and told me about the army chief six hours earlier. "They are coming into town from their bases."

"What do they want?"

"Revenge," he said, and stepped on the gas. We made it to the center of the shattered city ahead of the army and he deposited me at the only hotel in town a European would be wise to stay at. Then he left in a hurry to return to his wife and family to lock themselves in. Considering that he knew about the assassination, it was extremely decent of him to have come to the airport at all.

I checked myself in, went to my room, and tried to sleep. But to no avail. At four a.m., I put on the bedside light, hauled myself upright, and started to read a paperback I had already started on the airplane. At four thirty, about five hundred yards down the street, there was one almighty bang.

There are three reasons for noises that big in an African city in the darkness before dawn. One is the first thunderclap of a tropical storm. The second is a head-to-head crash between two speeding vehicles. The third is a bomb. This was a bomb. Only later was I able to piece together the events of the night.

The local authorities—army, navy, port and harbor, customs, police—were all on the Colombian payroll, but the payoffs are not in the worthless local currency but in a "skim" of the cocaine shipments themselves. It looked as if the chief of staff had been skimming too much, and paid for it. But for the Balanta tribesmen who made up the army, it was the Papel president they wanted. So they left their out-of-town barracks and came to get him.

The poor old booby was fast asleep in his bed. Because the once-grandiose presidential palace, former home of the Portuguese governor, was a ruin, his residence was a low-build hacienda-style complex in a walled garden. The bedroom was on the ground floor.

The army trucks smashed down the gate and someone put a rocket-propelled grenade through the bedroom window. That was the bang. The seventy-one-year-old politician must have been tough. As his bedroom wing collapsed around him, he stumbled through the rubble and out into the garden. The soldiers put three bullets through him.

But still he would not die. Then they realized what a foolish mistake they had made. He clearly possessed a juju that kept him immune to death by bullet. But there is one thing that no juju can proof against. They went to the gardener's store, got a machete, and chopped him to pieces. Then he died. The soldiers went off into the night to break into a bar or two and celebrate. And Bissau City waited for dawn.

Before dawn arrived, the rest of the government had vaporized and headed for their indigenous villages where they would be safe. I descended to the dining room and asked for breakfast. Jan appeared an hour later to say the city was quiet, apart from patrolling jeeps of army men looking for Papel victims but not interested in whites. So we got into his SUV and drove to his home.

Business would be very slight that day, he opined, so he could drive me out into the area of the creeks and swamps to get an idea where the cocaine cargoes came in and see the Colombians' mansions by the beach. This we did. While we were away, other things happened. At sub-politician level, various functionaries closed both the land borders, north and south, and the airport. The tiny republic was sealed off.

In London, my wife, Sandy, knowing nothing of this, e-mailed a girlfriend to set up a lunch date. Part of her text read: "I'm free this week 'cos Freddie is in Guinea-Bissau."

Someone in Fort Meade, Maryland, or maybe Langley, Virginia, intercepted this and her screen went berserk. Her message disappeared. Things flashed up with the insignia of the Great Seal of the United States warning her not to use her laptop under any circumstances. She had not the faintest idea what she had done. I was later advised it was those two words "Guinea-Bissau" that did the trick. Word had leaked out. You can close borders nowadays, shut the telephone switchboard and the cable office, but you cannot silence the Internet.

Meanwhile, I was in the creeks peering through the undergrowth at the white sculpted mansion of the Colombians. Never one to look a gift horse in the mouth, I figured this coup was too good to ignore, so the passages in *The Cobra* are not simply accurate but autobiographical.

Back at Jan's house, I borrowed his communications technology to contact the *Daily Express* in London and offer them the story. To their utter bewilderment, I insisted I wanted a copy taker on the other end of the line with headphones and a keypad or a typewriter. Of course I was talking to youngsters who had never heard of any of these things. But eventually the lovely Gladys came on the line and I dictated a thousand-word despatch, old style, the way it used to be.

Dinner that evening was most convivial. Next to me was the Dutch forensic pathologist. Part of the foreign aid from Holland was a state-of-the-art mortuary adjacent to the general hospital. It was well placed, because patients tended to enter by the main doors but only exit in a horizontal box straight into the morgue.

The kindly pathologist was in retirement, but serving a three-year stint in return for a nice, plump pension when he got home. I asked him if he had had a busy day.

"Extremely busy," he agreed.

"What were you doing?"

"Putting the president back together again," he said.

According to custom, the dead head of state had to be presented in an open casket, which was not easy because none of the bits recovered from the garden actually fitted. That problem solved, we tucked into our veal escalopes.

After two days, I had all my research done, and the next day the airport opened. The TAP flight from São Tomé dropped in and picked up the few of us returning to Lisbon. From there, I could take a BA flight back to London.

My wife's laptop remained unusable for five days and then suddenly cleared as the mysterious ban-on-use was removed without explanation. But I retain a silly fantasy of the morning conference at Langley when the news came through.

"No, Mr. Director, sir, we don't know what is going on inside. The borders are closed, ditto the airport. There's some weird Limey in there who has a bit of a track record on coups in West Africa and he seems to know what is going down. Yes, sir, we have tried to contact him, but to no avail. He doesn't have a laptop and he won't use a cell phone."

"Oh, well, let's just screw up his wife's lunch dates."

PEACE HOTEL AND TRACERS

This time, my wife, Sandy, was in serious voice and she had a point.

"You are an old fool to be even thinking of going to a place like that," she said.

"Calm down," I advised. "You could be a rich widow."

"I don't want to be a rich widow," she replied.

I thought that was rather touching. There are quite a few women on planet Earth who would do the trade. But that did not solve my problem. I was in the last stages of the research for the last novel I intend to write. It already had a title, *The Kill List,* after a document that really exists and in which are written the names, continuously updated, of all the terrorists the United States intends to "terminate" without benefit of the habitual formalities.

The usual travels had taken me around the "official" tour of agencies, ministries, technical establishments, weapons stores, and a score of experts in their various fields. That was all in note form. But there is one thing that is too often missing.

As a reader, I am disagreeably picky. When reading about a place in someone else's work, I cannot avoid a nagging question: Has he actually been there? There is a reason.

Reading about a place is one thing, going there is another. A personal visit, it is my long-held view, reveals a whole range of discoveries that is not available from reading research, and certainly miles more than is on the Internet. The next best thing, if a personal visit is not feasible, is spending hours with someone who knows the place intimately.

When I needed to describe Iraq under Saddam Hussein for *The Fist of God*, I was advised that if I slipped in, the dictator's secret police would take about an hour to work out who I was, what I was doing, and that it was not going to be complimentary to the tyrant. The occasional risk is tolerable, but suicide is just stupid. So for Iraq I relied on a score of people who had lived, worked, and traveled there for years.

But this was going to be different. I had tried academic sources, including the Internet and passages from other fiction writers, and it was clear none of them had been near the ravaged city that had to occupy a whole chapter in *The Kill List*. Not many people had been to Mogadishu, the notional capital of the permanently-at-war Somalia.

The country appeared to be pirates in the north, Al-Shabaab terrorists in the south, and a capital under siege in the middle. And my wife had a point. Seventy-four is getting on a bit for bullet dodging. One slows up. So we agreed on a compromise. She would not blast it all over the Internet in her e-mails about lunch and I would go in with a bodyguard for the first time ever.

Through a few contacts, I got in touch with a specialist agency run by Rob Andrew out of Nairobi. He agreed to lend me Dom, who had escorted whiteys in there before and brought them out again. Dom was British, ex–Special Forces, knew the terrain, and was steady as a rock if things got lively.

There was one airline servicing Mogadishu, or "Mog," as everyone called it. Turkish Airlines ran a flight out of Istanbul, with a stopover at Djibouti (formerly French Somaliland, still run by the French with a huge American air base), a stopover at Mog, and a final leg to Nairobi. Then a turnaround and back. Passengers could get on and off at Mog. Dom agreed to be there to meet me on the tarmac. It was a night flight arriving at dawn, already blazing hot at seven thirty a.m., and there he was.

He saw me through the formalities of passport control and customs, with the usual gratuities to the unpaid officials and outside in the shade explained to me the local layout.

Mog has two quite different zones: the inner zone, and the city zone. The former is hemmed in by sandbag blast walls, razor wire, guarded gates, and an entire garrison of soldiers from AMISOM—the African Union Mission in Somalia. These are almost all Burundians and Ugandans. They are armed to the teeth, but have taken casualties that would cause government-toppling scandals in a European country, but are shrugged off in Africa.

Colloquially, the inner zone is known as the Bancroft Camp, or the Camp. It encloses the entire airport, all the (not many) embassies, the HQ of the African military mission, and the living quarters of everyone else who is not Somali. These include mercenaries, bodyguards, technical aides, and relief workers—in a word, the whites.

Separate at one end of the single runway is the highly secretive American embassy, also walled, with its huge CIA mission, suspected UAV drones, and a training school for young Somalis destined, hopefully, to become US agents when they qualify. The point is, no one can pretend to be a Somali who is not a born Somali, so no one can infiltrate "the bad guys" except a Somali.

Somewhere in the undergrowth, there is a British embassy pretending not to be. And right in the heart of the Camp is the cluster of lodgings, bars, and mess halls where the non-military, non-diplomatic whites hang out. The hutments are converted steel sea containers, the bar chairs are plastic rejects, the beer supplies are constant (the place would be in revolt without them), and the atmosphere is raucous. Dom and I spent a few hours there and then, in our rented jeep, headed out of the guarded gate and into town. What I needed, I had explained, was to spend time in the Mog City that my Mossad agent in the novel would be visiting on a covert mission.

Our Somali driver weaved his way through the donkeys, camels, and ubiquitous pickup trucks, known as "technicals," and deep into the heart of Somali Mogadishu. We finally arrived at a side street and, driving up it, found a sealed gate. Dom exercised his linguistic magic, and it slowly opened to reveal a courtyard, into which we drove as the gate closed behind us. We had arrived at the Peace Hotel, charmingly named as it was in a war zone.

The AMISOM troops attempt to hold the outer perimeter of the capital city, while beyond their ring of garrison strongpoints the country belongs to Al-Shabaab, who attack fairly regularly. That is where the casualties occur. But many jihadist fanatics are also inside the cordon. That apart, there are the gangs. There are no police—the life span would be too short. As Dom explained to me after we checked in, "It's not so much that they want to kill you, though the fanatics might. The danger is kidnap. Most of these people are living on a dollar a day, if that. With your face, you are two million dollars on the hoof. So a snatch is what I am here to prevent."

Thus reassured, we dumped our luggage in the pretty spartan rooms and headed back out to explore the real Mog. I had just two days, then the Turkish airliner would come in from Nairobi at dawn of the third day to head north to Istanbul—hopefully with me on board.

And the two-day tour was really fascinating. We had the jeep with its Somali driver, and behind us a second jeep with four Ugandans. They were happy to be earning enough to go home at the end of their contract of service with enough to become wealthy in their villages, with wives and cattle as befitted their new status.

I had noticed that Dom was carrying something metallic under his left armpit and was confident he knew exactly how to use it. The Ugandans had rifles, though I was not quite so confident of their expertise.

Dom took us to the principal mosque, untouched by shot or shell despite twenty years of civil war that had reduced most of the once-handsome Italian-designed colonial city to rubble. We saw just one of the sixteen pitiful refugee camps, where the destitute and homeless lived in urine-wet squalor beneath tarpaulins and sacks; the old fishing port; and the Portuguese quarter.

At one point, we found the crossroads where the U.S. helicopter in the film *Black Hawk Down* was grounded and besieged by the fighters of the warlord Aideed. Eighteen Rangers died there, so it seemed the decent thing to stand and say the Lord's Prayer for them. Until the growing crowd became rather disagreeable and Dom thought it wise to move on.

That first night we were sitting in the hotel window, relishing our camel stew, when something red and feathery drifted past the window. I remarked that it seemed odd that someone was celebrating with fireworks. Dom looked at me pityingly and said, "Tracer."

Then I recalled that with tracer fire only about one bullet in six or seven is illuminated. The rest you cannot see. Fortunately, these rounds were going left to right and not straight at the glass.

Nevertheless, I fingered my lucky bullet, worn on a gold chain round my neck. It passed through my hair one day in Biafra and lodged in the doorpost behind me. After the firefight, I dug it out, brought it back to London, and had it mounted on a chain. Though not particularly superstitious, I adopted the habit of wearing it around my neck if going into any "rough" environment.

Before bed, I tried to shower off, but the tap had the strength and capacity of a urinating rabbit, so I settled for a bowl and a scrap of towel.

We checked out the next morning, spent part of the day completing our tour of Mog City, and withdrew to the ramparts of Bancroft Camp. There at least we could check into a steel container, enjoy a few beers, and be free of camel stew. Or it might have been goat, but it was rich and sustaining. We still settled for imported steak.

The next morning Dom saw me back through the airport formalities and onto the Turkish airliner. He later found his way back to his family in Nairobi on a small chartered flight.

When I returned home I had a warm welcome. "That's it," said Sandy, "the next time you pull a stunt like that, I'm going to see Fiona."

She was referring to a mutual friend and the best divorce lawyer in London. But of course, she doesn't really mean it. Anyway, I agreed that those days really are over, and then a year later . . .

DREAM COME TRUE

———◆———

It was a very small news item and one might have missed it. Down in the heart of the county of Kent, where I came from long ago, is a grass airfield called Lashenden, just outside the pretty town of Headcorn. Lashenden is the home of several clubs including a branch of the Tiger Club, flying Tiger Moth biplanes, plus a skydiving club and another dedicated to classic aircraft called Aero Legends. The item that caught my eye revealed that Lashenden wished to upgrade all its buildings and facilities and sought donations.

I had an idea and made a call; that was in August 2014. I mentioned the news item to the voice that answered and said I was prepared to be very generous, but there was a condition. The voice replied he doubted it would be possible, but he would ask. Four weeks went by. My seventy-sixth birthday came and went. Then the phone rang. Her name was Andrea.

"Are you free tomorrow?" she asked. "We have one flying in from Duxford."

I know RAF Duxford; it is the aeronautical end of the Imperial War Museum, a collection of classic and revered warplanes, some still flying. Including a Spitfire. Of course I was available. I had been available for seventy years. So I motored down, parked, checked in, and waited. I was issued a flying suit and a cup of coffee. There was a problem. Morning mist hung over the Weald of Kent, but the sun of our Indian summer was burning it off. Up in Cambridgeshire, where Duxford is situated, the fog was worse. Would old Fred's luck still hold? It held. The mist lifted, and she took off and headed south, over the Thames and into Kent. She landed just before noon. A Spitfire Mark 9, green-and-brown RAF combat camouflage. And she was beautiful; an icon that had once changed the history of Britain, Europe, and the world. And she had been adapted with a second cockpit for a single passenger.

She taxied into the apron near the dispersal huts and closed down. Her pilot, Cliff Spink, a professional who flies classic warplanes for a living—ex-RAF, of course—came over and introduced himself. "Who's first?" he asked. There were two donors awarded a flight. I was ready. He nodded and we walked out into the sun.

She was just as I had remembered her from seventy years earlier, when, aged five, I was dropped into an open cockpit at Hawkinge field and became mesmerized by the power and beauty of the Supermarine Spitfire. The long, lean lines, only slightly degraded by the bubble Perspex dome behind the pilot's cockpit; the recognizable-anywhere elliptical wings, the genius of designer R. J. Mitchell. The four-bladed propeller, stark against the Kentish late-summer sky the same cerulean blue it had been in the summer of 1944. That was when I swore my little boy's oath; that one day I, too, would fly a Spitfire.

One is older and stiffer than long ago. It took a hefty shove to get me onto the wing, and thence I could step into the tiny rear cockpit.

Helpful hands belted on the parachute and then the seat straps. A brief lecture on how to bail out if need be. Unhook the seat straps but *not* the parachute straps as well. Jettison the canopy, stand, turn, dive. Of course. But that was not going to happen.

Cliff climbed up front, his head disappeared out of sight. I used the seat-height adjuster and rose out of the cavern into the bubble dome itself. The Rolls-Royce Merlin engine, all thirty-seven liters of her, coughed once, then roared and settled down to a throaty growl. Chocks away. A bit more power. She moved away from dispersal and taxied to takeoff. Cliff turned her into the wind and checked with the tower. Clear to take off.

The engine note rose smoothly from low growl to maddened roar and the Spitfire threw herself across the grass field, bumping over the ruts. Then the vibration stopped, the grass drifted downward, clunk clunk, wheels up, a lurch forward as the impediment vanished. Cliff held her low over the field as the speed built up, then hauled back.

A raging climb into that blue, blue sky. Kent dropping away like a discarded map in a gale. At three thousand feet, Cliff's voice on the intercom: "You have her." His hands raised to head height, visible through two layers of Perspex to prove it. So I gripped the control column and flew her.

Just as I had been led to believe. Ultrasensitive to the touch, eager, willing, wanting to obey before the order was complete. It had been an awfully long time, but as with the bicycle it never quite leaves you. Diffident at first, confidence growing. Bank, turn, climb, twist, correct. I pulled into a rate-two left-hand turn and looked down.

There was the Weald of Kent as it had been since the times of the Crusaders. A patchwork quilt of woods and fields, manors and meadows, farms and streams, hop oasts and orchards, ancient villages clustered around the cricket green, timbered pubs, Norman churches. The same Weald I had pedaled through as a boy, just as it was in 1940, when Spitfires and Hurricanes hurled themselves at the oncoming Luftwaffe. Enough to make even a cynical old journalist choke up. England, our England.

It was over too soon, but it was done. The seventy-year-old promise was fulfilled and the little boy's dream had come true.

PHOTO CREDITS

Every effort has been made to trace copyright holders, but any who have been overlooked are invited to get in touch with the publishers.

FF: author's collection

Credits read clockwise from top left.

SECTION ONE

Spitfires of the No 91 Squadron lined up at Hawkinge, Kent, 5 May 1942: courtesy Imperial War Museum/CH5429

Dewald family: *FF*; Hanna Reitsch with Bozo Komac at the German glider championships held at Oerlinghausen, Germany, 31 July 1953: © TopFoto.co.uk; all RAF photos: *FF*; Tonbridge School from the air and Big School, Tonbridge School: both courtesy Tonbridge School

Frank Keeler: © Archant Ltd; Doon Campbell in the Reuters newsroom, Fleet Street, London, 1950s: Reuters; newsmen at the scene of the attempted assassination of President Charles de Gaulle, Petit Clamart, 22 August 1962: Keystone-France/Gamma-Keystone via Getty Images; Kurt Blecha, Press Secretary to the Politburo at a press conference in Berlin, 1 February 1962: Koblenz, Bundesarchiv, Bild 183-90187-0008/photo Heinz Junge; President de Gaulle's bullet-riddled car, August 1962: ©1962 Rex Features; East German border guards at Checkpoint Charlie, Berlin, April 1963: Ullstein via Getty Images;

reconstruction of the assassination attempt, August 1962: Patrice Habans/*Paris Match* via Getty Images

Lt Col. Yakubu Gowon holding a press conference, August 1966: Priya Ramrakha/The LIFE Picture Collection/Getty Images; posters warning of the threat of war, Enugu, 9 June 1967: Associated Press; bridge at Onitsha, June 1969: ©RIA Novosti/TopFoto; FF and Col. Emeka Ojukwu: David Cairns, *London Daily Express*; Col. Ojukwu giving a press conference during the war: AFP/Getty Images

David Ben-Gurion at Sde Boker, October 1965: © David Rubinger/Corbis; Ezer Weizman: UA/Israel Sun/REX Shutterstock; King David Hotel, 22 July 1946: Fox Photos/Getty Images

SECTION TWO

Children, Biafra, June 1968: David Cairns, *London Daily Express*

Trip to Biafra with army escort, 1968; FF and Biafran, 1968; Biafran mother and baby, 1968; malnourished Biafran baby, 1968: all David Cairns, *London Daily Express*; protest rally, Speaker's Corner, Hyde Park, London, 1968: *Evening Standard*/Getty Images; shell, Biafra, 1968: David Cairns, *London Daily Express*

FF and his parents; FF and sons hunting and scuba-diving: all *FF*; FF and his wife, Sandy, at Buckingham Palace, London, 4 April 1997: Fiona Hanson/Press Association; FF, Carrie Forsyth and their first son, Stuart, 14 June 1979: Philip Jackson/Associated Newspapers/Rex; FF, Carrie and their second son, Shane, 1979: Mike Forster/Associated Newspapers/Rex

FF at his typewriter, *c.* 1970: Hulton Archive/Getty Images; FF and Michael Caine, 14 February 1986: Mirrorpix; FF in Guinea-Bissau, 4 March 2009: Associated Press; FF at a book signing, London, 25 September 1972: Wesley/Keystone/Getty Images; Edward Fox and Fred Zinnemann on the set of *The Day of the Jackal*, 1973: Snap/Rex

FF flying, August 2014: all *FF*

PUTNAM EST. 1838 | Penguin Random House